D1603618

Educating Feminists

Life Histories and Pedagogy

Educating Feminists
Life Histories and Pedagogy

Sue Middleton

TEACHERS
COLLEGE
PRESS

Teachers College, Columbia University
New York and London

Published by Teachers College Press, 1234 Amsterdam Avenue, New York, N.Y. 10027

Library of Congress Cataloging-in-Publication Data
Middleton, Sue, 1947–
    Educating feminists : life histories and pedagogy / Sue Middleton.
        p.   cm.
    Includes bibliographical references (p.) and index.
    ISBN 0-8077-3234-6 (alk. paper). — ISBN 0-8077-3233-8 (pbk. :
alk. paper)
    1. Feminism and education.   2. Critical pedagogy.   3. Women-
-Education—Social aspects.   4. Women educators.   5. Sexism in
education.   I. Title.
LC197.M53   1993
    376—dc20   92-43007

Printed on acid-free paper
Manufactured in the United States of America
99 98 97 96 95 94 93   8 7 6 5 4 3 2 1

Contents

Foreword

*I*n June 1990, I was fortunate enough to receive a Fulbright award for a brief lecture tour of New Zealand universities. At the end of the first week, in the course of a conference at Victoria University in Wellington, I had my initial encounter with Sue Middleton. Perhaps I should say that her presence and her presentation encountered me—reached out to me in a way not easy to forget. She talked about life history and presented chapters from her own life history in a carefully wrought context, both sociological and political. I do not think I had ever experienced such an authentic, rhythmic account of what it is to be a contemporary woman—teacher, wife, mother, writer—existing in a problematic world. Nor do I think I had anticipated the feeling of recognition that Sue Middleton's talk aroused. Here was a woman from rural New Zealand, a boarding school graduate, a guitar-playing wanderer, a young mother writing a doctoral dissertation in Hamilton, more than half a world from my New York City home. And here I was, a life-long New Yorker reared on city streets, in city schools, feeling wholly identified with someone technically a stranger.

I began to learn something this book has carried further: It has to do with connections among women reaching across boundaries, with networks of women who risk self-knowledge and critique, and with companies of women concerned as much with social change as they are with their own liberation. Sue Middleton's text speaks in tones that resonate far beyond her own beautiful, complex country. Those of us who teach, those of us who engage in research, and those of us who are trying to live full and varied lives even as we do our work will see more and perhaps know more through engagement with this book.

Sue Middleton begins with a vivid personal account of her day-to-day living and communicates, as few can, a sense of place. At once reaching beyond the personal, she talks about marginality along with the possession of "cultural capital," putting so many academic women in a contradictory position that this author works to resolve. Describing the "fault lines" created by the Maori presence in her country, she may contribute to our own discussions of multiculturalism by enabling us to look, from an unfamiliar direction, at the new perspectives on our own lived cultures that the stories of those from other cultures provide, especially if we allow them to tell their own stories without imposing academic or social scientific frames.

With extraordinary originality, Sue Middleton presents various approaches to the understanding of feminism and the discourse of the "sociology of women's education" through an account of her own effort to develop and introduce a course on women and education in her particular university. Such problems as the relevance of the traditional disciplines and the theories and knowledge maps considered acceptable are dealt with in a manner that cannot help but hold implications for people in this country who are still working to institute or preserve women's studies. Moreover, because of Dr. Middleton's fidelity to the life-history approach, her treatment of what happened reads the way that well-wrought narratives read. True to her belief that the writer and the teacher must make visible their own vantage points and their own lived orientations, she succeeds in wedding a clearheaded discursive account to an equally clear personal account. We always know where she stands, and she helps us, her readers, discover where we stand.

Her offering of materials from what she calls researching encounters not only opens unfamiliar doorways to an understanding of the significance of sexuality and its relationship to women's professional lives, but it also helps readers make sense—often in novel ways—of women's powerlessness and power. Reading Sue Middleton, we cannot help but be struck by the exploration of themes that lead into a veritable history of contemporary and postmodern feminist theory. The tensions between liberal feminism and critical theory are made clear; so are the disclosures of the importance of discourse in the development of the sociology of women's education. Readers are likely to feel like participants in the ongoing conversation among some of the best known and most scholarly feminists of our time. Issues like the so-called androcentrism in familiar educational theories, the problematic character of liberal constructions of the individual and individual autonomy, the need to pay heed to childbearing and child rearing in widening cultural contexts, and the implications of feminist thought for teaching are all examined and discussed within a dramatic and personalized rendering of changing—and sometimes conflicting—feminisms. Readers of whatever gender are challenged over and over to choose.

However, there is even more in this book. In her role as public intellectual, Sue Middleton has served on the New Zealand Indecent Publications Tribunal. She writes about this introduction to the countless ways that there are and have been of making objects out of women, mutilating them, and disposing of them. Of course, she faces the matter of censorship, but she also draws all sorts of implications for educational restructuring and gender equity. Writing from an experience similar to that of American feminists, she struggles to create a discourse that will deconstruct and expose the uncaring, often patriarchal assumptions of what may be called, in both our countries, the New Right. This book moves further than many that have explored the life stories of hitherto silenced women. In exploring her direct experience and describing the actual and metaphorical rooms she has created, Sue Middleton points toward ways of resisting encroachments and confinements, remaking humane communities, battling plagues, and becoming free. Sue Middleton's voice is one to savor; her argument feeds necessarily into our informed unease.

Maxine Greene

Acknowledgments

*T*his book originated on a recent visit to the United States. From March to May 1991, I was in the United States on a Fulbright grant, and I am grateful to the New Zealand-U.S. Educational Foundation for this support. For part of this time, I was a visiting academic in the Department of Curriculum and Instruction at the University of Madison, Wisconsin. My thanks to Michael Apple and others who shared ideas with me, welcomed my participation in seminars, and gave me feedback on some of the papers that have been transformed into this book. A wonderful month in New York was made possible by Maxine Greene, whose friendship and encouragement have sustained and inspired me throughout this book's creation. Much of the first draft was written at the Department of Educational Policy and Leadership at Ohio State University. My thanks to Patti Lather and other staff in that department for organizing superb office and technical facilities, keeping me on task, and helping me to have fun. Many other American colleagues supported me professionally and personally during my American visit; I would especially like to thank Rima Apple, Courtney Cazden, Elizabeth Ellsworth, Nancy Lesko, Mimi Orner, David Schaafsma, and Kathleen Weiler.

Academic writing is both cumulative and collective: It builds on the ideas of those who have gone before and those with whom we network. There are many colleagues with whom I have engaged in collaborative writing and editing projects. There are those who have influenced my thinking through sharing their writing in progress, through formal interchanges at conferences and in informal conversations. There are colleagues who have looked after me on my overseas and New Zealand travels. In particular, I acknowledge the support of Sandra Acker, Madeleine Arnot, Phillida Bunkle, John Codd, Rosemary du Plessis (formerly Novitz), Kathie Irwin, Alison Jones, Geraldine McDonald, Helen May, Logan Moss, Jock Phillips, Peter Ramsay, Shaista Shameem, Sandra Taylor, Gaby Weiner, and Lyn Yates.

I would like to thank my colleagues in the School of Education at the University of Waikato for their good-humored tolerance of my moods and absences. The career development seminars held in local restaurants have been particularly therapeutic; my thanks to the women staff of T Block and K Block for these.

It was important to make this book student-friendly, and a number of graduate students in education and women's studies have helped greatly by reading the various drafts. Kay Edwards and Roseanne Mathieson gave me detailed comments on an early draft, and my graduate students' reading group—Gail Cawkwell, Wendy Drewery, Kay Matthews, Justine Cameron, Jane Gilbert, Elizabeth McKinlay, Brenda Taitoko, Rose McEldowny, and Sen Wong—proofread and commented on the final draft.

I am grateful to all those who have allowed me to use their taped and written life histories and comments in my writing over the years. My thinking was transformed by the feminist teachers and students who were in my doctoral thesis and subsequent academic papers (chapters 3, 4, and 5). Chapter 6 includes interviews with members of school boards of trustees; I thank them for their contributions. I also thank David Mitchell and the other members of the Monitoring Today's Schools Research Team for permission to use the project's research data in this book. I also thank the students in the 1991 undergraduate "Women and Education" course, who allowed their written work to be used in chapter 7. All my students over the years have helped give form to the pedagogy that is described in these pages.

My husband George and daughter Kate have nurtured me throughout. I dedicate this book to them and to the memory of my niece, Carla Cardno.

Educating Feminists

Life Histories and Pedagogy

Introduction

*F*or feminist teachers, education has been an object of demand, a source of ideas, a means of employment, and a site of political activism. Teacher education has become an important arena of feminist activity. In university education departments and colleges of teacher education, courses on women and education or gender and education have been established. Since 1981, I have been designing and teaching such courses.

This teaching has taken place over a period of rapid change. There have been major theoretical shifts within disciplines such as women's studies and sociology of education. The schools and universities in which we teach and study have been restructured. This restructuring has influenced both the context and the content of our teaching and research. For example, the economics and politics of the New Right have not only shaped our material circumstances but have also become the objects of our academic inquiries. In the past decade, feminists and other educational writers of the Left have produced a large literature that argues that the atomized, competitive individualism of the New Right is antithetical to collectivist notions of social justice or equity, which we have taken as our central concerns (Apple, 1986, 1989; Arnot, 1991a; Aronowitz & Giroux, 1987; Flude & Hammer, 1990; Greene, 1988; Lauder & Wylie, 1990; Livingstone, 1987).

Like many of today's feminist and Leftist educators, I attended university during the 1960s and began teaching in high schools in the early 1970s—times of full employment and hope. Today, as a university teacher in the 1990s, I watch my students and my daughter moving into adulthood in times of economic recession and despair. The kinds of feminism and progressive educational theories that offered possibilities to my generation of teachers may seem to today's students to be irrelevant and quaint anachronisms. As Maxine Greene (1986) has posed the question: "What might a critical pedagogy mean for those of us who teach the young at this peculiar and menacing time?" (p. 440). How can we, middle-aged and older teacher educators, develop feminist courses that are appropriate for the lives and times of today's students? It is this question that this book addresses.

I hear a door bang . . . the mutter of a distant radio. George, my husband, is awake and listening to the news. I become conscious once more of my surroundings. I love this room—my own small space, my study at home. The timbered walls are painted a glossy avocado green. It is August 21, 1991, a wet Wednesday dawn in an early New Zealand spring. I have been writing since 5:00 a.m. I seize for myself the dawns, late nights, and weekends. I try to stay at home on Mondays—the day on which I do not teach. To write, I must separate myself from my family and stay out of reach of the university—meetings, students, and administration. This is the beginning of a 3-week, end-of-term, nonteaching recess. I can create for myself the time and space to write.

I am privileged to be able to indulge in the luxury of writing. As Virginia Woolf (1978) explained, "A woman must have money and a room of her own if she is to write . . . " (p. 6). As a tenured academic, I can—with the mortgages, credit cards, and overdrafts extended to today's professional classes—purchase a computer and create study space. I gaze at the grey luminescent screen of my Macintosh, grateful for the clear black type that appears as I press the keys. Grateful for technology and tenure. Grateful for the salary that has bought release from the typewriter on the kitchen table, surrounded by scraps of food and children's comings and goings.

A cold southerly blast hits the wall of my room. This room—the new study I had converted from a laundry—faces south, the cold side of the house. But it is well heated; I feel snug and protected. The rain has eased; briefly, I hear a sparrow. Buds are appearing on the swaying hibiscus bush outside the window.

I sense slight shocks and jolts in the taken-for-granted worlds of my northern hemisphere readers. I know your orientation to the world is different from mine. I have read your books, visited your countries, and grown up with your movies and popular songs. To you, it is wrong to have spring in August, for the south to be the origins of biting winter winds. I grew up with your sense of the wrongness of our seasons. Spring, April showers, and snowy Christmasses were taken for granted in the books I read, the songs I sang, and the movies I watched. Our Christmasses were spent at summer beaches. We stayed in *baches*—holiday shacks or cottages—a word I must translate, a further reminder of my otherness. As we sweated in the sultry sun, we ate the Christmas fare—hot turkey and plum pudding—of English ancestors. We festooned our Christmas trees with tinsel icicles.

But there are also points of recognition—affinities—between us. You recognize the structuring and the fragmentations of my life. You know the dissonances and disharmonies between the domestic and the academic. You recognize the political situation I have described: the New Right revolution and the antifeminist backlash. You recognize the computer on which I write. Many of you live and work in old houses. You, too, have renovated, juggled mortgages and overdrafts, and built spaces to make your writing possible.

My location in a converted laundry room may seem strange. My New Zealand house is a 1930s, one-storied wooden bungalow; the laundry is a room at the back. We have no need of basements. I live in the warmer, northern part of the country. We do not need furnaces or central heating and do not have tornadoes from which to hide. My mother—and many of your mothers—would have needed this space for washing, for ironing, and for drying clothes in wet weather. When my mother started married life immediately after World War II, she had to boil her washing in a copper.[1] It took many hours of her working week. In the late 1950s, she obtained a washing machine—an agitator with a wringer that required constant supervision and interaction. My modern appliances—American brands that you would recognize—are tucked away behind the back door. They take up little space or time. I can do the washing by pushing a button. As I write this, I am doing the washing. I can hear the machines whirring outside my door.

Through my study wall, I hear a clatter in the kitchen. George is making breakfast. He is a teacher. He was made "redundant" last year when the government's restructuring of the Social Welfare Department closed down his school. He was principal of Whaiora Special School. He taught girls who were short-term residents in the Hamilton Girls' Home—victims of sexual abuse and rape; glue sniffers, truants, and kids in trouble. Now they are deinstitutionalized—cared for in the community. George has only a temporary position in an intermediate school (junior high). Unemployment is up to nearly 10%.

I hear a blues bass. Kate is in the shower listening to Contact FM, our local university student radio station. She is 14, in high school, but is already on the fringes of university student subculture—a theater crowd. She listens to New Zealand and alternative rock bands. She loves my old records—Moody Blues, the Doors, Jethro Tull. She likes to wear 60s originals from *op shops* (thrift shops): psychedelic minidresses and black tights. Boutique clothes—accoutrements of yuppiedom—are uncool.

Kate expects to be able to choose whether or not to go to the university. She is an only child with university-educated parents. She has bourgeois "cultural capital" (Bourdieu, 1971a, 1971b). Her chances of having such a choice are very high. Until very recently, university education in New Zealand was virtually free, and students could win bursaries—living allowances—on passing the Bursaries Examination in their final year of high school. University students could mostly be free of parental support. In July 1991, fees were increased and living allowances were removed for students whose parents earn high incomes (set somewhere between NZ$30,000 and $35,000 [US$17,400 and $20,300] a year in total). Free hospital care, education, and welfare—taken for granted in my country since 1938, when the first Labour government passed the Social Security Act creating the welfare state, including the public health system—are being eroded away. My generation of parents never expected to pay, never saved, and never planned for these things. Many of Kate's peers may not make it to the university.

I was born in 1947. I grew up in a welfare state, New Zealand, during the prosperous years of the post–World War II era. Like many of those who were to become the radical sociologists, critical pedagogues, and feminist educators of the 1980s and 1990s, I found teaching to be a route to social mobility (Nash, Harker, & Charters, 1990; J. Watson, 1966). My parents did not have the opportunity to attend institutions of higher education. My father had finished high school; my mother had only 2 years in a shorthand/typing course in a technical high school. Many New Zealanders of my parents' generation did not attend high school.

Many of us—today's feminist and socialist educators—are children of parents from the working or lower middle classes, of ethnic/cultural minority backgrounds, and from rural areas or small towns (Heron, 1985; Middleton, 1990b; Walkerdine & Lucey, 1989; Weiler, 1988). In New Zealand, during the 1960s and 1970s, teaching opened up for such students the possibilities of higher education and of a profession. Teacher trainees were paid a salary during their university and teachers' college study.[2] There was a shortage of teachers and a strong government recruitment campaign to attract young people—and mature students—into teaching.

As I shall argue in the early chapters of this book, such students—especially those who were among the first in our families to attend institutions of higher education—often felt marginalized within them. My generation's radical sociological and/or feminist perspectives on education had been at least partly theorizations of our experiences of marginality or alienation within it although—as individuals who were to become academically successful—we had sufficient "cultural capital" (Bourdieu, 1971a) to enable this marginalization to become the basis of an intellectual critique rather than of educational withdrawal or failure. The simultaneous experiences of marginality and the economic circumstances of full employment and teacher shortages created in many Western educationists who had been students in the 1960s and early 1970s a sense of both the desirability and the possibility of progressive or radical educational and social change.

Our responses to the New Right have been more than mere intellectualizations. They are underpinned by deep feelings of outrage and loss. The kinds of social-democratic collectivism or socialism that are being attacked and dismantled had characterized the educational and social policies that had made possible, for many of us, our own educations and academic careers. We now see for our children's generation the erosion of such possibilities (Apple, 1986; Secada, 1989).

George brings me coffee and toast. We chat about today's arrangements for after school. Kate has a drama rehearsal. She calls out to ask me if I've seen her math book. They leave, and the front door slams shut. Silence.

This room is a repository of dreams and remembered travels. On the walls are French artists' impressions of some of my favorite cities—visited in hippie backpacking days or, more recently, on sabbaticals. Monet's London, Leger's New York. There is a watercolor I painted as a teenager of duffle-coated students in an urban cafe. I grew up in a tiny country town, but my mother subscribed to *The New Yorker*.

There are statements about land. In front of my computer is a pencil sketch of two women hiding their faces, exiled from the land. It was drawn by a feminist artist from this town, Hamilton. Our region was, in the nineteenth century, the scene of bloody land wars between *Maori* (indigenous Polynesians) and *Pakeha* (New Zealand–born whites). Next to this hangs an Aboriginal land rights poster from Queensland, Australia. They are constant reminders that I am the descendant of colonists. Behind me is another of my teenage paintings: a country dance. The band, all males—two Maori and two Pakeha—have Beatle haircuts, wear black skivvies (turtlenecks), and green V-necked jerkins. The dancing couples—some of mixed race—are doing the twist. In the next chapter, I will share with you these paintings. They say much about the imagery, the themes, and the mainsprings of my pedagogy.

I can read my room as an archaeologist would decipher a site. I can read my intellectual genealogy (Foucault, 1979), my academic life history. I can retrace my personal voyage through the theoretical currents of my discipline. To my left hangs my doctoral degree from the University of Waikato. It is framed ceremoniously in red, gold, and black. It hangs over a small bookcase. Most of my books are stored in my office at the university. These shelves contain only the immediate and the intimate. There are four shelves.

The top two shelves contain academic books. On the second shelf are books I plan to read soon, but from which I am too often pulled away—by teaching, by meetings, and by grading of papers. There are biographies of women painters and musicians—Frida Kahlo, Alberta Hunter—waiting for leisurely summer beaches. There are several much-underlined texts on feminism and postmodernism that I brought back with me from my recent sabbatical in the United States: useful to me and much borrowed by my master's and doctoral students. But these abstracted conversations between overseas intellectuals are beyond the reach of my undergraduate students: feminism receding into terrifying reifications; writing about the personal in ways that disembody, mystify, and alienate.

On the top shelf, within easy reach, are the textbooks I use in my undergraduate courses. There is my own edited collection, *Women and Education in Aotearoa,* which I use for my "Women and education" course (Middleton, 1988c). There is a text that I coedited with friends—our immediate rejoinder to the New Right economists' encroachments on educational thinking (Middleton, Codd, & Jones, 1990). I use this, along with other readings, in my interdisciplinary "Education and Society" course. Beside this are the texts I use in my undergraduate course, "Sociology of Education" (Codd, Harker, & Nash, 1990; Jones, 1991).

Although these texts have New Zealand content, you would recognize many of the issues and perspectives they address. You would be familiar with many of the texts and authors cited in these books. They address similar themes and use many of the same references as their northern counterparts. Like sociologists of education in the Northern hemisphere and in Australia, New Zealanders' Leftist or radical responses to the individualism of the New Right had diverse theoretical origins and orientations. All were, however, based on the analysis of educational institutions as having played a part historically in the construction and reproduction of inequitable power relations between groups of people. Marxists and neo-Marxists emphasized class relations and feminists emphasized gender relations. Maori writers—like black, ethnic/cultural minority, Third World, and indigenous writers elsewhere—brought into the foreground racism and colonial relations. More recently, postmodernists have emphasized people's simultaneous positionings in multiple power relations. These theorists—overseas and local—have substantially influenced my thinking.

This book draws on works of Marxists, feminists, black and indigenous writers, and postmodernists. However, my reading of all these theories is feminist in that it brings into the foreground what Dorothy Smith (1987) has termed my "standpoint" as a woman. Like some other feminist educators, I make visible the positionality or situatedness of my analysis. I locate or contextualize it within its biographical, historical, and cultural setting (D. Smith, 1987, 1990; Steedman, 1986; Walkerdine & Lucey, 1989). I bring into focus the environment in which my sociological and educational activities are carried out. My everyday life in a sexist society—my life as a woman, an academic, a mother, and a citizen—is studied as sociologically relevant in that it is generative of my pedagogy.

I become aware of the phone ringing in the distance. One day, I will succumb to the pressures to get a phone installed in this room. I resist having a phone, a modem, or a fax—resist technological intrusions into my privacy, my space. For the conveniences of the electronic cottage bring also the possibility of monitoring and surveillance, of increased regulation of one's time, and of invasions by memoranda, inquiries, and demands (Foucault, 1979; Haraway, 1990a). It is a call from Wellington, from my other life. I have to locate a file and, somewhat reluctantly, search the bottom shelf of my bookcase.

There, hidden away at floor level behind the electric radiator, are folders full of papers and several sealed plastic envelopes—red, white, and yellow—with the name of a courier company emblazoned on them. They contain a paperback novel, *American Psycho* (Ellis, 1991) and magazines with titles like *Legs and Asses, Tits and Snatch, Baby Dolls, Black and Lusty,* and *Lusting Geisha.* Pornography. You might recognize these publications; most are imported from Britain or the United States. They are hidden—hidden from visitors, from my daughter Kate, and from Pat who comes to clean on Thursdays and—as far as possible—suppressed from my own consciousness. Why does my sanctuary—my archive of memories, ideas, and dreams—contain lurid depictions of sexual violence and of women's sexual degradation?

Like many academic feminists, I am involved in feminist activities in the community outside the university. Women's studies has always been organically connected to the work and pains of women involved with grassroots activism: in rape crisis centers, battered women's refuges, and feminist health groups (Bowles & Klein, 1983). As academic feminism becomes respectable, it is becoming less connected, more abstract, and increasingly remote from everyday sexual oppressions. It becomes easier for tenured feminist academics to become remote, sheltered from such horrors. One becomes complacent when one lives in one's head. It becomes more and more difficult for feminist academics to make time for grassroots activities. There are ever-increasing pressures to publish in the proper places, to attend and chair committee meetings, and to become available more often to more and more students. As Michael Apple (1979,

1986) has expressed it, the labor of academics is intensifying.

My community work is not particularly grassroots. I hold an official post. In my "spare" time, I am employed by the government—the Ministry of Justice—as a censor for printed materials; books and magazines. I am a representative of the community, a citizen, on a statutory body known somewhat anachronistically as the Indecent Publications Tribunal. I was chosen because of my expertise in education. We decide, for the whole country, which publications should be age-restricted (R 16 and R 18 ratings), otherwise classified, or banned.[3]

The contradictions in this work tear me apart intellectually and emotionally. As a liberal and a rational intellectual, I am opposed to censorship. As a woman and a feminist, I feel sick when I read pornographic writing and see pornographic photographs. I do this job as a civic duty. I do it to stay in touch with the gross sexism of a violent patriarchy. At first, I tried to keep it separate from my family and my working life. But like a poisonous gas, it oozed into my nightmares and into my fears for my daughter's safety. I saw connections between these images and the experiences of people with whom George has worked in schools and in community groups: victims and perpetrators of sexual assault. Girls who have been raped, males who have violently offended. Sexual violence—bracketed out and invisible in most sociological and educational writing—has become an ever-present theme in my research and teaching.

Woven into this book are references, ideas, and images from all of the shelves of my bookcase: the sometimes arid rationality of top-shelf sociological theory, images of sexual violence from the bottom shelf, and feminist narratives and theories from the second shelf.

My bookcase has a third shelf. Beneath the rational layers of academic texts and above the hidden images of sexual violence is a shelf crammed with sheet music; a little Bach, a little Chopin, but mainly jazz—Ellington, Monk, and Brubeck. To the right of my computer table is a small and vibrant watercolor from Bloomington, Indiana: a young red-haired woman playing a classical guitar. She wears a purple skirt. My guitar—a battered relic of coffee-bar folksinging days—lies abandoned in a corner. It has broken strings. Beside it is my much-played digital piano, and a 50-watt amplifier for performances. Japanese brands that you would know. On the wall beside the piano is a menu from the Blue Note jazz cafe in New York and a space reserved for a poster of Janis Joplin, when I find one.

When I work in here, I move continually from one keyboard to another—from computer to piano. My music surfaces in my pedagogy. In my school-teaching days, I often used the singer poets of the times: Dylan, Baez, and Donovan. More recently, in university classes, I have played tapes of songs about education: Pink Floyd and Herbs (a New Zealand–based Polynesian reggae band). I encourage my students to study the popular culture of their time: rock videos, soap operas, and comics. I play keyboards at feminist gatherings and at staff social functions. My music is woven through the fabric of my academic life.

This book is like a counterpoint—a polyvocal score (Lather, 1991). Woven through my theoretical deliberations and my struggles with feminist and sociological theories in education are reflections on the everyday practicalities of my experience—as a teacher of university courses in the sociology of women's education, as a feminist educational researcher, as an educator involved in processes of institutional reorganization and wider political upheaval during times of economic crisis and administrative restructuring, and as a woman whose maternal and civic responsibilities have come into conflict with the demands of a professional life. You will also hear the voices of other feminist teachers, of school administrators, and of students. They speak through taped life histories and group discussions, written assignments, and questionnaires. Through a focus on what C. Wright Mills (1959) and others have termed "biography, history, and social structure," I explore relationships between individuals' educational life histories, their historical and material contexts, and the broader patterns of power relations (such as those of class, race, and gender) that shape and constrain our possibilities and that release our educational imaginations.

Each chapter focuses on one of the activities that characterize the work of a feminist teacher educator. Chapter 1 demonstrates my teaching—a life-history approach to feminist pedagogy. Using paintings from my own childhood, I identify some of the "generative themes" (Freire, 1971) of my pedagogy and of my generation's versions of feminism. I take you through the first lesson in my "Women and Education" course. Chapter 2 explores the problems of mapping curriculum content for courses in the sociology of women's education. It revises the traditional taxonomies and typologies through placing these within the historical and political circumstances— the power relations—of their construction. In chapter 3, I explore the process of making sociological knowledge by means of life-history research techniques. I raise questions about methodology, ethics, and politics.

Chapters 4 and 5 explore some educational experiences and perspectives of feminist teachers of my post–World War II generation. Chapter 4 is a collective life history of the 12 feminist teachers who participated in my doctoral research in the early 1980s. In this, I explore the processes of becoming feminist and the ways in which we, as feminist teachers, have experienced continuing contradictions and marginalities in education. In chapter 5, I use my own experiences as a feminist academic in the 1980s to further study the marginalization of feminist knowledge in educational settings. I contextualize my "Women and Education" course within the wider women's studies program of which it is a part, discuss ways in which my community work with pornography has influenced my teaching in the wider program, and use this as a basis for analyzing relationships between academic and grassroots feminism.

Chapters 6 and 7 focus on some feminist educational questions that are of central concern for our students in the 1990s. Chapter 6 draws on some of my recent research as a basis for an exploration of the ways in which issues of equity are being conceptualized by those who are presently, or soon will be, my students' employers—the parents and teachers who have been elected to their schools' boards of trustees. In chapter 7, I construct a conversation from the writings and taped comments of New Zealand and American education students. Students of different age groups discuss their experiences as women in education, their responses to the life-history techniques used in the course, their ideas about feminism, and their application of the sociology of women's education to their own lives in schools. In the epilogue, I raise questions for feminist teacher education in the 1990s.

Throughout this book, I bring into focus the everyday world within which my pedagogical and sociological activities are carried out. My sociology and my pedagogy are studied as constructed within the constraints and the possibilities of my particular circumstances. From the vantage point of my analysis of the personal, historical, and social/cultural circumstances that helped generate or made possible my own generation's feminist critiques of education, I raise questions about how we, as feminist teachers and researchers, can best approach our activities in the age of the New Right.

Notes

[1]A copper was a large copper tank set in a concrete case. There was a fire grate underneath; wood fires were lit in this.

[2]Teacher-training salaries were much more generous than the ordinary student bursaries, which have varied greatly over the years. Teacher-training salaries were later abolished, and student teachers were given the same range of living allowances as other tertiary students.

[3]This tribunal handles only printed materials. Films and videos are dealt with by different groups and come under separate legislation. This situation is about to change, and all forms of material will come under the one piece of legislation.

A Life-History Approach to Feminist Pedagogy

A new semester. A new course begins: "Women and Education." I have been teaching a course with this title for 10 years now. But it is never the same.

I have not yet met my students, but I already have expectations about them. I have studied the class list. There are 45 students, all undergraduates and all women. Most of them are in their final year of a Bachelor of Education (B.Ed.) program—a 4-year undergraduate degree. These students have completed 3 years of study in the Hamilton Teachers College, on the other side of the campus, combined with university courses on my side. They have completed 3 years of practical teacher training and have passed their teachers' college qualification (a diploma in teaching). The majority of the students in my class are completing their university degree by studying full-time for a year at the university or by combining this with full-time or part-time teaching. If they teach successfully, they will become certified teachers, eligible for registration. As a university teacher, my role and my course are classified as purely academic—I am not involved in the supervision, evaluation, or certification of their practical teacher training.[1]

About one third of my students are enrolled in other degree programs: bachelor of arts or social science. Some will be taking this course as part of an education major or minor for such degrees. Some are already teaching and completing their degrees part-time. Others may intend to enter 1- or 2-year teachers' college diploma courses as university graduates. Or they may have no intention of becoming teachers. They might be studying education for many other reasons: just for interest, because it fits in well with psychology or sociology or some other subject, or because it helps them to understand their own children or their voluntary work in schools. Some students are taking the course as part of the women's studies program. These students—a minority—will probably identify themselves as feminists. Some of the others will be suspicious or fearful of my generation's versions of feminism—a problem that is of concern to many of my contemporaries in Britain (Arnot, 1989), in the United States (Ellsworth, 1989; Lather, 1991), and in Australia (Yates, 1990). In this chapter, I demonstrate the use of a life-history technique that is helping me to address some of the ethical, methodological, and political questions that this situation raises.

The chapter falls into four sections. The first positions my teaching within the political and historical circumstances in which it is taking place. By means of a sketch of policymakers' changing conceptualizations of equity during the recent restructuring of New Zealand education, I identify contradictions between socialist or collectivist models of society and the New Right versions of liberal individualism. These contradictions have characterized educational debates in recent years throughout the Western[2] world but have been thrown into particularly stark relief in the New Zealand setting.

In the second section, I identify the international discourses and debates in the sociology of education—critical and feminist pedagogy—that are relevant to the approach I am developing. In particular, I focus on some implications for "Women and Education" courses of recent writing—especially feminist writing—within curriculum theory: that which discusses the audibility (or otherwise) of the voices of teachers.

The third section takes up the challenge that this literature poses to feminist teacher educators. I undertake an historical and materialist analysis of some personal texts (my own childhood paintings and school exercise books from the 1950s and 1960s) as a basis for constructing a contextualized autobiography; a narrative that grounds or positions my voices (as teacher, as author, as feminist, and as sociologist) within the biographical, historical, and cultural circumstances that have made them possible. I will use my contextualized personal narrative as a means of identifying some of the "generative themes" (Freire, 1971) that have been of most concern to the feminist educational theorists of my generation, both internationally and within my own country, New Zealand.

In the fourth and final section, I take up one such generative theme—biculturalism—as it has been defined and developed within the New Zealand feminist movement. I argue that in some of the countries of the Southern hemisphere, the juxtaposition of Western—or, perhaps more accurately, Northern—feminist and other social theories with those of indigenous peoples (such as New Zealand Maori) throws into question, or makes problematic or strange, the taken-for-granted assumptions of white feminists about gender relations, about the nature of women's oppression, and about the directions that women's liberation should take through education. Such a juxtaposition can help to "make questionable the categories that have contained feminine lives and, by so doing, . . . alter the other labels and categories that compose the taken-for-granted " (Greene, 1988, p. 57).

The contradictions within New Zealand's feminist movement between imported Anglo-American feminisms and Maori women's perspectives can make visible the colonial power relations that are inscribed in the white modes of feminist thought that have come to dominate our teaching and research in women's studies. This theme will be developed further in subsequent chapters.

Feminism and Educational Restructuring

New Zealand's fourth Labour government (1984–1990) undertook a radical restructuring of school administration. Following recommendations in a document that has become popularly known as the Picot report (Taskforce to Review Educational Administration, 1988), policymakers devolved responsibility for many major educational decisions from central government authorities to elected boards of trustees. The powers of the boards were listed in school charters, which contained detailed statements of broad objectives and specific goals. School successes and failures in achieving these were to be monitored regularly by state[3] educational review officers.

New Zealand's left-wing critics identified similarities between these reforms and those in Britain, North America, and Australia (Codd, Harker, & Nash, 1990; Lauder & Wylie, 1990; Middleton, Codd, & Jones, 1990). They claimed that New Right economic theories were having an undue influence—that the language of competitiveness, efficiency, effectiveness, and accountability was dominating the new policies. Education was being increasingly conceptualized as primarily an economic—not a social, political, or moral—activity.

However, alongside its libertarian economic policy, the Labour government had also made a strong commitment to equity. In contrast to the individualistic, free-market ideas that have been so frequently described as characterizing the educational reforms, Labour's view of equity involved conceptualizing the population as groups. Certain groups rather than individuals were seen as having been disadvantaged educationally—through no fault of their own—in the past. Compensation was owed. Schooling became a site for the bringing about of "compensatory justice" (O'Neill, 1977). "Equity objectives" were to "underpin all school activities" (Ministry of Education, 1989, p. 8).

During 1989 and 1990, the boards of trustees of all state educational institutions, including universities, were required to write their charters. In this, they were—in the words of the school charter guidelines—to ensure that their

> . . . policies and practices seek to achieve equitable educational out-
> comes for students of both sexes, for rural and urban students; for stu-
> dents from all religions, ethnic, cultural, social, family and class back-
> grounds, and for all students irrespective of their ability or disability.
> (Ministry of Education, 1989, p. 8)

With respect to gender, school boards of trustees were required to develop specific targets for bringing about equal opportunities, to provide role models along nonsexist lines, to develop a nonsexist curriculum, and to provide freedom from sexual harassment. Boards were also required to develop policies on biculturalism: "The board of trustees accepts an obligation to develop policies and practices that reflect New Zealand's dual cultural heritage" (Ministry of Education, 1989, p. 6). For teacher trainees, taking courses on Maori education or women's education could be seen as being a smart career move in this context.

However, in October 1990, New Zealand had a general election, and the National party defeated Labour by a landslide majority. During the election campaign, Lockwood Smith (now minister of education) announced: "Under National schools will be free to re-negotiate their charters if they wish to do so. They will no longer be compelled to adhere to Labour's 'Orwellian' social agenda" (New Zealand National Party, 1990b, p. 8).

During the first weeks of its administration, National announced that equity provisions in educational institutions were to be optional. In terms of National's view of society as consisting of autonomous competitive individuals, Labour's collectivist requirements to bring about social equity for disadvantaged groups were constituted as social engineering. In describing their paramount educational aim as being the creation of an enterprise culture, National conceptualized education as an economic, not a social, activity (Middleton, 1992c). During the early months of 1991, the National government attacked other women-oriented social policies: pay-equity legislation was repealed and social welfare benefits cut. The New Right had gained ascendency.

For feminist students and teachers, the political and educational climate with respect to gender was thereby suddenly and radically changed within the final few weeks of 1990. Whereas Labour, with its strong feminist membership, had heeded many feminist concerns, National rejected these as unimportant in all but the most individualist, nointerventionist, equal opportunities sense. In the 1990s, student teachers may decide that taking feminist courses could disadvantage their careers. To many of them, the possibilities and dreams of our generation of Left and feminist educators may seem neither desirable nor possible. "They" cannot see themselves or their concerns in "our" feminist theories. To put it another way, like many forms of academic knowledge, our feminist and other radical theories can constitute their generation as "other." As Ellsworth (1989) and others (Lather, 1991) have argued, such feminisms and socialisms can appear to our students as oppressive rather than as empowering.

Sociology of Education, Critical Pedagogy, and the Teacher's Voice

What does the literature of our discipline offer (in terms of pedagogical theories and strategies) to us as teachers of the sociology of women's education? Until recently, the dominant perspectives in the sociology of education construed educational institutions primarily as sites of social and cultural reproduction. Rejecting the liberal view that schools and institutions of higher education were agents of social mobility and human emancipation, many sociologists studied how such institutions constructed and reproduced the oppressive power relations of class, racism, and gender in the wider society (Bowles & Gintis, 1977; Willis, 1977). During the late 1970s to mid-1980s, many feminist sociologists of education adopted similar perspectives. Black feminists prioritized racism and colonialism as the bases of their oppression (Awatere, 1984; Davis, 1981); Marxist feminists asserted the primacy of class (Wolpe, 1978); radical feminists brought into the foreground patriarchal gender relations (Spender, 1982b); socialist feminists explored interactions and contradictions between women's experiences of class, gender, and in some cases, race (Anyon, 1983; Arnot, 1982; Jones, 1990; M. McDonald, 1980).

Theoretical debates among feminists and between feminists and sociologists of other persuasions often centered on which of these was the primary oppression—the cause, or the basis, of the others (Eisenstein, 1981; Hartmann, 1981; Segal, 1987). It became customary for feminist teacher educators to teach students about the various feminist discourses and debates and to expose them to the kinds of educational research that such liberal, radical, Marxist-, and socialist-feminist perspectives had generated. To help in this task, we produced textbooks of readings that brought together examples of studies that represented each of the dominant discourses within the discipline (Acker, 1989; Arnot & Weiner, 1987; Middleton, 1988c; Weiner & Arnot, 1987). Many of our students—themselves aspiring, preservice, or practicing teachers—found the reproduction theories profoundly depressing. If the educational institutions in which they studied and taught merely reproduced existing social and cultural inequalities, they as teachers were mere agents of oppression and preservers of privilege.

Perhaps partly as a response to the pessimism of reproduction theories, many leftist and feminist educators paid increasing attention in their writing to radical or critical pedagogy. They argued that radical teachers could make visible to students the patterns of power relations that constrained their own and others' lives and could help make audible the voices of students from oppressed and marginalized groups (Freire, 1971; Giroux, 1982, 1986). Writers such as Giroux suggested that teacher educators could teach their students life-history techniques to enable them, as prospective teachers, to develop

> . . . the concepts and methods to delve into their own biographies, to look at the sedimented history they carry around, and to learn how one's cultural capital represents a dialectical interplay between experience and history. (Giroux, 1982, p. 24)

At first, the ideas of the critical pedagogues seemed compatible with feminist uses of personal experience as a basis for generating theory. As many feminist writers (Spender, 1981; Tobias, 1978) have observed, the women who spearheaded the second wave[4] of feminism found little published writing that could help them to explain and to theorize their "sense of something wrong" (Mitchell, 1973) with their lives as females. Discussion of such experiences in consciousness-raising groups became a means of translating the personal into the political, the public, or the social. As Ellsworth (1989) has observed, "these voices have never been solely or even primarily the result of a pedagogical interaction between an individual student and a teacher" (p. 311).

Recently, some feminists have expressed reservations about the usefulness of the approaches taken by some of the critical pedagogy theorists. Although these theorists recommended teaching techniques that required students to analyze their lives, many such writers rendered invisible their own biographies. Similarly, reproduction theorists—who may themselves have come from educationally marginalized backgrounds and yet have been empowered and politicized by means of their own education—usually bracketed out in their writing, the conditions of their own intellectual production. Somewhat ironically, this was also true of some feminist postmodernist writers, whose topic was how people's positions in multiple power relations were productive of their subjectivities. Authors such as Chris Weedon (1987) positioned themselves as "masters of truth and justice" (Lather, 1991)—as knowers or revealers of the truth about others' oppressions—through addressing such questions at a purely rationalist level while omitting to mention the problem of what made their own ideas possible. As Linda Nicholson (1990b) has argued, academic feminism has shared the

> . . . failure, common to many forms of academic scholarship, to recognize the embeddedness of its own assumptions within a specific historical context. Like many other modern western scholars, feminists were not used to acknowledging that the premises from which they were working possessed a specific location. (p. 1)

A feminist pedagogy requires us as teachers to make visible to and explore with our students the aspects of our own life histories that impact on our teaching. We must analyze relationships between our individual biographies, historical events, and the broader power relations that have shaped and constrained our possibilities and perspectives as educators. As Ellsworth (1989) expressed it, "a relation between teachers/students becomes voyeuristic when the voice of the pedagogue . . . goes unexamined" (p. 312). As feminist teacher/educators, it is important for us to explore the power relations between ourselves and our students by researching the ways in which we as feminist researchers and teachers are "produced by what [we] are studying"; and by recognizing that we "can never stand outside it" (Dreyfus & Rabinow, 1986, p. 124). Our academic perspectives are viewed as historically, socially, and biographically constructed. As Dorothy Smith (1987) has expressed it, the everyday world is viewed as problematic and is studied as that in which our research and pedagogical questions originate.

Within the academic subject of education, feminist methodologies subvert traditional social science approaches, which, following the dictates of natural science, have required what Smith (1987) referred to as "the suppression of the personal" (p. 146). Because such a scientific world view is said to be detached from the social world and to provide an objective bird's-eye view of reality (Harding, 1987), researchers and teachers are required within such a tradition to "begin outside themselves" (Smith, 1987). The reliance of women's studies on the personal is antithetical to such approaches, and its apparent subjectivity is therefore frequently used by academic gatekeepers as a basis for its exclusion from or devaluation within what counts as high-status or proper academic knowledge (Acker, 1989; Bowles & Klein, 1983; Martin, 1987; Spender, 1981, 1982b). Making visible to students aspects of one's biography lays the feminist academic open to accusations—from students as well as colleagues—of being unscholarly. Developing a feminist pedagogy involves taking professional as well as personal risks.

A Teacher's Voice

In this section, I have written up what I do in the form of an oral presentation and color slides (reproduced here as black and white photographs) in an early part of my course.[5] This precedes students' directed reading of formal theories in the sociology of women's education. For the first few sessions, the students read published personal accounts of women's educational experiences. In this, I hope to avoid the partiality or fragmentation of experience that comes about when the various feminist grand narratives (Marxism, radical feminism, and so on) dominate personal accounts. For example, because of its neo-Marxist orientation, the literature of critical pedagogy has often designated class as the primary oppressive social relation and rendered invisible or marginal people's experiences of other power relations. As Valerie Walkerdine and Helen Lucey (1989) have observed, "It is only the left and the women's movement that splits and fragments our history this way, as though we did not live our class, our gender and our race simultaneously" (p. 206).

In this respect, my approach is compatible with those postmodernist feminisms that focus on peoples' simultaneous positionings in multiple power relations and on the personal experiences of contradiction that such multiple positionings bring about (Arnot, 1989; Henriques, Hollway, Urwin, Venn, & Walkerdine, 1984; Walkerdine & Lucey, 1989).

Theoretical Beginnings

When I was a child growing up in small-town rural New Zealand, I knew of few New Zealand writers, intellectuals, or artists. At the age of 13, I read *Spinster* by Sylvia Ashton-Warner (1958). Sylvia, I gathered, was the subject of much adult disapproval. Although she was a married woman with a "good" husband, she worked and "neglected" her husband and children. A selfish woman. She also drank.[6] And, I suspected from the hushed innuendoes when her name was mentioned, she was associated with immorality (her novels did not condemn sex outside marriage). Inevitably, the book captivated me and stimulated fantasies of imaginary futures. Like Sylvia herself and like the central characters in her novels, I loved to write, to paint, and to play the piano. I dreamed of becoming an artist and escaping to the enchantment of big and glittering cities. Her books portrayed aspects of Maori life—which then seemed to me romantic but which now appear condescending. But I knew of Maori life only through its portrayal in my book, *Maoriland Fairy Tales,* and the stories told to me by the local district nurse,[7] a neighbor, about the Maori children who lived up the valley in distant bush-clad hills.

Like so many bright, rural girls from unpropertied families without means, Sylvia had had to earn her living through teaching. But rather than give up her art, she turned teaching itself into an art form. Many rural girls wanted to be artists—writers, painters, musicians, actors, or dancers—but knew that instead they would have to go teaching or nursing. Sylvia seemed to have it all. "Asylums," she wrote, "are full of artists who failed to say the things they must and famous tombs are full of those who did" (Ashton-Warner, 1960, p. 169). She inspired in me and in many of my contemporaries a sense of *possibility* in realizing our fantasies and dreams.

Today, I would regard Ashton-Warner's work as my introduction to feminist pedagogy, although Ashton-Warner would not have used the term "feminist" to describe herself. Like contemporary feminist educators and researchers, she urged that we start with the personal—that we explore our native imagery.

From Native Imagery to Feminist Scholarship

I begin with images from some of the school exercise books and paintings that I produced in the late 1950s and early 1960s during my schooling in New Zealand, in a rural primary school and a state girls' secondary school in a provincial town. These give access to my native imagery—to my interpretations of the world in which I grew up and to my dreams, wishes, and fantasies.

They are of interest in this text not as personal memorabilia but as examples of ways in which the grand narratives and historical events of my childhood and adolescence contributed to the development of my adult perspective as a feminist educator. More broadly, they identify several of the generative themes of the academic women's studies created by my post–World War II generation of Pakeha academic feminists.

Figure 1.1

Colonialism and Racism.   The first paintings illustrate my positioning in the grand narrative of colonialism as reproduced in my reading of what the social studies curriculum of the late 1950s was about (McGeorge, 1981). Figure 1.1 shows the title page of an 11-year-old rural schoolgirls' social studies exercise book in her first-form year[8] in 1959. The "good ship social studies" bears, in descending order, the signs of the Christian cross, the British crown, and the Union Jack—God, king, and country. On the beach stand "hostile natives"—black men in grass skirts brandishing spears. What counted as school knowledge (the social studies curriculum) rendered legitimate this way of knowing colonization. Indigenous peoples were constituted as "other."

We learned about the history of exploration—how Europe "discovered" and "took possession" of much of the rest of the world (Figure 1.2). The poems we studied reinforced the ideology of our glorious empire and male battles. We learned that New Zealand had been part of this process. However, during the years of my schooling—the 1950s and early 1960s—it was believed that modern New Zealand was a truly egalitarian society. We were taught that equal rights and opportunities for Maori and Pakeha had been guaranteed in 1840 with the signing of the Treaty of Waitangi by Maori chiefs and the colonial government (McGeorge, 1981).

At primary school, we never questioned the rightness of colonialism. However, during our secondary schooling, our glorious empire was to collapse. These momentous changes led many of my generation to question taken-for-granted ideas about the "nature" of races and the legitimacy of Pakeha domination.

It has proved very useful to discuss in classes these 1950s images of a child's interpretation of colonial relations. This was particularly true in 1990, for this marked the sesquicentenary of the signing of the treaty. Unlike Australia, which had marked its bicentenary with a huge celebration, New Zealand commemorated rather than celebrated its anniversary. For many Maori, as for Australian Aborigines, the birth of the colonial state was not cause for celebration. The 1980s had seen strong protests by Maori that the treaty had not been honored and that they had been dispossessed of their lands, forests, and fisheries. The treaty became one of New Zealand's most contested political issues (Orange, 1989). Today, its clauses are interpreted as including Maori rights to education in the Maori language and to cultural autonomy.

The text of my exercise book (Figure 1.3) is not accurate (all the chiefs did not sign it, for example). In New Zealand university education and women's studies courses, as in other educational and feminist settings, the treaty has been a central issue of debate. Issues of Maori-Pakeha relations have become increasingly prominent in New Zealand Pakeha feminist theory and in women's studies courses. Some of the contradictions this raises will be addressed in a later section of this chapter.

Maori people make up about 10% of the total New Zealand population. The term "biculturalism" in the New Zealand setting usually refers to relations between Maori and Pakeha. The term is used in various senses. In its less radical sense, it refers to bicultural individuals (e.g., Pakeha attempt-

Admirals All

Effingham, Grenville, Raleigh, Drake,
Here's to the bold and free!
Benbow, Collingwood, Baron, Blake,
Hail to the Kings of the Sea!
Admirals all, for England's sake,
Honour be yours and fame!
And happy, as long as waves shall break,
To Nelson's peerless name.

Drake nor devil or Spaniard feared,
Their cities he put to the sack,
He singed (ha) his Catholic Majesty's beard,
And harried his ships to the wrook.
He was playing at Plymouth, a rubber of bowls
When the great Amada came,
But he said, "They must wait their turn, good souls,"
And he stooped and finished the game

Splinters were flying above, below,
When Nelson sailed the Sound
"Mark you, I wouldn't be elsewhere now,"
Said he, "for a thousand pound!"
The Admiral's signal bade him fly
But he wickedly wagged his head,
He clapped the glass to his sightless eye
And, "I'm damned if I see it," he said.

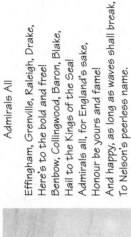

Figure 1.2

1. The Maoris recognized Queen Victoria as their Queen
2. The Maoris could sell their land only to the Queen, (the government!)
3. The Maoris were promised the Queen's protection, and the rights and privileges of a British Subject.

The treaty could not come into force until all the chiefs had signed it and it took several months for this to be done.

Figure 1.3

ing to learn Maori language and customs). In its more radical sense, it refers to the restructuring of major social institutions (schools, hospitals, social welfare, justice, and so on) according to Maori values. Separatist institutions—controlled by Maori and often funded with public money—are also seen as a way of achieving a bicultural society. A more extreme view is one that argues that Pakeha are visitors *(manuhiri)* on Maori land (Awatere, 1984). Throughout this book, numerous examples are given of bicultural ideas and strategies in education—especially in chapters 2, 4, and 6.

Gender, Work, and Female Sexuality.   The next set of pictures gives access to the possibilities and constraints experienced by Pakeha rural girls of that time and place. The paintings construct images of genderedness in work and leisure activities. In these childhood impressions of everyday life in a rural town in the 1950s, clear gender relations are apparent in the work force. Although the details in the paintings suggest a childhood fascination with machinery, the images I presented were of a *gender-segregated work force.* Access to certain kinds of technical knowledge and occupations was not at that time seen as suitable for girls.

For example, Figure 1.4 shows an 8-year-old girl's impressions of a small-town garage (drawn from memory) that suggest a great fascination with machines and technology. As the daughter of a stock agent (a person who buys and sells livestock on behalf of farmers), I was around farms and machinery a great deal. However, the painting suggests, by the absence of women figures, that the garage was a man's domain.

Figure 1.4

The local agricultural and pastoral show (equivalent to an American county fair) was a highlight of the country child's year (see Figure 1.5). Again, my fascination with machinery is evident, but the person looking at the machines is male. In the foreground is a woman on a horse show, jumping. As young girls, many of us read books by Pat Smythe, the British Olympic equestrienne, who wrote novels about girls our age. Her central female characters possessed great physical courage. Fantasies about sporting success were acceptable for New Zealand girls. Sports, however, were in general segregated. Competitive horse riding—show jumping, one-day events, dressage—were a rare exception and provided girls with models of equality between the genders.

The following two paintings were done at secondary school. To be able to take the academic subjects that had high status at the time (Latin and French), I had to leave home and board at a state girls' school in a nearby provincial city. During this time in adolescence, sexuality became an important concern. Sexuality and intellectuality were often constituted as being in conflict or contradiction (Middleton, 1987b). This is evident in Figure 1.6, a painting done when I was a junior at the boarding hostel.

Figure 1.5

"Seniors swotting" (cramming for exams) shows girls reading "love comics," setting one another's hair in rollers, and perfecting their suntans.

We were prepared for heterosexual coupledom through regular school dances. In Figure 1.7, only heterosexual couples are dancing. At school, our sexuality was closely regulated and monitored (Foucault, 1980a): We were taught very specific modes of conduct and of dress. Although I was a keen pop pianist, it is evident from the painting and from documented histories that dance bands were a male preserve. Being part of a rock band was closed to girls. And only European classical music—by long-dead, white, male composers—was included in the formal school curriculum. Black music—jazz or Maori music—was relegated to the margins in our schooling.

As children of the post–World War II baby boom, we were members of the first generation to be *promised* equality of opportunity in education. Children of both sexes, all races, and all classes were promised equal opportunities to what the policymakers had described as "a free education of the kind for which he is best fitted and to the fullest extent of his powers" (Beeby, 1986, p. xxxii). The promise was one of meritocracy. However, at the same time, it was believed that the morality, stability, and cohesion of

Figure 1.6

society rested on women's domesticity. Girls' experiences, then, were con-tradictory. On one hand, within the discourse of liberalism, we were equal to—the same—as men. On the other, within the discourse of patriarchy, we were expected to become domestically feminine. Our intellectuality and our feminine heterosexuality were construed as contradictory.

Dreams, Wishes, and Fantasies.   My fantasy life was centered on escape to the city. Many rural daughters of the petit bourgeoisie in the 1960s joined the rural-urban drift in search of higher education, work, or glamour. As a young child, I had adored ballet, theater, and other activities I associated with the city. My mother had been brought up in a city and had a love of urban culture. As a primary school child, I was therefore taken to ballets, galleries, and concerts (Figure 1.8). I was given bourgeois intellectual "cul-tural capital" (Bourdieu, 1971a, 1971b).

   Although being a professional full-time artist was not financially possi-ble for women like me, escape to the city was made possible by the educa-tional provisions of the first Labour government. Academic girls could

Figure 1.7

attend institutions of higher education on salaries if they were prepared to commit themselves to nursing or teaching. I went for teaching because I wanted to go to the university. My image of this had been shaped at secondary school through women like my French teacher, through whom I had discovered existentialism, beatniks, and the Left Bank. The painting in Figure 1.9 was done in my first year at Victoria University. "The cafe" is a place for intellectual debate rather than eating!

Pedagogical Applications

As a middle-aged, middle-class, white, feminist teacher, I am aware of my "otherness" to many of the students to whom I am presenting this material—younger students, Maori students, students from overseas, and working-class students beginning university study at a mature age. As Ellsworth (1989) has observed, "There are things that I as a professor could *never know* about the experiences, oppressions and understandings of other participants in the class" (p. 310).

Figure 1.8

For example, as a white woman, I cannot know directly what it means to experience racism as a brown or black woman. At this early stage of the course, the students read life histories of other women of my age group whose experiences have differed from mine. My own personal account, together with published life histories, are used to orient my students to a research assignment on women's educational life histories. This assignment requires each student to interview two women, one of whom is to be of the post–World War II generation (aged in her late 30s or early 40s) and the other of whom is to be either about 20 years older or 20 years younger. The students are to compare and contrast the two women's experiences of education, taking into account not only their individual biographies but also the historical events, educational policies and provisions, and relevant power relations (e.g., race, class, gender, and town/country) characteristic of that time and place. In C. Wright Mills' (1959) terms, the focus of the assignment is simultaneously on "biography, history and social structure."

I use my own generation as a reference point for several reasons. First, today's remnants of the kinds of collectivism or socialism that had influ-

Figure 1.9

enced the educational policies and provisions of the postwar era are coming under attack from the New Right of the 1980s and 1990s, and an understanding of these helps students to come to terms with present-day educational debates. Second, many of my mature students are themselves of this age group, and many of my younger students have parents of the postwar generation. In fact, many of the students choose to interview their mothers or their grandmothers for this assignment.

Third, studying the experiences of other women of my age group gives students a counterbalance to my life history—a means of testing the voice of the pedagogue. I tell the students that I am sharing with them my understanding of my own theoretical origins—developing a sociological analysis of my own sociological position as a feminist educator.

Fourth, it was the educational experiences of our generation that provided the momentum for the second wave of feminism as a mass social movement. If students are to understand feminist educational theories, it is important that they understand the educational conditions and wider social circumstances of their production. By means of further case studies (women's autobiographies, biographies, and sociological life-history research), I contextualize the origins of my own feminism historically, generationally, and in terms of my social class origins.

Using material such that which will be summarized in Chapter 4, I show how, at the time, generous incentives from a benevolent welfare state enabled many of my generation and class—unlike our parents or previous generations—to attend both secondary schools and institutions of higher education. Although promised equal opportunities that would be limited only on grounds of merit or ability, many were to experience marginality or alienation from the culture of the academic. As rural, as Maori, as working class, as female—as combinations of all or some of these—many experienced a distancing and an exclusion from what counted as advanced educational knowledge. We lacked some of the academic cultural capital of the urban bourgeoisie. We sensed "something wrong" (Mitchell, 1973)—something unfair—about the education we were receiving.

In the late 1960s, some gained access to radical ideas—about class, about race, about gender, and about sexual orientation—through academic studies or through radical social movements of the times. Within these movements, people's personal experiences of discrimination or oppression were translated from mere personal problems into broader public or political issues (Mills, 1959). The sense of discomfort that such people felt made change seem desirable. The social theories to which we gained access and the security of such times of economic prosperity and full employment made such change also seem possible.

Fifth, I offer aspects of my educational life history as an example of a technique that students might like to explore with respect to their own lives. I tell them that if they wish, they can use themselves or each other as case studies for the essay. But I do not require them to do this because I respect their right to privacy. I do not wish to pry—to engage in monitoring and surveillance of their private lives (Foucault, 1980a). I do not wish to be what Ellsworth (1989) termed a pedagogical "voyeur."

However, immediately after my session on my schooling, I run one class based on the students' official personal texts—photographs, school reports, and exercise books—an archaeology of our schooling. As official records, these depersonalize, objectify, and make public aspects of personal biographies. Because I have used such texts as part of my own biographical narrative—made aspects of my schooling visible to them—the students do not seem shy about doing this. They choose whether to provide texts and what to provide. We discuss these documents in small groups whose membership is determined by the ages of the students. This enables the younger students (aged 19 or 20) to speak freely—many in previous years had felt intimidated by what they saw as the greater experience of the mature students. As a woman in her early 40s, I found that my own life history and my writing about the radicalization of postwar feminist teachers spoke to the mature students but alienated some of the younger students—construed them as "other." I have tried to provide for them a space in which my generation's analysis and experience do not silence or distort theirs. Within the groups, the students discuss how their educations were similar to and different from one another's. We then report back and bring together the experiences and documents from the different generations. This becomes a basis— a grounding for our theorizing during the course.

In our feminist pedagogy, as Dorothy Smith (1987) has argued with respect to sociology, "Opening an inquiry from the standpoint of women means accepting our ineluctable embeddedness in the same world as is the object of our inquiry" (p. 127).

Feminist Educational Theorizing in the 1990s: A New Zealand View

An understanding of our own and other women's life histories involves going beyond the personal. It requires that we also make accessible to our students the various theoretical tools that are available to feminists and to sociologists. It is important that such teaching does not take the form of an initiation into feminist theory as a disembodied form of knowledge. We must devise ways of teaching students about the various feminist perspectives in ways that focus them on students' everyday personal, intellectual, and political dilemmas. I will develop this theme further in chapter 2. Here, I shall illustrate this theme with one example: the question of biculturalism in the New Zealand feminist classroom.

As will be discussed in the next chapter, the sociological and other disciplinary theories available to social scientists have been seen to conceptualize as "other" all people who are not middle-class white men (Greene, 1978; Martin, 1987; D. Smith, 1987). Similarly, some Western feminist theories have rendered invisible or marginal women who are not of the dominant class, race, culture, sexual orientation, generation, and so on. In emphasizing sisterhood—the shared nature of women's experiences— some radical feminist discourses neglected or underemphasized our differences. Socialist feminists have sought materialist explanations of differences between groups of women—those of different classes and, to a lesser extent, ethnicities and cultures. Postmodernists emphasize the multiple

and contradictory power relations experienced by individual human subjects—"the fractured identities modern life creates" (Harding, 1987, p. 28).

However, a focus on multiple subjectivities does not preclude single-
issue analyses that bring into the foreground or highlight racism or class. By
means of a brief discussion of biculturalism, feminism, and education in
New Zealand, I shall argue, like Lyn Yates (1988) that

> we should not always defer to the call to look at "class, sex and race" in
> interaction. Studies of the interaction of these issues are needed, but there
> is a need also to attempt to isolate issues and to attempt to theorize each as
> an issue in its own right. (p. 41)

In the 1970s and 1980s, those of us who were researching, writing,
and teaching in New Zealand about women's lives found little published
local feminist analysis to build on. We therefore imported our feminist
grand theories and fitted our analyses into the Northern typology of feminisms: liberal, classical Marxist, radical feminist, socialist, and black and
Third World feminisms (Jaggar & Struhl, 1978). However, these theories—developed in other contexts—did not always fit our local circumstances. For example, British Marxist- and socialist-feminist perspectives
were derived from the experiences of working-class women in a country
with a vast urban industrial proletariat. The lives of New Zealand rural
women, for example, were difficult to conceptualize from within this perspective. Some Maori women saw Marxism as yet another European discourse that marginalized or rendered invisible their experience of
racial/colonial oppression (Awatere, 1984). Similarly, the Northern hemisphere's liberal and radical feminist analyses were in many ways alien to
New Zealanders' everyday realities. For example, American liberal feminist portrayals of girls' socialization into a sex-role stereotype of simper-
ing, passive, suburban femininity (Friedan, 1963) did not describe the
reality of the boisterous, tomboyish New Zealand girl. Those from
marginalized groups within the feminist movement felt alienated from
feminist perspectives.

Some Maori women who had grown up within their tribal traditions
argued that white women's analyses of female gender roles as oppressive
and of women as socialized for submissiveness did not articulate their experiences. For example, writing about her own extended family, Rangimarie
Rose Pere (1983) stated:

> My Maori female forebears, prior to the introduction of Christianity, and
> the "original sin of Eve", were extremely liberated as compared to my

English tupuna [ancestors]. With the exception of slaves (male and female), the women were never regarded as chattels or possessions; they retained their own names on marriage. Retaining their own identity and whakapapa (genealogy) was of the utmost importance and children could identify with the kinship group of either or both parents. (p. 9)

Several Maori women who identify themselves as feminists have written of the multiple marginalities and contradictions they experience within Maori and Pakeha feminist and nonfeminist settings: as Maori, as Maori women, as feminist women, and as Maori feminists (Irwin, 1989, 1992a; Te Awekotuku, 1984, 1988, 1992).

Within the New Zealand feminist movement, contradictions between Western feminism, Maori protocol, and bicultural politics are central dilemmas. During the 1980s, it became increasingly customary for New Zealand educational and feminist gatherings to assume some degree of biculturalism in their procedures. For some Maori ceremonial protocols to take place, both genders must be present to play their differentiated parts in the ritual. This means that—in contrast to the gender separatism (the women-only convention) of Western feminist gatherings—men must be present. In certain communities or tribal groups, only men may speak on the *marae* (the tribal gathering place where visitors are received and formally welcomed) (Irwin, 1992b; Papakura, 1983; Pere, 1983; L. Smith, 1992). In some schools, Maori women who are principals choose to follow their tribal traditions by having men speak on their behalf in ritual greeting situations. In such settings, Western feminism and antiracism/biculturalism come into conflict.

New Zealand Pakeha feminists have, in the main, accepted this cultural difference and view issues such as who should speak on the marae as a matter for Maori women and men to resolve. In this, Pakeha feminists have come to accept that Western feminisms—like other modes of Western thought—can embody imperialist power relations.

In New Zealand education, biculturalism is a strongly contested issue. Theories of pluralism or multiculturalism in state schools are rejected by many Maori and by some Pakeha New Zealanders on the grounds that because the object of these is to combat Pakeha ignorance and racism, they benefit Pakeha rather than Maori students and do little, if anything, to alleviate the disenchantment, unemployment, and imprisonment of Maori youth (Walker, 1985). Viewing previous forms of public schooling as reproductive of their oppression, many Maori are arguing for separate, Maori-controlled, state-funded educational institutions. These are seen as a means of reviving Maori language, protecting cultural autonomy, and developing curricula that teach tribal knowledge and approach the academic disciplines from Maori perspectives (Awatere, 1984; Irwin, 1990; Smith & Smith, 1990; Walker, 1985).

It is Maori educational movements rather than Western-style feminist activities that many Maori women educators have chosen as their priorities. The *kohanga reo* (Maori-language preschools) have been largely an initiative of Maori women. They have been an outstanding success, not only in the teaching of Maori language to preschool children but also in their empowering and politicization of Maori adults—mainly women (Irwin, 1990). Maori parents have been able to exert considerable pressure on state primary schools to provide bilingual or total-immersion Maori-language classes for children coming through from kohanga reo. However, racism and opposition in some communities make integrated versions of biculturalism difficult (Middleton & Oliver, 1990). Separate Maori-language schools *(kura kaupapa Maori)* are preferred by many Maori parents (Smith & Smith, 1990). Maori withdrawal from the Pakeha educational system and the establishment of separate Maori educational systems are the project of many Maori women and men in the 1990s.

Similar trends are evident in university programs, including women's studies. University women's studies programs have been, in the main, run by Pakeha women and dominated by Anglo-American feminist theories. Women associated with such programs are struggling with ways of making them bicultural. One strategy that has been discussed on some campuses is the appointment of Maori women to tenured positions within women's studies programs. Such appointees would teach courses in Maori women's studies and would contribute Maori perspectives to more general core theory courses. Such proposals have been regarded with suspicion by some Maori academic women and men on the grounds that Maori women's studies courses should be based in Maori departments. To employ, for example, one Maori woman academic within a Pakeha-dominated women's studies center would be to isolate her, to constitute her as individual, and to sever her from the Maori academic community that could provide her with a collectivist epistemological base. Such appointments, it has been argued, would be of more benefit to Pakeha than to Maori women. At present, there are discussions about the possibilities of designing structures that are appropriate to the educational requirements of both groups. Some argue that in our university women's studies programs, as in New Zealand education more generally, both separatism and bicultural forms of intellectual encounter are necessary. Perhaps in this respect, New Zealand women will be able to develop theoretical positions that contribute something unique to the international debates within the discipline.

Conclusion

Many students may find that feminist courses, like those in other disciplines, comprise

> practices of thinking and writing . . . that convert what people experience in their everyday/everynight world into forms of knowledge in which people as subjects disappear and in which their perspectives on their own experiences are transformed and subdued. (D. Smith, 1990, p. 4)

The use of life-history methods as pedagogical techniques can help teachers and students to understand the circumstances of one another's possibilities. To develop pedagogies that are authentic to our personal and collective histories, we must explore the ideas and imagery that are indigenous to our circumstances—geographical, cultural, historical and material, and generational. This provides teachers and students with ways of understanding how our own subjectivities have been constituted and with ways of making visible the alienations that can result from interpretations of our personal and collective histories purely through the eyes of theorists whose perspectives have arisen elsewhere.

Notes

[1]As I revise this for publication, Hamilton Teachers' College and the University of Waikato are amalgamating. This will break down the theory/practice split that has characterized New Zealand teacher education and will break down the my side/their side duality of the B.Ed. degree. The National government recently announced that teacher registration is to be made voluntary. However, the students in my 1991 class—the subjects of this analysis—come under the earlier regulations. Boards of trustees will be permitted to employ unregistered and unqualified teachers. Centrally determined salary scales and conditions of employment are also under threat (Gordon, 1991).

[2]The term "Western" is problematic for the nations of the Southern hemisphere. The former Eastern Bloc nations and what Europeans have termed the Far East or the Orient are to the west of New Zealand. The English language is imbued with geographical imperialism.

[3]New Zealand does not have a federal system of government. We use the term "state" to refer to all government agencies. While Americans speak of public schools, New Zealanders use the term "state" schools.

[4]The first wave of feminism is the mass movement that organized in the 19th century around issues such as suffrage. The second wave is the late 20th-century movement.

[5]The autobiographical material in this section was originally compiled for a seminar presentation, "A day with Maxine Greene," held at the Stout Research Centre, Victoria University of Wellington, in 1989. A modified version of the talk and slide presentation is published in du Plessis, Bunkle, Irwin, Laurie, & Middleton (1992). I would like to thank Anne French of Oxford, New Zealand for permission to revise and publish this material in the present volume.

[6]For studies of gender and alcohol in New Zealand, see Phillips (1987) and Park (1991).

[7]District nurses are employed by the New Zealand Department of Health and provide health care to the needy in rural areas.

[8]New Zealand schools do not use the term "grades" in the sense of classification of students by age level. In primary shoools, what Americans call "grades" are called "primers" (ages 5-7) and "standards" (ages 8-10). The term "forms" refers to the grades of intermediate (junior high) and high school classes. Form one is the first year of junior high.

two

The Sociology of Women's Education as Discourse

*I*n 1980, my first year of employment as an academic, I proposed my new course, "Women and education." I was the first and only woman academic staff member in my university's education department. At first, my male colleagues expressed grave reservations about my proposal. Some argued that their courses already covered women's issues through lectures on stereotyping. Others were worried that a narrow focus on women's issues would be damaging for me professionally. Their most prevalent concern, however, was that there was too little content on which to base my curriculum. There was no sound theoretical or disciplinary base.

Accordingly, I set about reviewing the literature to prove that there was indeed a discipline—a set of theories, concepts, and debates—into which my students, like those in other disciplines, could be initiated (Hirst, 1975). At the same time as I was developing this curriculum, I was struggling to write a proposal for a doctoral thesis on feminist teachers (chapters 3 and 4). To satisfy the relevant committee, I had to position my research questions within an acceptable body of theory. My literature review would serve a dual purpose: I was simultaneously positioned as an academic staff member and as a doctoral student. I would have to begin my teaching and my research in a conventionally academic manner. I would have to draw a map of knowledge and teach my students how to read this map. This would serve as a navigation guide for my own and my students' inquiries.

The education major of which my course would become a part was structured according to requirements that students cover courses in the history, philosophy, psychology, and sociology of education. There was little space for interdisciplinary courses or for courses that were based on alternative conceptual frameworks (such as feminist theory) and that were not considered mainstream. To make the course available to as many students as possible, I had to classify it as a disciplinary course. It was institutional politics as much as epistemological considerations (Goodson, 1988) that led to its development as a course in the sociology of women's education rather than as a women and education course.[1]

To gain institutional acceptance and professional legitimacy for the course, I would have to follow academic conventions. For, as Dorothy Smith (1979) has argued:

> The canons of science as a constitutional practice require the suppression of the personal. . . . We begin from a position in the discourse as an ongoing process of formally organised interchange. We begin from a position within a determinate conceptual framework which is identified with the discipline . . . and by virtue of our training and of what it means to do work in our discipline we begin from outside ourselves, to locate problematics organised by the sociological, the psychological, the historical discourse. (p. 146)

I begin this chapter by retracing the processes of drawing maps of the sociology of women's education—creating curriculum content for a new discipline—during the early 1980s. Second, I discuss how my location in New Zealand—both inside and outside the Anglo-American discourses that dominated the new discipline—exposed the constructedness of such typologies and the broader colonial power relations in which we, as international academics, participate. I use this experience to introduce some recent postmodernist ideas about academic knowledge and power. I then develop this theme further by means of an exploration of the ways that my own schooling and that of other post–World War II feminist sociologists of education were structured by the gendered sociological theories of the 1950s and 1960s. My overall aim in this chapter is to construct a theoretical framework and to sketch a historical setting for the life-history narratives in the chapters that follow.

Mapping the Field

The term "sociology of women's education" was coined by Madeleine Arnot (then writing as Madeleine McDonald, 1980) to refer to feminist scholarship within the sociology of education.[2] As an academic subject, it has developed since the mid-1970s, when the ideas of the second wave of feminism were increasingly influencing the thinking of many academic women. From our dual location as feminists and as sociologists, we developed critiques of male-centered (or androcentric) sociology, engaged with one another in feminist theoretical debates, and began to develop new methodologies. As we engaged in research and developed courses in the subject, we found it necessary to bring together the literatures of the sociology of education and of women's studies.

Such reviews of the international literature were being developed simultaneously within various countries—by feminist sociologists and curriculum theorists[3] who were often working in isolation or in small networks and who had not yet discovered one another's writing. For example, during the late 1970s and through the 1980s, such work was being done in Australia (Kenway, 1990; Taylor, 1984; Yates, 1987); in Britain (Acker, 1981; Arnot, 1981; David, 1980; M. McDonald, 1980); in Canada (Eichler, 1980; Gaskell, McLaren, & Novogrodsky, 1989; D. Smith, 1974, 1979); in New Zealand (Jones, 1990; G. McDonald, 1980; Middleton, 1982, 1984, 1988b); and in the United States (Anyon, 1983; Grumet, 1988; Lather, 1991; Lesko, 1988; Weiler, 1988). Through our published writings and through feminist, sociological, and educational research conferences, we became aware of one another's work. From within our various scattered insularities, we had produced overviews of the field that displayed a great deal of congruence.

Methodologically, we usually approached our task as one of "marrying" (Hartmann, 1981), or bringing together, two fields of study: sociology of education (and/or curriculum theory) and feminist theory. Similarities were perceived between the theoretical divisions and debates that were commonly described as characteristic of sociology of education (Apple, 1979; Giroux, 1982; Lawton, 1975) and those that feminists had identified within academic and grassroots women's studies (Eisenstein, 1981; Jaggar & Struhl, 1978; Segal, 1987). With minor variations in categorizations and terminology, we saw the sociology of women's education as characterized by three or four major sets of theoretical perspectives.

During the 1950s and 1960s—before feminism had reemerged as a mass social movement—educational sociologists were primarily concerned with measuring the extent to which postwar egalitarian visions of equality of opportunity were being achieved. British researchers had focused on the underachievement of working-class children, and American researchers had focused on that of black and Hispanic students. Theories of cultural deprivation or disadvantage dominated the sociological literature; such children, it was argued, failed at school largely because of deficits in their socialization (Keddie, 1973).

Liberal feminists (Byrne, 1975) extended this analysis to apply to girls and women. They applied existing sociological concepts of disadvantage to women's socialization (Eichler, 1980). Women were seen as disadvantaged by our socialization—by sex-role stereotyping—and as in need of measures of compensatory education and affirmative action. Liberal feminism is centered on women's individual rights and opportunities. Its political aim is the equitable distribution of the genders across the various divisions of labor and throughout existing social hierarchies. Because liberal feminism did not overtly challenge conventional assumptions or research methodologies, those espousing or using[4] liberal feminist ideas readily entered what Dorothy Smith (1990) has referred to as "the governing mode of our kind of society" (p. 17). Liberal feminist strategies of adding women into conventional sociological research and educational policy agendas earned government funding in many countries and facilitated the development of official equal opportunities projects.

A second major set of theoretical tendencies integrated concepts and methods from the interpretive[5] sociologies with the analyses and politics of radical feminists. The interpretive perspectives became very influential in educational sociology during the early 1970s—when many of my generation of feminist academics were university students or were beginning our careers. Leading sociologists of education were questioning assumptions such as deprivation theory. They argued that sociologists should shift their focus from viewing children and their communities as the problem. Instead, they should problematize education—for example, what counted as school knowledge and how it had come to be provided (Young, 1971). How, they asked, did academic knowledge connect with students' everyday or commonsense knowledge? Aiming to depict the world from the point of view of those studied, sociologists increasingly employed the kinds of qualitative methods—such as ethnography—used by anthropologists (Keddie, 1973). Interpretive perspectives focused on the socially constructed nature of everyday life and on the discontinuities experienced by the marginalized between their commonsense realities and the academic knowledge valued in educational institutions.

The various theories and methodologies that characterized this approach were useful to radical feminists. Rejecting liberal feminist analyses of women as the problem, as disadvantaged, or as in some way deficient, radical feminists sought to understand and celebrate women's differences from men (Gilligan, 1982; Grumet, 1988; Spender, 1982a, 1983). The curriculum—what had come to count as academic knowledge—was of particular concern: the rediscovery and study of lost works by women, the design of women-centered curricula, and the valuing of "women's ways of knowing" (Belenky, Clinchy, Goldberger, & Tarrule, 1986; Grumet, 1988; Spender, 1982a). Although they found interpretive sociology useful, such writers were critical of the gender blindness of many of the male sociologists of education who worked within such traditions; these male sociologists had not included gender in their analyses or had looked at and represented women and girls through men's eyes (Clarricoates, 1976; Greene, 1978; Spender, 1982b).

Some sociologists developed more radical analyses. They argued that although the interpretive sociologies provided rich descriptive data of students' and teachers' lives in schools, they could not explain why various forms of inequality continued to exist. They ignored questions of power (Sharp & Green, 1975). The inequalities between pupils needed to be contextualized in and explained by an analysis of the power relations between groups in the wider society. Neo-Marxists argued that such inequalities needed to be explained by an analysis of class relations. The hierarchical structures of schools (Bowles & Gintis, 1977) and their middle-class cultural biases (Willis, 1977) served to reproduce the class relations of capitalism. Many feminists were strongly influenced by Marxist arguments. However, some feminists rejected Marxism in favor of arguments that were centered on questions of *gender* and power. Such radical feminists had found that interpretive sociologists' focus on consciousness—people's interpretations of the world—could not explain men's violence (physical, psychological, and ideological) against women.

Although the more revolutionary feminist theories differed according to whether they were grounded in Marxist or in radical feminist assumptions, they shared a rejection of the individualism of liberal approaches that were seen as merely "adding women in" (Yates, 1987) to hierarchies that were inherently inequitable. Marxist feminists researched the ways in which women's education served to reproduce the sexual division of labor and the class differences between women (Deem, 1978; Wolpe, 1978). Radical feminists, emphasizing women's oppression by men, studied how schooling reproduced women's sexual subordination and how patriarchal curricula served to alienate us from our own experience (Spender, 1983). Marxist feminists criticized radical feminists' treatment of women as a homogeneous category and brought into the foreground the class differences between women. Radical feminists, who emphasized issues such as male sexual violence, accused Marxists of ignoring or underemphasizing patriarchal power (Lees, 1986; Mahony, 1985).

Socialist feminism emerged as a drawing together of these positions as we struggled to integrate the increasingly dominant neo-Marxist ideas in sociology with our feminist concerns. Students and teachers were studied as simultaneously and contradictorily positioned within the social relations of class and gender (Anyon, 1983; Arnot, 1981; David, 1980; Jones, 1990; Kenway, 1990; Lesko, 1988; McRobbie, 1980; Middleton, 1985a, 1985b, 1987b; Taylor, 1984; Weiler, 1988; Yates, 1987). Socialist feminists developed critiques of the ways many male neo-Marxists had rendered women and girls invisible and marginal or had depicted us only through the eyes of men and boys—as, for example, in ethnographies that represented girls as "birds, scrubbers, and hangers on" (Llewellyn, 1980, p. 42).

These were the major theoretical tendencies that sociologists of women's education identified in the typologies written during the early to mid-1980s. Many such typologies assumed this form, progressed through a similar sequence, and were written from within a socialist-feminist problematic. By mapping our field in this way, we conceptualized the sociology of women's education as a conventional academic discipline (Acker, 1981; Arnot, 1981; Arnot & Weiner, 1987; Middleton, 1987b; Yates, 1987). With respect to our teaching in "Women and Education" courses, we had produced curriculum content—a map of the sociology of women's education— that could be taught as received knowledge. It was necessary for us to do this to gain approval for our courses within the university system. As Chris Weedon (1987) has explained it, "Liberal, radical and socialist feminist theories developed in the context of existing accounts of social relations" (p. 19).

Although many have disagreed with the ways that the various typologies and taxonomies have classified feminist sociological and educational theories, some have attacked the very idea of a taxonomy (Haraway, 1990a, 1990b; Hutcheon, 1989; Lather, 1991; Weedon, 1987). First, by dividing feminism into neat categories, taxonomies imply that feminists are theoretically monogamous, whereas most of us are theoretically promiscuous, or pluralist. Second, the ordering of the categories—from liberalism through radical feminism to socialist feminism—implies a chronology or evolution when, in fact, the various perspectives have coexisted and interacted. Third, there were feminisms that did not fall into these categories; by constructing an official list, the taxonomies served to "police deviations" (Haraway, 1990a, p. 198). As Patti Lather has argued (1991): "To put into categories is an act of power" (p. 125).

Fourth, in accordance with the conventions of Western academic rationality, most typologies were constructed as if their authors were standing outside them—as if we were looking from an eye-of-God position. In this, we assumed the standpoint of the scientist, the grounds from which "sociologists have sought to practice an objectivity constituted in relation to an 'Archimedian point'—that is, a point external to any particular position in society" (D. Smith, 1987, p. 71). Such writing, however, is not objective; we are in our texts (Jones, 1992). Such accounts can be read as resting on teleological (evolutionary, or progressive) assumptions: that our analyses have been getting us nearer to the truth. For example, by concluding with socialist feminism, some of us had implied that this position was the evolutionary apex of feminist theory and thereby positioned ourselves within it. As Donna Haraway has argued (1990a), such typologies tend "to make one's own political tendencies appear to be the telos of the whole" (p. 198). The overviews we sketched, then, were not views from the skies but were landscapes drawn from our own perspectives.

When such typologies are used as a framework for curriculum design, the students are positioned outside the theories. They are like spectators, looking in. Theory is presented as a map—a chart drawn by those with the expertise to depict objectively what is there in the theoretical terrain. The international debates in the sociology of women's education appear to students as "abstracted from particular participants located in particular spatio-temporal settings" (D. Smith, 1987, p. 61). Theories appear as disembodied and decontextualized abstractions. Rather than presenting theories as a flat, or two-dimensional, map, we can study the ways in which we—as teachers, as students, as social researchers—are positioned inside the social and educational phenomena that are the object of our inquiries. The various feminisms are studied historically and sociologically as knowledges that have been constructed by particular people in particular circumstances and that are variously and unequally related to the apparatuses of power (such as schools) in which we experience both possibilities and contraints and plan and live our lives.

A Voice From the Margins

In 1979, Phillida Bunkle, one of the founders of university women's studies in New Zealand, wrote that "feminist ideas have come to New Zealand from overseas; their dissemination has been uneven and their assimilation to the New Zealand context has been haphazard" (p. 24). In 1981, I taught my "Women and Education" course for the first time. As outlined above, at first its content and organization were those of a conventional academic discipline. I systematically initiated my students into its major theories and explored the implications of those theories for research design (Hirst, 1975). The texts I used were of British and American origin (Deem, 1978; Jaggar & Struhl, 1978). As New Zealanders, my students and I found ourselves positioned both inside and outside the Anglo-American discourses that dominated our new discipline. This contradictory positioning generated questions about colonial power relations in which the sociology of women's education was inscribed.

During the late 1980s, I edited a textbook (Middleton, 1988c)—a collection of readings by different authors—that was designed for New Zealand university undergraduate courses on women and education and the sociology of women's education. While editing, I faced the structural problems that are common to the task. How could I sequence the chapters in a way that was pedagogically appropriate? Where should such a book start? I considered the common editorial strategy of beginning with an authoritative overview of the literature and placing the various papers in the book within the theoretical and methodological traditions of the discipline. But to do that with this text would be to remove myself conceptually and spatially from my lived world—to locate myself within the abstracted interchanges of scholars of the Northern hemisphere.

Although I wanted my students to become familiar with such ideas and debates, I wanted them to learn about these "authentically" (Freire, 1971; Greene, 1973)—to approach them organically, from the vantage point of their own "native imagery" (Ashton-Warner, 1973). I wanted my students to feel part of a lineage of educational theorists, to locate themselves within their indigenous traditions, and—from that base—to engage with the ideas of feminist scholars from elsewhere. As Maxine Greene (1986) has argued with respect to American academic and imaginative writing: "We cannot and ought not escape our own history and memories, not if we are to keep alive the awarenesses that ground our identities and connect us to the persons turning for fulfillment to our schools" (p. 427).

I needed to discover and make audible the voices of those described by Keri Hulme as the "ancestral figures" of New Zealand feminist, sociological, and educational writing (interview in Kedgley, 1989). However, as many New Zealanders have observed with respect to their education (Kedgley, 1989; Roberts, 1989), such works were not visible. Academic works, works of art, and ideas came from elsewhere. There was a national amnesia where women's—especially feminist—writing was concerned. Like New Zealand children's author Margaret Mahy (Kedgley, 1989), my "reading imposed a distance between me and my natural environment. I was made the inhabitant of a country that didn't exist" (p. 137).

To write the first chapter of my indigenous text, I asked Rangimarie Rose Pere—a prominent educator and Maori woman who had been brought up within a traditional tribal setting and whose native language was Maori. The first page of her chapter is a *waiata* (a chant or poem) written in Maori. This is translated into English on the opposite (right-hand) page. Although some Maori genealogies (whakapapa) are traced back to the canoe in which the person's ancestors migrated to Aotearoa[6] from Polynesia, Pere's waiata began with the primeval ancestors of the earth mother (Papatuanuku) and the sky father (Ranginui). Writing from her tribal perspective as a "descendent of the heavenly mist maiden," she began (1988):

> Observe, behold the descendents, grandchildren
> Of Papatuanuku, Ranginui, the parental universe
> Observe ever so closely
> Observe, behold the modern world that changes,
> Divides, consumes and challenges;
> Observe ever so closely. . . . (p. 7)

Indigenous feminist thought was thereby positioned both within Aotearoa and in the continuities and dissonances of human history.

The following chapters, by Pakeha historians, introduced the colonial perspectives of the 19th and early 20th centuries. As the title page of my first-form social studies book suggested, colonial knowledge came in ships. Education was grounded in the intellectual and commonsense theories of elsewhere. My textbook reproduced the disjuncture, the fissure, and the epistemological chasm between Maori knowledgeand Pakeha knowledge. This "line of fault" (D. Smith, 1979) in New Zealand feminist educational thought presents possibilities for new perspectives in the sociology of women's education. As one overseas reader of the book observed, the Maori women's writings offered

> . . . relatively familiar issues of colonialism and racism . . . [but] as well can be read a different sort of story: of the feminist strengths that are drawn from a Maori cultural background, and an implicit questioning of the assumption that European norms are the landmark of progress for women. (Yates, 1989, p. 310)

The perspectives of the women of colonized indigenous populations can throw into question for white women "the hegemony of the Eurocentric academy over what is legitimated as 'feminist theory' in women's studies" (Lather, 1991, p. 89). My Pakeha feminist assumptions are challenged by, for example, Pere's statement (1988) that "my Maori female forebears, prior to the introduction of Christianity, and the 'original sin of Eve', were extremely liberated as compared to my English tupuna [ancestors]" (p. 9).

As a teacher of women's studies, I also hope that such writing makes the Eurocentric assumptions of my Pakeha students seem strange. I hope that such writing will be organic to the experiences of my Maori students, whose tribal traditions and ancestral figures may vary.

But I cannot claim this as *my* intellectual and spiritual heritage. Maori knowledge is transmitted and developed in tribal communities of which I am not a part. Mine is an outsider's knowledge, from secondhand accounts. Much academic knowledge about Maori women has been distorted by the mediations of European male anthropologists. I therefore encourage my students to read writings by Maori women. Such writers include academics (Irwin, 1989, 1992a; Papakura, 1983; Pere, 1983; L. Smith, 1992; Te Aweko-tuku, 1984, 1992) and writers of novels. Because teaching was, for many of the marginalized, their route to higher education, many Maori women fiction writers and other artists have also worked as teachers and have written about it.

New Zealand also has a strong Pakeha feminist history. New Zealand women won the franchise in 1893 (Bunkle, 1980; Grimshaw, 1972). I recently discovered that we have a heritage of early women novelists whose writing was grounded in strong feminist theoretical positions (Roberts, 1989). For example, in 1908, Edith Searle Grossman wrote a novel about battered women. In the story of Hermione, a battered wife who flees a brutal marriage and joins the feminist movement, Grossman described education as a route to liberation.

> As with most "advanced women," her first ambition was to gain knowledge, not to be led blindfold through the world. She was free from tyranny; now she wanted her own powers developed. In receiving education she had a vague instinctive feeling that she was preparing for warfare. (p. 62)

In the 1920s, Jean Devanny had applied her Marxist insights to the study of women in indigenous societies: "Civilized woman is really comparatively inferior to savage and barbarian woman . . . [who] occupied a relatively higher position in the social life of her day" (Roberts, 1989, p. 59). In Devanny's novel (1928/1981), *The Butcher's Shop*, one of the characters argues, "In the past woman has been the slave of man. The working man has been a slave, but woman's place in society has been lower than that of the working man, for she has been a slave even to them" (p. 206).

There is, then, a long tradition of New Zealand feminist theorizing. But like those of other Western countries, such works have long been out of print. Some were rediscovered and reprinted in the 1970s and 1980s by feminist presses. Most, if not all, remain outside the canon of what counts as "good New Zealand literature" (Roberts, 1989). Although the possibility for an indigenous New Zealand curriculum on feminist theory exists, the materials are not yet sufficiently available to be used as the basis of university courses.

Within the sociology of women's education as an international field of study are evident colonial power relations between the Anglo-American nations and those of the South. Our positioning as New Zealanders made visible the "conceptual imperialism" (Stanley & Wise, 1983) of Western feminist theories. Those of us on the margins had long been aware that disciplines are "articulated to the ruling apparatus" (D. Smith, 1987). We could not see ourselves clearly in foreign texts that were based on the various master narratives of liberalism, Marxism, and so on. Life-history methods—telling our own and others' stories—offered ways of making knowledge that were grounded in our own native imagery.

As mainstream Northern academics began to hear the voices of those who had been inaudible or marginalized within their disciplines, the older monolithic or dualistic sets of categories (e.g., class and gender) were found to be too simplistic to work with. The "master narratives of the disciplines" (Aronowitz & Giroux, 1991, p. 18)—including feminist theories—began to collapse. The "larger cultural shifts of a post-industrial, post-colonial era" (Lather, 1991, p. 5) required theories that could accommodate people's multiple and simultaneous positionings in complex, changing, and often contradictory patterns of power relations—between races or cultures within countries, between the Anglo-American/European nations and those of the third world, between indigenous populations and those descended from former colonists, and between those of different sexual orientations, different religions, different abilities, and so on. Postmodernist[7] theories focus on such multiple and often contradictory positionings.

Postmodernists are primarily concerned with relationships between knowledge and power—for example, between academic disciplines and "the governing of our kind of society [, which] is done in abstract concepts and symbols" (D. Smith, 1990, p. 14). The dominant perspectives in the social sciences are seen as conceptualizing the social world from a vantage point of ruling. Although social scientists have traditionally been centrally concerned with the scientific accuracy, objectivity, or truthfulness of their disciplines, postmodernists are concerned with what Nancy Fraser (1989) described as "the processes, procedures, and apparatuses wherein truth, knowledge, and belief are produced" (p. 14). Such perspectives enable us to study *sociologically* the ways that academic disciplines and their associated professional or clinical practices are complicit in the monitoring, surveillance, and regulation of populations (Foucault, 1980a, 1980b; Henriques, Hollway, Urwin, Venn, & Walkerdine, 1984).

As I developed my course and read the various sociological, feminist, and educational theories for my doctoral research, I became fascinated by such sociological questions about sociology. What, I wondered, were the theories—about women, about education, and about women's education—that had informed the schooling of those of us who were to become feminist educators as adults? How did such theories influence the processes, procedures, and apparatuses by which we were educated? And how did these shape, constrain, and make possible the various feminist truths, knowledges, and beliefs that we were later to develop?

Sociological Theories in the Education of the Post–World War II Woman

The question that drove me through my doctoral research was this. I was reading the various feminist narratives (liberal, radical, Marxist, and so on) in the women's studies and sociology texts. When I attended women's studies conferences, I found myself in debates with women who used these ideas in their everyday intellectual and grassroots activities. What was the relationship between the academic theories in the overseas texts and the ideas of real women in the New Zealand feminist movement? How did real-life feminists of my own generation come to adopt such positions? How did those who had also become teachers live their various feminisms in the course of their educational activities? What, if any, part had our own schooling played in making all this possible? And how could I, as an educating feminist, help my "Women and Education" students to develop their own feminist educational theories?

Life-history interviews (chapters 3 and 4) were crucial in helping me to address these questions. However, I also needed a knowledge of the historical settings in which our ideas as feminist teachers had come to form. To help in this, I read the key education policy documents and the major sociological, historical, and biographical writings concerning the 1950s and 1960s; the time we were at school.[8] In studying these texts, I found Foucault's version of postmodernism particularly helpful because he analyzed relationships between academic and professional knowledge, state power, and the specific institutional apparatuses (such as schools) in which our everyday lives are monitored and regulated. I shall briefly outline his analysis here because I shall use it as a basis for my contextualization of the life histories in chapters 4 and 6.

Foucault and Women's Education

According to Foucault, the social science disciplines are, to varying degrees, "articulated to the ruling apparatus" (D. Smith, 1987). Using the example of demography, Foucault argued that in modern societies, social scientists have shared with governments a top-down or disengaged view of the social world. From the vantage point of governing, societies are conceptualized as populations—"population as an economic and political problem: population as wealth, population as manpower and labour capacity, population balanced between its own growth and the resources it commanded" (Foucault, 1980a, p. 25). Such an analysis is useful in studying the ways in which theories about society, about women, and about education become regulatory practices within schools—with real, material consequences for students' lives. Foucault used the term "discourse" to conceptualize theories in action.[9] As Dorothy Smith (1987) has explained, a discourse is like "a conversation mediated by texts that is not a matter of statements alone but of actual ongoing practices and sites of practices " (p. 214).

For example, Valerie Walkerdine (1984) studied British primary school classrooms that, like many post–World War II schools, were structured according to the progressivism of Piagetian developmental psychology. Although a more conventional approach would be to study the strengths and weaknesses of Piaget's theory, Walkerdine's (1984) postmodernist approach was to study Piagetian developmental psychology as discourse by researching its social technologies or apparatuses "for the modern scientific normalization and regulation of children" (p. 173). Questions such as what counts as progress, what is normality or intelligence, what constitutes data for pupils' official dossiers, how such information is recorded, and to whom it is made available are decided according to the criteria of the discourse. Within the various textual representations of their progress, the individual student is constituted as an assemblage of discursive[10] data. As in other clinical or professional practices, "the structuring of the case history" of students in schools "is articulated to an organization of power and position" (D. Smith, 1990, p. 91).

Although Foucault himself did not address questions of gender, his analysis of sexuality and power is useful for feminist studies of social policy. According to Foucault (1980a), within various state "organizations of power and position," sexuality is of particular concern to policymakers because it "concerns characteristics that are at the intersection between the discipline of the body and the control of the population" (Giddens, 1982, p. 219). In *A History of Sexuality,* Foucault (1980a) argued:

> At the heart of this economic and political problem of population was sex: it was necessary to analyse the birth-rate, the age of marriage, the legitimate and illegitimate births, the precocity and frequency of sexual relations, the ways of making them fertile or sterile, the effects of married life, or of the prohibitions, the impact of contraceptive practice. (p. 26)

In what ways were our girlhood educational and sexual experiences structured by the apparatuses of monitoring and regulation? And what kinds of sociological theories[11] informed such practices?

Prefeminist[12] Theories in Postwar Education Policy

In 1963, as a senior student in high school, I was assigned an essay on the topic "New Zealand: God's Own Country?" In this essay, I wrote, "We all have equal opportunities. Any individual with initiative, perseverance, willpower and intelligence can succeed in his or her chosen vocation, regardless of wealth or rank." What influenced me, a 17-year-old schoolgirl, to develop such a perspective? What were the theoretical possibilities and constraints of my circumstances? Were such ideas likely to have been shared by others like me?

Probably, the majority of present-day tenured sociologists of education and teachers of academic women's studies attended primary and secondary schools during the 1950s and 1960s and began their undergraduate degrees during the 1960s and 1970s (Middleton, 1990b). In many Western nations, this was the time of the postwar baby boom, the establishment or consolidation of welfare states, the expansion of free and compulsory secondary schooling, and increasing opportunities to enter higher education. The concerns of policymakers and the investigations of social scientists were centered on bringing about equal opportunity (Beeby, 1986).

The premises on which New Zealand's first Labour government (1935 to 1949) was to base its postwar educational policies were outlined in 1939.

> The government's objective, broadly expressed, is that every person, whatever his level of academic ability, whether he be rich or poor, whether he live in town or country, has a right, as a citizen, to a free education of the kind for which he is best fitted and to the fullest extent of his powers. (Beeby, 1986, p. xxxii)

This remained the rationale for New Zealand's education policy until the fourth Labour government undertook its restructuring of schooling in the late 1980s (McKenzie, 1975; McLaren, 1973; Renwick, 1986).[13] It was the official ideology during the period that I, like many of today's sociologists of women's education, was at school. My adolescent view of the social world—shaped within the close confines of a boarding school—was, as Dorothy Smith (1987) would express it, "positioned from within the ruling apparatus."

The education policy-making of the immediate post–World War II period was strongly influenced by progressivist[14] models of society. Education was seen as reconstructionist—as the means of developing in individuals the kinds of rationality that would form a sound basis for democracy and for preventing the resurgence of fascism. The policymakers' intentions were later explained by Beeby (1986), the head of New Zealand's Education Department at the time: "Our overriding interest in educational equality for the individual would, we thought, itself contribute, through the next generation, to the growth of a more equitable society" (p. xxxii).

Such ideas were the theoretical rationale for the "Thomas report" (Department of Education, 1944), the document that was the blueprint for the postwar secondary school curriculum. This report, together with similar American texts *(General Education in a Free Society,* 1946), were read by many teachers in training in university education and society courses during the late 1940s and the 1950s. Within the sociological study of education and in policy statements, education was conceptualized as an instrument of social transformation. The population that was to be governed would be both democratic and rational. Such ideals applied to both genders. However, the Thomas report also rested on clear assumptions about gender roles within the family. To understand these, it is necessary to explore women's work and sexuality as they had been constituted in the policy texts and in the regulatory practices of wartime and postwar society.

During World War II, many New Zealand women of our mothers' generation—like their counterparts overseas—had volunteered for or been manpowered into noncombat duties in the armed forces or sometimes in nontraditional civilian jobs. After the war, they were expected to leave their wartime jobs and devote themselves to domestic duties. Policymakers and social scientists of the time saw this as essential (Ebbett, 1984; May, 1992b). Women's domesticity, argued psychologists and doctors, was necessary for the psychological well-being and rehabilitation of returned servicemen. Before and during the war, there had been concern about a falling population. The postwar wife and mother could ensure a growing population of stable, well-adjusted children. Women who did not conform to such maternal images were seen as deviant, neurotic, or disturbed; as likely to produce delinquent children; and as in need of the curative powers of medical science (Ehrenreich & English, 1979; Friedan, 1963; May, 1992b). As Valerie Walkerdine and Helen Lucey (1989) have argued in the case of Britain, "the guarantees of democracy were to be assured by a science of mothering that held women responsible for the next generation" (p. 42).

These ideas remained in the educational policies of the 1950s and 1960s. For example, the Thomas committee had assumed that certain curriculum subjects were suited to particular genders. Although the schools' clientele were spoken of throughout most of the report as pupils, in discussions of some subjects (e.g., agriculture and engineering), they were "boys," and in discussions of other subjects (e.g., shorthand, typing, and domestic science), they were "girls." Girls would be prepared for marriage and motherhood through a curricular component of compulsory domestic science: "An intelligent parent would wish a daughter to have the knowledge, skill and taste to manage a home well and make it a pleasant place to live in" (Department of Education, 1944, p. 7). The Thomas report, then, was based on gendered assumptions about the ways that individuals would be educated as "workers, neighbours, homemakers and citizens" (Department of Education, 1944, p. 5).

The gendering of women's education was evident not only in the ways that women's work was conceptualized, but also in the ways that sexuality was perceived and regulated. By placing lessons on human reproduction within the general science syllabus, policymakers "medicalized" sex (Foucault, 1980a), removed it conceptually from the anarchy of passion, and placed it in the realm of scientific reason. Within the sex education literature of the time, such as that produced for girls by the New Zealand Department of Health (1955), a sexual double standard was evident: " . . . sexual desire is much more easily aroused in boys. . . . The responsibility of controlling our desires lies with us [women] and we find that boys respect girls who have a natural dignity and control" (p. 7). Female sexuality was seen as controllable and women were seen as responsible for curbing the natural lust of the male (Hollway, 1984). The "discipline of the body" would ensure "the control of the population" (Foucault, 1980a; Giddens, 1982).

Prefeminist Sociology of Education

According to postmodernist theorists, sociologists and other social scientists have provided policymakers with the kinds of language they need to conceptualize the population as "governable" (Foucault, 1979, 1980a, 1980b; Fraser, 1989; Walkerdine, 1984; Walkerdine & Lucey, 1989). Relations between policy-making and sociology are both direct and indirect.

Relationships are direct in the case of government-commissioned or -sponsored research. For example, New Zealand's Department of Education had its own research and statistics division. A more subtle relationship has been pointed out by Dorothy Smith, who argues that traditional sociology has shared the vantage point of policymakers: the view of a society as a population to be governed. Sociological perspectives enter the relations of ruling through university and teacher-education curricula (the professional training of administrators and researchers); through processes of consultancy between government agencies and outside researchers; and through the various professional and personal networks that bring academics, administrators, and politicians into contact with one another. Sociological theories about women's education become "articulated to the ruling apparatus" by "transposing the actualities of people's lives into the conceptual currency with which they can be governed" (D. Smith, 1990, p. 11).

The kinds of assumptions about gender that I have described as characteristic of the educational policies of the postwar years were also evident in the educational sociology of that time. New Zealand educational sociologists were strongly influenced by American ideas (Beeby, 1986; Middleton, 1990b; Moss, 1990). Before World War II, there were few New Zealand sociological analyses of education. Crawford Somerset's *Littledene* (1938/1973) was New Zealand's classic text—a qualitative study of a small South Island town researched and written by its school's headmaster. Other textbooks of the time were highly theoretical, such as those by Robert McIver (1924/1960), a prolific Scottish theoretician who had spent most of his long career in the United States. As Beeby (1973) explained, "It was still possible to look with a trained eye at a total community, and to write about it in a language that would be intellectually respectable and yet intelligible to the layman" (p. xvi). However, by the late 1950s, such "enlightened subjectivity" (J. Watson, 1973, p. 4) was rendered unscientific. Beeby (1973) has described the transition: "Sociology hovered for a period between the weighty theoretical generalizations of a McIver and the statistical generalizations and no less terrifying vocabularies of the younger generation of sociologists" (p. xvi).

Within the new scientific perspectives, education was conceptualized as a means of socializing or governing the population. In 1950, an Auckland University master's course, "Principles of Sociology," had been described as focused on "the influences of educational agencies upon social structure." However, by 1961, the object of analysis in "Educational Sociology" was described as "the social forces that influence education." This shift from an emphasis on schools as agencies of social transformation to one on schools as instruments of social reproduction was characteristic of the rise of functionalism and "technocratic rationality" within the sociology of education (Giroux, 1982).

Within this technocratic discourse, people became manpower units, human resources, or personnel. For example, in a paper on the shortage of university graduates in science and technology, Eric Braithwaite (1967) argued that "education in developed countries has become a sector of the economy . . . everything that happens and will happen in education must be considered in relation to the needs of the economy" (p. 54). Similarly, Musgrave (1965), a British sociologist, whose textbook was widely used in New Zealand education and sociology of education courses during the 1960s, asked:

> What part does education play in the balance between stability and change, in maintaining a democratic political system, in ensuring the full use of talented people in our society and, finally, in supplying trained manpower to the economic system?" (p. 12)

Many functionalists saw schools as instruments for the maintenance of social cohesion, stability, and what Logan Moss (1990) has described as "social efficiency." As will be shown in chapter 6, such a technocratic discourse has, since the 1980s, assumed increasing prominence with the ascendency of the New Right.

During the 1950s and 1960s, the topics such researchers studied were often those that policymakers saw as social problems—as issues of social control. For example, studies measured the "rate of juvenile delinquency." Statistical measures of socioeconomic status were developed so that correlations could be established between variables such as socioeconomic status and examination success. The research methods of the physical sciences were assumed to be appropriate for the study of social phenomena. Such sociology "converts people from subjects to objects of investigation" (D. Smith, 1987, p. 31). It was written from a vantage point that was implicitly or explicitly positioned within the apparatuses of ruling (Delphy, 1981; Eichler, 1980; Friedan, 1963; D. Smith, 1974).

During the 1970s, the ideas of the second wave of feminism stimulated feminist critiques of such sociology (Lengermann et al., 1978; Oakley, 1974; D. Smith, 1974). Such writers argued that the functionalist and technocratic discourses that dominated the field were inherently masculine or androcentric. A 1966 study on the marriages of New Zealand women teachers serves as a useful example (J. Watson, 1966). During the 1950s and 1960s, there was a severe shortage of teachers due to the increasing numbers of baby-boom pupils and the raising of the school leaving age to 15. As in wartime, the labor of married women—the "reserve army" of workers (Marx, 1867/1976)—was required by the government in a national emergency. This problem was of interest to sociologists such as John Watson (1966). Although Watson was not working for the state, his conceptualization of women was typical of the functionalist perspective that characterized the sociology of education of the time (Bernard, 1973; Eichler, 1980; Friedan, 1963).

Watson (1966) wrote that "for a man, an occupation or profession is his dominant 'social role,' but for a woman it is her marriage that is pivotal" (p. 159). Without interviewing or surveying the women or men concerned, Watson asserted that there was

> a strong and consistent tendency for the career plans of men teachers to be related primarily to factors intrinsic to their work (pay, social status, working conditions, etc) while those of women are related primarily to factors extrinsic to their work (marriage, family plans, needs of relatives, etc). (p. 160)

This typifies the kinds of sexist functionalist theory that Betty Friedan (1963) saw as dominating the textbooks of American college social science courses during the 1950s. The message, she argued, was prescriptive as well as descriptive. Students were learning that such patterns were normal (in the sense of healthy, necessary, and desirable)—deemed by science as essential for social well-being.

Similarly, measures of socioeconomic status were designed from a male-centered perspective. The status of women was measured according to the status of the man to whom she was most closely connected: her father or her husband (Delphy, 1981; Eichler, 1980). The following example—also taken from J. Watson's study—usefully illustrates the androcentrism of such perspectives. Here, Watson (1966) is thinking about whether women teachers move up the social hierarchy when they marry and how this could be measured:

> For the purposes of the present analysis the occupations of the fathers of teacher-brides have been classified into five categories, and compared with the classification of their husbands' occupations: (a) professional-administrative-technical (b) clerical (c) highly skilled or skilled (d) semi-skilled, and (e) farmers. It could be argued that this is an unsatisfactory form of comparison since husbands at the time of their marriage are likely to occupy a more lowly position than that which they might reasonably expect to attain during the subsequent ten years or so. Again, it

could be argued that because of the age factor, occupation at time of marriage is not a very satisfactory index of status vis a vis that of the father in law. (p. 156)

Such androcentric analyses focused only on the men in women teachers' lives; a woman's social mobility was measured only in relation to her father and her husband. These analyses rendered invisible the achievements, influence, and cultural capital of her mother. As will be illustrated in case studies in the following chapters, the educational achievements and cultural capital of a student's mother are often major influences on her or his educational performance and aspirations. Furthermore, the actual processes of education were bracketed out of such researchers' inquiries. As Madeleine Grumet (1988) has argued with respect to similarly framed research in the United States, "all those hours in classrooms" were thereby "collapsed into an equation that indicates whether the child has maintained or surpassed the socio-economic status of [the] parents" (p. 175).

Summary

Within various political and social science discourses of the 1940s to the 1960s, women were contradictorily positioned. On one hand, within the discourse of liberal individualism, we were designated as potentially rational. We were educable individuals who were to be accorded equal opportunities with men. On the other hand, within the discourse of patriarchy, we were females. Our domesticity within the patriarchal nuclear family (with the husband/father as breadwinner) was seen as essential to the maintenance of social cohesion and stability. Our education and our socialization would prepare us for our natural functions as wives and mothers. This was the official ideology in educational policy and the dominant sociological discourse of the time. Our girlhood educational and sexual experiences were structured by the sociological theories that were later to become the object of our adult feminist critiques. We were "produced by what we are studying" (Dreyfus & Rabinow, 1986, p. 124).

In chapter 4, I will explore how such ideas were productive of specific professional practices or "technologies of the social" (Henriques, Hollway, Urwin, Venn, & Walkerdine, 1984) that served to classify, regulate, and rank female students in New Zealand secondary schools at the time. Using a life-history method, I shall show how, for some of us, the contradictions we experienced in the course of such monitoring and regulation—together with the alternative possibilities that our historical and biographical circumstances made visible to us—generated our feminism.

Conclusion

In studying the complicity of disciplines in the ruling of populations, I adopted a Foucauldian perspective. Some feminists have criticized such analyses (Fraser, 1989). Within a Foucauldian framework, individual human subjectivities are bracketed out. People become mere passive victims of their regulation and monitoring within various discourses. Dorothy Smith (1990) accuses Foucault of linking power and knowledge "in some mystical conjunction" (p. 79). "Knowledge," writes Smith (1990) should "be investigated as the co-ordinated practices of actual people" (p. 62). The addition of life-history narratives to this analysis will enable me to focus on the creative strategies devised by the post–World War II generation of feminist teachers as we resisted and resolved contradictions and wove our way through the constraints and possibilities of our biographical, cultural, gender, historical and material, and generational circumstances. For, as Maxine Greene (1988) has expressed it, "Human beings . . . devise their life projects in time—against their own life histories and the wider human history into which those histories feed" (p. 23).

Many of our students, especially younger women without teaching experience, feel alienated—not only by theory but also by talk about policy, which they see as dull conversations and texts produced by grey-suited men in remote offices. The life-history techniques that I outline in the following chapters make policy three-dimensional as students study the educational choices of individual women of their own and other generations as contextualized in the constraints and possibilities of their circumstances, and as they come to see the part played by policymakers in these choices. As discourses, educational theories and policies are constitutive of our subjectivities. As sociologists of women's education, we are positioned within, produced by, and productive of that which is the object of our inquiries.

Notes

[1]In fact, after a few years, I changed the name of the course back to "Women and Education" and accepted its status as a noncore course within the major. The requirements to cover "male-stream" sociology would have marginalized the feminism in the course. The emphasis in the course remains sociological/historical because of its life-history focus on "biography, history, and social structure" (Mills, 1959). I also teach a master's course entitled "Sociology of Women's Education."

[2]In this section, I shall define the field as Arnot did—to refer to a field of study that integrates feminist theory and sociology of education. In the chapter as a

whole, I have included nonfeminist (e.g., 1960s functionalist) sociological research on women and education.

[3]Many sociologists of education, including myself, became interested in sociology through our contact with the sociology of knowledge (or sociology of the curriculum) as a branch of curriculum theory (Apple, 1979; Bernstein, 1971, 1975; Giroux, 1982; Lawton, 1975; Young, 1971). Writers such as Madeleine Grumet (1988) and Patti Lather (1991) are curriculum theorists rather than sociologists. Because of the overlap between these disciplines, I have incorporated both into my analysis.

[4]Feminists of more radical persuasions (radical, Marxist, and socialist feminists) may choose to employ liberal feminist language and strategies as a means to more radical change. For example, within a liberal feminist framework, getting more girls to study science would be seen in terms of advantages to the individual such as pay, status, personal fulfillment, and so on, and in terms of the role modeling that female scientists can provide for other women. A more radical position would be that such women could revolutionize the nature of science (Harding, 1987).

[5]The interpretive paradigm in sociology includes theories and methods based on phenomenology and ethnomethodology. For a detailed general explanation, see Bates, 1978; Giroux, 1982; Lawton, 1975; and Wilson, 1971. More details of the interrelationship between such perspectives and feminist scholarship in education are in Middleton (1988b).

[6]Aotearoa (literally the land of the long white cloud) is the Maori name for New Zealand. Today, it is often used by Pakeha as well as Maori to signify the precolonial society and/or an imaginary noncolonial or nonracist nation. Sometimes academics use the term "Aotearoa/New Zealand."

[7]Patti Lather (1991) defines postmodern as "the larger cultural shifts of a post-industrial, post-colonial era" and poststructural as "the working out of those shifts within the arenas of academic theory" (p. 5). Many writers do not make such a distinction. My own work draws substantially on Foucault, who is often described as a poststructuralist rather than a postmodernist (Weedon, 1987). Poststructuralism is often seen as a subset of postmodernism, and because this book is written at a general level, I shall subsume all such categories under the generic term "postmodernism." I understand this to mean a disbelief, skepticism, or suspension of belief in universal truth or in the possibility of a totalizing master narrative and, instead, a focus on the various master narratives, disciplines, or theories as regimes of truth—as historical and socially constructed knowledge with varying and unequal relations to various apparatuses of power. The languages of some disciplines are seen as inscribed in the apparatuses of ruling and, by means of various social technologies such as clinical or professional practices, as having material effects on the monitoring, surveillance, and regulation of populations (e.g., school pupils). Postmodernist writers define the characteristics of modernity or the modern age as follows: an emphasis on rationality as the rationale of governing (as distinct from feudal hereditary powers and positions), the belief in science as a basis for truth, and a belief in the individual as the basic unit of society (Dreyfus & Rabinow, 1986;

Fraser, 1989; Harding, 1987; Henriques, Hollway, Urwin, Venn, & Walkerdine, 1984; Hutcheon, 1989; Lather, 1991; Nicholson, 1990a; Poster, 1984).

[8]The research from which material in this section is drawn was a study of American influences in the sociology of New Zealand education, which I undertook as part of the 40th anniversary celebrations of the Fulbright program in New Zealand. My study, which covered the years from 1945 to 1988, included analysis of information about education staffing and courses from university prospectuses, a content analysis of prescribed texts and of publications by New Zealand sociologists of education, and a postal questionnaire sent to those who were then teaching the subject (Middleton, 1990b). This study was developed in consultation with a colleague, Logan Moss, who undertook analysis of the development of New Zealand sociology of education before 1945 (Moss, 1990). I would like to acknowledge his help with my own part of the project.

[9]The definition "theory in action" was used by Linda Smith (1992)

[10]"Discursive" is the adjective from "discourse." Discourse refers to both theories and practices. In Walkerdine's example, "discursive data" means that "what counts as data" is decided according to the conceptual framework or system of relevances of developmental psychology.

[11]I am using the term "sociological theory" to include both the formal theories of trained, professional sociologists and the theories about society that informed social, including educational, policy.

[12]I am using this term to distinguish the sociological theories about women (e.g., functionalism) that informed the education policies of the postwar years from those that followed the second wave of feminism in the 1970s. See note 2. Feminist sociological theories are also articulated in various ways to the ruling apparatus. In this chapter, I have given the example of colonial relations. In Chapter 6, I will explore the incorporation and marginalization of the various feminisms in New Zealand's recent and current educational restructuring policies. In this, they materially shape the schools in which my students teach.

[13]The statement was written by Dr C. E. Beeby, who was director general of the Education Department during the time of the first Labour government. It was incorporated into the 1938 annual report to Parliament of the minister of education, Peter Fraser. The statement has been widely quoted as encapsulating postwar egalitarian ideals—as being the accepted foundation of state schooling in New Zealand (see Beeby, 1986; Renwick, 1986; Shuker, 1986). Even the New Zealand Treasury (1987) cited this statement—in a largely New Right economic analysis—as fundamental to the state system.

[14]There are many definitions and versions of progressivism. All share a belief that education is a means of bringing about social progress—the betterment of the human condition. As yet, there is not a systematic history of progressive movements in New Zealand education, although several works are in progress. During the 1920s and 1930s, the ideas of John Dewey and of various psychoanalysts were highly influential in New Zealand, especially in early childhood education (May, 1992a). The New Education Fellowship Conference was held in New Zealand in 1937 (Moss, 1990). Progressive ideas were highly influential in the educational

policies of New Zealand's first Labour government (Beeby, 1986). However, the extent to which such ideas were put into practice in schools remains an issue to be researched in depth.

three

The Politics of
Life-History Research

W hen I took up my present university appointment in 1980, I was aware that to gain tenure 4 years thereafter, I would be required to have made substantial progress on a doctorate. I had been appointed to a full-time lectureship (the equivalent of assistant professor in the United States). It was my first university position. Like many of my contemporaries, I would have to fit the researching and writing of my dissertation into a full-time teaching load, the administrative tasks and politics involved in a university department, and my private life as a mother and a wife.[1] I would have to snatch whatever fragmented moments I could. Certain kinds of methodologies—such as those involving long and continuous observations in classrooms—would be out of the question.

As the first and only woman teaching in my department, I felt marginal—alienated from the collegial culture. This sense of otherness bonded me closely to feminists in other social science departments. I became involved in the women's studies program and started my undergraduate course entitled "Women and Education." Very little indigenous material on which to base my curriculum was available. My students— mainly New Zealand women, many of them about my age— could not see themselves in the curriculum. I could not see myself in what I was reading or teaching. Like other academic knowledge, feminist knowledge was from elsewhere. I wanted our stories as New Zealand feminist teachers to be part of my curriculum. I would have to make this knowledge myself.

As a doctoral study, my research was brought into being within particular power relations—with my supervisors, with my colleagues, and with the women in my research. As with my research, its questions, its methods, and its theories had their origins in the biographical and historical circumstances of my own life history.

Asking the Questions

I wanted to understand my own situation as a feminist and a teacher. I was also strongly reacting to the pessimism in sociology of education at the time: its emphasis on the relationship between schooling and inequality. As a teacher educator, I wanted to understand the part played by education in helping people to develop "a concern for the critical and the imaginative, for the opening of new ways of looking at things" (Greene, 1988, p. 128). As a feminist, I wanted to understand why so many women teachers of my own generation had—despite the conservative intentions of policymakers—rejected patriarchal constructions of our femininity and come to see the world through feminist eyes. I was a feminist educator who was both experiencing and studying the contradictions, tensions, and joys of being a feminist educator. My questions came from inside what I was studying. In studying the lives of other women, I was also trying to understand myself. As Dorothy Smith (1990) expressed it, "as thinking heads—as social scientists—we are always inside what we are thinking about; we know it in the first place as insiders" (p. 51).

[Throughout the volume, beginning below, text is incorporated that reflects shifts in the author's consciousness—e.g., flashbacks in time, or dramatic lateral changes in theme due to interruptions in the writing/thinking process. The idea behind integrating these entries is to capture the stream of consciousness and the rhythms and disruptions of a writer's life. The following is the first of such entries, which are distinguished from the main body of text by presentation in an alternative typeface.]

My research questions did not "start" with my university career. They had their origins in the conscious and subconscious tensions and conflicts of a lifetime. In the first chapter, I traced these to my schooldays. There had also been unarticulated feelings of "something wrong" in 1969 when I attended a 1-year secondary teachers' college course (because I already had a B.A. degree, I was required to do only a 1-year credentialing course at teachers' college) where teaching was made out to be a set of scientific/technological problems. We were taught to prepare our "lesson plans" according to a set formula. We learned about Behavioural Objectives (BOs) and Topic Analyses (TAs). To teach successfully, one had to analyse one's "topic," conceptualize it as a hierarchy of concepts, and present it in a form appropriate to the child's "level of readiness." We had to design in advance hierarchies of questions which we would ask the children. If the lesson "failed," we were told, it was because we hadn't prepared the topic or the questions correctly or had pitched them inappropriately to the pupils' "levels of readiness." I felt alienated from this approach, but could not yet articulate my reasons. Problems such as what should count as "worthwhile knowledge" were not raised.

My first teaching position was in a large school in a country town about half an hour's drive from a major city. I was given a heavy teaching load: a class of fifth formers repeating School Certificate English and another class of repeaters for geography; the agriculture and technical stream[2] boys for social studies; the fourth form "commercial girls" for English; the fifth stream third form for French; and various groups for current events discussions. I taught guitar in the lunch hours and helped with the school musical. I worked late into the night on my TAs and BOs, but they couldn't help me deal adequately with Janice in 3D who slashed her wrists with broken glass, or Sally, the petty thief. There were uniforms and rules and children were punished for wearing the wrong coloured socks. It snowed. I became ill and left.

I took a position in another co-educational school in a city. I had heard of the "student-centred" program they were running—one where the students chose their topics of study. Remembering Sylvia Ashton-Warner, repelled by the "technocratic rationality" of teachers' college and the authoritarianism of my first school, I instinctively felt at home with this approach. It just felt right. At this school, I found wonderful support from several older women teachers. One in particular fed me educational theory. At first I resisted—"No—I hate theory. They rammed it down our throats at teachers' college." But the theories she fed me were those of the neo-progressives of the early 1970s—John Holt (1974); Postman and Weingartner (1971); Ivan Illich (1971) and books about cultural pluralism in language teaching. My "sense of something wrong" with technocratic rationality was being named, articulated. The stress I experienced in schools was understandable as a theoretical/political/social conflict, not a "personal problem" such as being weak or unable to cope. There were others on the staff, even within the same departments, who strongly opposed our progressivism. The dialectical engagement of the opposing discourses of technocratic and neo-progressivist versions of liberalism—those which I was later to encounter in the university as the "positivist/functionalist versus phenomenological/interpretive debate"—were lived within my school (Schubert, 1991). I developed a passion for educational theory.

I had a year of "travel and adventure" (Firestone, 1979). I sat "in the Gods" (in the cheapest seats in the highest balconies) at West End shows, ate escargots on the Left Bank, helped out with drama and music in a South London "free school," busked with my guitar—sang protest songs in London tube stations. . . . On returning to New Zealand in 1973, I returned to teaching—this time in an "Intermediate" (junior high) school in a multicultural, working-class neighborhood. There was poverty and violence and malnutrition. The children wanted their teachers to be "tough"—to "make them do things." It took them a long time to accept a female teacher who wanted them to choose their curriculum, to make movies and tape-slide sequences as part of "school work," to write books illustrated with their own photography. Again, I was accused by administrators of being "soft." "These children," they said, "had no background." "These children" could not "handle freedom." "These children" needed "discipline."

There was also conflict within the school over challenges to the dominance of the Pakeha/Western canon. Each year the school gave a concert. Some Pakeha staff expressed concern at the undervaluing of "Pakeha culture" in the curriculum. The man who took the choir decided to put on a rock opera. It was not until the dress rehearsal that we saw what he had done. It was the Bible story of Elijah. The choir children (mainly Pakeha) were cast as the followers of Yaweh, the One True God; the Polynesian Club children (in Maori costumes bought at great expense for the school by parents) were the worshippers of Baal, the "heathen god." Then—in the mid-1970s—we lived the debates between the advocates of pluralism and those who upheld the curricular hegemony of "Western culture."

I returned to university to take a Master's degree. I wanted "theoretical ammunition." I wanted the confidence that "theoretical security" could give me in my work. At first, I used the analytic philosophers as a basis for theorizing my student-centred teaching practice (Peters, 1966). Then, in the mid-1970s, the "new sociology" and the phenomenological perspectives in philosophy created for me a "sense of theoretical possibilities." Maxine Greene's *Teacher as Stranger* (1973) was the book which most articulated for me my experiences in schools of the multiple marginalities and alienations of teachers and students. She gave names to my sense of otherness while at the same time rekindling my hopes. And—so unusual for the time—this was an education book written by a woman. Sylvia Ashton-Warner—the only other I knew—was invisible in the university curriculum.

I had a pre-school child. At the university creche I became close friends with other "mature" women students who had children the same age as Kate. We spent many afternoons in each other's houses, drinking coffee, talking, attending to our children's intermittent demands. We talked at length of experiences of childbirth, of children's illnesses, of how to cope with the conflict we experienced between our worlds as graduate student intellectuals and as mothers.[2]

When I wrote my dissertation, I traced the origins of my life-history methodology to books—such as C. Wright Mills's *The Sociological Imagination* (1959). But there were no recipes in the books. The methodology was grounded in my experiences with these women—our friendships. It was for me a natural thing to ask other women—other feminist teachers of my age group—to talk about their lives. We often talked this way with one another. Such sharing of stories had been the method of making knowledge of the consciousness-raising groups of the 1970s.

> In 1979 I went with one of my "creche friends" (a lecturer in women's studies) to a huge feminist convention. I was not then part of any feminist groups. Previously, I had read Germaine Greer (1972)—her anarchistic message of "do your own thing" appealed to my "hippy mentality." I had read Betty Friedan (1963) but saw the problems she wrote about as those of my mother's generation and the stereotyping she saw in college students as characteristic of American, not New Zealand, society. I saw myself as a liberated woman. I had a career; I had travelled; I had freely chosen in my late twenties to marry and have a child; I was enjoying my post-graduate study. I had not yet made connections between feminism and education.
>
> At the convention there were over 3,000 women. I met lesbian separatists who wore purple arm bands and who confronted bourgeois heterosexism with vigorous demonstration. I heard my first feminist concert, saw my first feminist art. There were workshops at which women discussed unmentionable things—sexual violence, psychiatric treatments, sexual experiences, pornography. In a huge plenary session, an American speaker, Charlotte Bunch, spoke of the importance of developing rigorous feminist theory. I had never heard the term before. I knew then that that was what I wanted to do—to develop a feminist theory of education. I returned to my Master's thesis re-charged. It had begun with the title, "A Phenomenological Perspective for the Classroom Teacher." After the convention, I added to the title "and its Application to the Education of Women." Immediately after the completion of that thesis, we moved to Hamilton so that I could take up the position I had been offered at the University of Waikato.[3]

The genesis of my research questions, then, lay deep in the tensions and conflicts of my everyday life. The origins of my methodology were the ways we women related to one another—the ways we made knowledge about our lives as women. There was no split between my personal and my intellectual dilemmas. I lived my feminism. I was inside my own questions and methods, positioned within the object and the process of my inquiries.

Power and Knowledge in Life-History Analysis

In constituting ourselves as inside what we were researching—as simultaneously the authors (subjects) and the objects of our analyses—feminists challenged the orthodoxy of the scientifically detached observer, which at the time pervaded the social science disciplines. Foucault's concept of the confessional provides a useful perspective on the form such researching encounters often took. He argued that "Western societies have established the confession as one of the main rituals we rely on for the production of truth" (Foucault, 1980a, p. 58). For Foucault, the confession, like the sociological research interview, is "a ritual of discourse in which the speaking subject is also the subject of the statement" (p. 61). Such a form of encounter is "also a ritual that unfolds within a power relationship" (p. 61). Within the social sciences, as in other professions,

> the work of producing the truth was obliged to pass through this relationship if it was to be scientifically validated. The truth did not rely solely in the subject who, by confession, would reveal it wholly framed. It was constituted in two stages: present but incomplete, blind to itself, in the one who spoke, it could only reach completion in the one who assimilated and recorded it. It was the latter's function to verify this obscure truth: the revelation of confession had to be coupled with the decipherment of what it said. (p. 66)

During the 1970s, feminists in many disciplines had researched the ways in which the narratives of those who spoke were reconstituted by those who assimilated and recorded. Within the feminist movement, the androcentrism or male centeredness of academic and other professional discourses were by then generating a large literature (Ehrenreich & English, 1979; Spender, 1982b). Feminists had argued that within the discursive practices of male-dominated professions—within all the regulatory apparatuses of modern states—women's experiences had been appropriated, reconceptualized in androcentric terms, and entered into the record as scientific data. The abstracted case histories that were entered into the various professional and academic records were "articulated to an organization of power and position in which some have authority to contribute to the making of the textual realities and others do not" (D. Smith, 1990, p. 91). The hierarchical relationship between researcher and researched, on which was based the production of sociological knowledge, was almost always bracketed out or rendered invisible in the written analysis.

At the time I began my research, I was strongly influenced by Dorothy

Smith (1974), who argued that if sociology were "to accommodate feminist analyses and to make visible women's experiences," it would require

> a methodological reorganization . . . which . . . changes the relation of the sociologist to the object of her knowledge and changes also her problematic. This reorganisation involves first placing the sociologist where she is actually situated, namely at the beginning of those acts by which she knows, or will come to know; and second, making her direct experience the ground of her knowledge. (p. 11)

My writing would be directed at two audiences: sociologists and feminists. I was a doctoral student; if my writing was to pass, it would have to fit the conventions of the dominant sociological and educational research communities. My case studies—women's personal narratives—would have to be entered into the professional and academic discourse.

As a feminist, I did not want to write in a way that would alienate the women from their own stories. I did not want to turn into abstracted data the rich emotionality of their narratives. I wanted my sociological account to be in some ways enriching to the women who were participating. How could I develop a methodology that was both sociologically rigorous and of value to the women who had participated?

Doing the Research

An initial problem in case-study research is selecting people to interview. In my study, the subjects had to be women born in New Zealand during the late 1940s or early 1950s who had their formal education in New Zealand, who worked as educators, and who identified themselves as feminists. As these women's *feminist* analyses of their lives were the center of interest, I wanted to explore how women positioned themselves with respect to the various different kinds of feminist discourse that characterized the academic and grassroots movements of the time. As outlined in Chapter 2, during this time, both academic and grassroots feminist publications identified these as liberal feminist, radical feminist, Marxist- and socialist- feminist, and antiracist/Maori-feminist positions. The women were to be chosen according to their theoretical perspectives.

The only way that a woman's theoretical perspective could be ascertained was if she had espoused it in a public situation. Without threatening confidentiality, it is not possible to be specific about actual examples. Generally, however, women's perspectives were visible if they had written them down (e.g., in publications or conference or seminar presentations), if they had spoken about them at feminist or other gatherings, or if they were known to me personally. I used my typology of feminisms—drawn from my reading of academic and grassroots feminist literature as well as experience within the movement—to ensure a variety of positions. I encountered one anomaly—an anarchist—and included her in the study. I was aware of the eclecticism or pluralism of the women's theoretical or political positions and used the typology only as a rough guide. To have chosen only Marxists or lesbian separatists would not have given me the breadth of feminist visions I wanted in my analysis.

At the time, I could find little sociological writing about the processes of gathering and interpreting life histories. Two issues that were commonly addressed in discussions of qualitative methodology had to be addressed: the accuracy and consistency of the stories that people tell and the nature of sociologists' interpretations of these.

Part of my thesis relied on people's descriptions and analyses of what had happened to them in their families and schools. It was possible for a woman to have been wrong in her interpretation of past events—for example, her mother's expectations, feelings, or motives or a teacher's prejudices. However, these adult memories and interpretations were accepted as valid because the central concern in the study was not the events themselves but the interpretations the women made of them and the importance the women attached to these interpretations in their becoming feminists and educators. As R. D. Laing expressed it (1971):

> The stories people tell . . . do not tell us simply and unambiguously what the situation is. These stories are part of the situation. There is no *a priori* reason to "believe" a story just because someone tells us it, as there is no *a priori* reason to disbelieve a story because anyone tells it. One may have good reason . . . to trust certain people's stories. The stories we are told and tell are always significant parts of the situation to be discovered. (p. 30)

In my study, I assumed that the women were telling the truth about their lives insofar as they understood and remembered the events. There was no reason for them to lie. The techniques of revising and reinterpreting the material in subsequent interviews, as outlined in the following, ensured that the stories were consistent.

It is important to bear in mind that the ways we tell our stories—the kinds of stories that we tell—are brought into being within particular power relations and are elicited by different audiences. For example, what I have divulged about myself in this book is the story both that I see as sociologically relevant to my topic and that I am prepared to divulge in a public forum. The kind of narrative I might construct in, say, a therapeutic situation could be very different. In my interviews, the women may have deliberately left out sociologically relevant information for very good reasons. In any research interview, people will only tell interviewers what they want them to know.

As someone who was a part of what I was studying—a postwar-born New Zealand feminist teacher studying what it was to become a postwar-born New Zealand feminist teacher—I wanted my sociological interpretations of the narratives to be a result of a collaboration between researcher and researched. Like Ann Oakley (1982), I wanted to replace "the methodology of 'hygienic' research with its accompanying mystification of the researcher and the researched as objective instruments of data production" (p. 58) with one that recognized "that personal involvement is more than dangerous bias—it is the condition under which people come to know each other and to admit others into their lives" (p. 58). In this study, the process of collaborative theorizing was helped by the women's theoretical sophistication; all had done some higher education studies in the social sciences and had been involved in academic and/or grassroots feminist theorizing. This helped in avoiding what Liz Stanley and Sue Wise (1983) have termed "conceptual imperialism."

> There is a continual contradiction between women's involvement in everyday experience and the "language of theory." The language of theory exerts a conceptual imperialism over experience. In effect, there is a power relationship between theory and experience, and one consequence is that women are not only alienated from theory but also from experience itself. (p. 163)

It was important to develop a methodology that would enable the women being interviewed to assist in the analysis of their own tape-recorded life histories and to try to avoid imposing alien constructions on their experiences.

This, however, was a doctoral dissertation. I was working with two male supervisors—both of an older generation and, although both were supportive of me, both with disciplinary and theoretical backgrounds that were very different from my own. As a doctoral student in the sociology of education, my "work of producing the truth was obliged to pass through this relationship if it was to be scientifically validated" (Foucault, 1980a, p. 66). My case studies—feminists' personal narratives—would have to "be entered into the professional and academic discourse" (D. Smith, 1987, p. 109). I also recognized that I had done more reading on the nature of the contradictions experienced by postwar-educated New Zealand women than had the women in the study and I believed that the kind of analysis I could construct would be of value to the women in the study without distorting or alienating them from their narratives. Like Dorothy Smith (1987), I believe in the worthwhileness of sociological theorizing.

> Though women are indeed the expert practitioners of their everyday worlds . . . disclosure of the extralocal determination of our experience does not lie within the scope of everyday practices. We can only see so much without specialized investigation, and the latter should be the sociologist's special business. (p. 160)

I wished to avoid both conceptual imperialism and a naive relativism. I attempted this by being as open as possible with the women about my theoretical orientation and the model I was developing in the course of analyzing their life histories.

I oriented the interviews around one three-part question: "I am writing a doctoral thesis about feminist teachers. I would like you to tell me how and why you became an educator, how and why you came to identify yourself as a feminist, and how your feminism influences your work and activities in education."

Few sociologists have written about the practicalities of conducting life-history interviews. One of the few texts available to me at the time was by Ken Plummer (1983), who likened the process and style to a nondirective counseling encounter:

> Often the subject is expected to take the lead rather than merely responding to a series of cues given by the questionnaire. Furthermore, it is not like a simple conversation, an analogy that is sometimes made, for the researcher has to be too passive for that. The image which perhaps captures this interview method most clearly is that of the non-directive, phenomenologically aware counsellor. All the rules of non-directive counselling . . . come into play here. Central to this view is the uniqueness of the person and the situation, the importance of empathy and the embodiment of "non-possessive warmth" in the interviewer. (p. 95)

Admittedly, my training a decade previously as a telephone crisis counselor for a voluntary organization was useful experience in interview technique. However, no interview—whether for counseling, research, or any other purpose—can be entirely nondirective. For example, the kinds of questions asked, the verbal and nonverbal reactions to responses, and even the physical setting in which an interview takes place will affect the content of the life history. Although my interviews were intended to elicit respondents' own analyses of their lives, they were also designed to test my developing and changing analyses of both the lives of the individual women and the events and structures of the wider sociohistorical context in which they planned and lived them. In this, it was important to be explicit about my position and to incorporate the feedback into my analysis.

At first, I limited interviews to 90 minutes—the length of one cassette tape. However, as this cut off some women in "mid-flight," I decided to allow them to talk as long as they wished; most talked for at least 3 hours in their first interview. To ensure that the interviews covered as much ground as possible, I suggested a chronological format and used a checklist (see Figure 3.1). When each first interview had been transcribed, I underlined it in five different colors to coincide with the five categories on the checklist. I photocopied an extra two copies of each transcript. I kept one copy intact. The second copies were cut up according to their dominant categories and were placed in the appropriate file—there was a file for each color category. As large portions of each interview were underlined in more than one color, these files were for quick reference and were very rough guidelines only. The third copy of each interview was sent to the woman interviewed, and she was asked to comment on both the interview and the color coding used. I sent each woman the checklist as a key, together with the explanation in Figure 3.1.

I received many written responses the women had made to their transcribed interviews when I interviewed them for the second time. All but two were interviewed twice; some were interviewed three or four times. Comments such as "that was an orange, not a blue experience" validated my categories: This was a sexual rather than a politicizing experience in her analysis of her own biography. I thus corrected my error of conceptual imperialism. Others made comments such as "I cried when I read that bit" or "Now I wouldn't put it that way—I'd explain it like this" as perceptions changed between the interviews. Because the women lived in several cities, there was no set time between the interviews.

The next stage was to write a preliminary sociological analysis for comment. I had been asked to write a paper on female sexuality and school cultures for an introductory textbook in the sociology of education (Middleton, 1985a). Because the paper dealt with childhood and adolescence, it was useful as a research tool in the initial phase of the analysis. In it, I theorized four case studies. The theory developed in the paper was strongly influenced by the writing of Bourdieu, whose work is discussed in chapter 4.

In this, I was influenced by an interview with a woman I shall call Joan. During her second interview, Joan, who had been studying the sociology of education, turned her knowledge of this to analyze her transcript. We discussed why it was that without University Entrance (a comprehensive high school exam that qualified students to enter the university), with preschool children, and living in a situation of domestic violence, she found the

Checklist for Life-History Interviews

Dear _____,

Enclosed is the transcript of the interview we did for my doctorate.

Your contribution has been very much appreciated. I am now working on the analysis of these transcripts. The copy I have sent you is yours to keep. The color code is as follows:

Pink	Family	parents
		siblings
		other "significant" relatives
		social class
		religion
		ethnicity
Orange	Sexuality	menstruation
		sexual relationships
		sexual morality
		marriage
		motherhood
Green	Career	ambitions
		influences (e.g., role models)
		paid work
		achievements (paid or unpaid)
Yellow	Formal education	primary school
		secondary school
		university/Teachers College
		other (e.g., WEA, Continuing Ed., Tech).
Blue	Feminism/ politicization	activities
		influences (e.g., reading, role models)

I am interested in your reactions to the categories I have used (influenced strongly by Juliet Mitchell's *Woman's Estate).*

Figure 3.1

strength, confidence, and desire to return to formal education as an adult and later to undertake teacher training and a university degree.

JOAN: Why were we good at school work, when Mum hadn't helped us much with our school work? I've made a note here—it was cultural capital! That's definitely what it must have been, because she'd been well educated—it was just an implicit passing on of values and language . . . and attitudes and all that sort of thing. But this [the first interview] was done over a year ago and I didn't know about cultural capital then.

SUE: Well, that's interesting that you should say that, because I'm using that, some of that Bourdieu stuff, because that was immediately what hit me about your interview. It's not just you, there's one or two others who left school, without having got their UE or in one or two cases without having got their School Certificate. And it was much the same, the cultural capital was *there.*

JOAN: I think the cultural capital was my Mother, I mean Dad had hardly any schooling. He had no academic anything to do with the school.

At the time of this interview, I had done little in the way of analysis of the transcripts, apart from the rudimentary interpretations of the color coding. This conversation motivated me to read more of Bourdieu's work. This usefully illustrates the process of collaborative theorizing that a life-history approach can engender.

The paper written for the textbook focused on the influence of parents and others and the influence of family marital strategies on the girls' subject choices and academic/professional motivations and aspirations—for example, aiming for the university in order to become an interesting, cultivated wife of some professional man. It explored the women's experiences of the social construction of femininity and intellectuality as contradictory and the sexual double standard (the virgin/whore dichotomy) as pervading the teenage subcultures of schools—for example, low-stream girls were typified by academic-stream girls as being both less intelligent and more sexually active. At least during their schooling, these women experienced sexuality and intellectuality as contradictory. My analysis of this had come out of the transcripts. Only later was I to read policy texts, such as the Thomas report, (see chapter 2), in which such contradictory expectations were inscribed.

The first draft of this paper was sent to the four women whose life histories had been used in it, and their feedback was incorporated into the second draft. I then used the same theoretical framework to analyze the schooldays of the other eight women and sent them each a copy of this and the original paper for comment. They responded to these in later interviews or in writing. Suggested alterations were of a personal nature, such as requests for changes of fictitious names or for refinement of ungrammatical or unclear expressions in the transcripts. Often, refinements were made to my interpretations of specific events or relationships between them— causal connections. The transcript material finally used in the thesis was okayed by the women concerned.

The interviewing took place over 3 years. The women's involvement included doing the interviews, reading and responding to the initial colorcoded transcripts, reading critically the paper on sexuality and school cultures together with any additional transcribed material, and commenting on these. There were times when I met my interviewees in unexpected social or professional contexts. This was sometimes problematic—what did I know about this person in this context? I have had to bracket out certain knowledge I have about people. My research information was an inviolable secret, as a result of my commitment to confidentiality. For example, once four of the women were speaking together with me at a feminist gathering, and one of them spoke openly about her involvement in the study. The others chose to remain silent. Several women have since talked openly about their involvement. I have taken great care to protect the identities of all the women.

A Case Study

For those being researched, research is an intervention in their lives. This is true of any social research—whether the researcher and researched meet face to face, as in an interview situation, or whether the relationship is more distant, such as via a postal questionnaire. Feminists in particular have argued that as a process of intervention, research can bring about change in the way people perceive their lives and may, in fact, stimulate them to make changes. For example, in her interviews with new mothers, Ann Oakley (1981) noted:

> Nearly three-quarters of the women said that being interviewed had affected them and the three most common forms this influence took were in leading them to reflect on their experiences more than they would otherwise have done; in reducing the level of their anxiety and/or in reassuring them of their normality; and in giving a valuable outlet for the verbalisation of feelings. (p. 50)

Presumably, filling in a postal questionnaire could bring about such changes, but they would remain invisible to the researcher. However, in the intimate relationship between researcher and researched in a sequence of long personal interviews, such changes may become visible to the researcher and become part of the data gathered.

During the early 1980s, some feminists described researching encounters as having consciousness-raising potential. The term "consciousness raising" has now been criticized because of the implications that somehow mature feminists can be conduits to revealed truths for oppressed peoples (Ellsworth, 1989; Lather, 1991; Miller, 1990; Weiler, 1991). However, in the course of the research process, people may describe their lives—their circumstances, their choices, their activities, their ideas—in ways they have not done before. In this, they may make connections between the personal (an event or an emotion) and the political or social. A personal problem may be reconceptualized as a social or political issue (Mills, 1959). The additional information and theorizations that the sociologist's analysis can provide may be helpful to the women who have told their stories.

> The most personal and intimate relationships can be seen in terms of relative power and powerlessness. A vital component of contemporary feminist activity is the consciousness-raising group in which the personal and unique experiences of women are shared in such a way that a pattern of common experience emerges. In certain respects life history analysis is similar. It involves looking at the life of an individual as a unique history, and the outcome of the historical, political and ideological context within which the person has lived. It essentially involves linking the personal and the political. (Novitz, 1982, p. 299)

I shall describe the case of Joan—how I selected her, the nature of some information she shared with me during the first interviews, and some consequences of those disclosures.

I had met Joan at a feminist party. In the course of the conversation, she began to discuss her schooling. She described feelings of marginality, observing that as a mature student at teachers college she felt different from the younger students, who had proceeded straight from school to college. She, in contrast, had "slept around" with boys as a schoolgirl, run away from home, and become pregnant at 17. She had later married and, while her children were young, took up the dropped threads of her formal education by returning to high school. Her husband opposed this. Inclined to domestic violence, he tore up her first assignments, forcing her to continue her correspondence studies secretly. Joan passed her University Entrance examination and was accepted as a teacher trainee. At teachers college, she had been introduced to feminism by other mature students. Joan agreed to be interviewed for my research.

During her first interview, she described her childhood on a farm, a lack of affection from her mother, and her later teenage pattern of sexual promiscuity. In the sixth form, she had run away from home and was living in a boy's flat. This was only the second interview I had done for the thesis. At that stage, my theoretical analysis was not clear. However, as a feminist, I believed that sexuality was relevant to my topic (the nature and development of feminists' educational theories). Had I not been both a woman and a feminist, the interview would not have gone the way it did. When Joan spoke hesitantly about her early sexual experiences, I pushed her to develop this further:

JOAN: I'd been sleeping with him at this flat and I got pregnant just after that.

SUE: Had you had any knowledge of sex before you started sleeping with guys, had you had any sex education, knowledge of contraception, anything like that?

JOAN: No, nothing. Mum never even did the little talk that you're supposed to have with your daughter.

SUE: Periods?

JOAN: No. When I got my period, I was too scared to go to Mum, because Mum had never even mentioned the word "sex" to us and I knew she absolutely disapproved of anything sexual because of hearing her with Dad and that sort of thing, you know. She was very anti-affection, anti-being-touched, everything like that, and there was a persistent "Get away, leave me alone," and we had the bedroom next door, so we heard it all the time. So my knowledge of sex really came from the boys on the bus.

SUE: School bus?

JOAN: Yes. We lived on the farm and traveled into school each day and that was sort of my main knowledge of it—and plus seeing the animals on the farm.

SUE: Oh yes. . . .

JOAN: A lot of the bull with the cows and all this sort of thing. I gathered a lot of what was going on from that. Um, also I had a few years of an experience with a relative who, um, what would you call it? More or less molested, but it was quite with my consent. It was more or less, not forced, but what do you call it when you're young and not really—

SUE: Taking advantage of you?

JOAN: Yes, it was really.

SUE: How old were you then?

JOAN: It started when I was twelve, and it went on till I was fifteen. And, um, he was giving me money. . . . It had happened to my older sister and I knew it was going on with her and my younger sister was too young, she was only about six when I was twelve. So—

SUE: Did you actually have intercourse with this guy?

JOAN: Yes. It didn't start off with that but it led up to it.

SUE: How old was he?

JOAN: He was in his, he would have been fortyish. Late thirties, forties, when it started off.

SUE: Married?

JOAN: And he was married with children and nobody knew anything about what was going on. You see, he kept saying to me, "Don't you ever tell anybody because I'll go to jail," and he kept saying this all the time. I knew what I was doing was wrong, but he used to give us money and, um, we used to say to Mum that the money came from helping him round the farm and helping him round the place and that sort of thing, so it was sort of money for helping.

SUE: He lived near you?

JOAN: Yes. And that went on for a long time, usually at his place around the farm. His wife used to go out quite a lot. I guess a lot of what went on— I don't sort of blame myself so much now, but I did for a long time; the fact of the money, kids, going back to get the money all the time. And of course we never had money at home, we never had hardly any pocket money or anything like that and—

SUE: He knew how to get his own way.

JOAN: Yes. As I got older, I was more and more scared it was going to be found out. I really was scared and, um, and I wanted it to stop, but at the same time I didn't know how to go about stopping it. But, um, it stopped once we sort of moved into town and that; I must have got to the stage when I just didn't see him. . . .

My being a woman had made it easier for Joan to share this information. Many other interviewees described sexual matters, such as menstruation, as socially constructed in the women's families and schools as a shameful and dirty secret. Despite the liberal intentions of the policymakers of the time in this regard (the policy of teaching in science classes the facts of reproduction, as seen in chapter 2), most of the women studied had been taught not to discuss such matters with others—even women—and certainly not with men. These observations are borne out in New Zealand research and women's autobiographies (Findlay, 1974; Frame, 1983; Glamuzina & Laurie, 1991). Had I been a man, I probably would not have seen the relevance of this information to the topic. Even if I had, the information might not have been shared in the interview. I knew this instinctively as a result of my own socialization. As Dorothy Smith (1974) expressed it, the feminist sociologist makes her "direct experience the ground of her knowledge" (p. 11).

At the end of this interview, after the tape had run out, Joan continued to talk of her childhood sexual experiences with the "relative down the road," describing these as incest. Apart from one woman friend in the past, she had not discussed this with anyone. She expressed the need for a support group or counseling situation but could not bring herself to take the necessary steps. At this stage, I was unfamiliar with the counseling services in her town but offered to put her in touch with someone I knew who was trying to come to terms with a similar experience. My involvement had changed from that of a mere researcher to that of a member of the wider feminist community. Her disclosure had come about as a result of my research.

Later that year, Rape Crisis Centres launched a nationwide publicity campaign to inform the public about the nature and prevalence of sexual abuse. At this time, I met Joan again. She had seen a television program on incest and was anxious to discuss it. Although she now felt ready for and in need of counseling, she was busy with higher education studies and felt unable to divide her time. As a teacher, I suggested to her that she write one of her assignments on incest—she was taking a course in an appropriate discipline and had been given a wide choice of topics to research. As students in several of my own courses had chosen this topic as a result of the recent publicity given the issue, I was able to share references, resources, and personal contacts with her. My involvement was now that of researcher, teacher, and counselor; her life and mine were intertwined through our mutual involvement in the small New Zealand network of feminists in education. In the process of being interviewed, Joan had shared something that had been personal and hidden. In beginning to analyze this as a social issue rather than as merely a guilty personal secret, Joan was going through a consciousness-raising process.

Some months later, Joan had her second interview. As requested, she brought with her the color-coded transcript of the interview and some notes she had made after reading it. At the end of this second interview, Joan discussed with me the essay she had written on incest for her course. She had visited her local Rape Crisis Centre for resources and information. Trusting the women who helped her with this, Joan had come out to them about her own experience and had entered counseling. She asked me if I thought it was possible to recover from such an incest experience, which was still adversely affecting her current sexual relationship. In reply, I commented that she was lucky it had been a relative down the road and not someone who lived under the same roof, such as her father. To this, she replied, "It *was* my father." We spoke for some time about the consequences of this for her life. At the time the thesis was being written, she was having counseling. In the course of this, she had encountered another woman who was in my research. As Penny Fenwick (1983) has observed, "The research *process* can provide a forum for strengthening women's networks."

Some Implications

In this as in all the case studies, much has had to be left out because the issue of confidentiality had to be the prime consideration. In a country the size of New Zealand, with a total population of three million, this can pose particular difficulties. To reveal someone as a Maori, a lesbian, and a kindergarten teacher, for example, would readily identify her to many people. Confidentiality had to be protected, as in the case of a woman who had never told her parents about a teenage pregnancy and adoption. Because of the priority of protecting confidentiality, some of the study's theoretical strength was lost. I could not use some women's adult experiences because they would be too easily recognizable because of their high public profiles in certain contexts. In these cases, only material from their childhoods could be used.

I had to use different names for the same women when discussing different aspects of their lives—for example, in the chapters relating to childhood, to sexuality, and to adult professional lives. The thesis had to be written in such a way that the women's sexual lives and professional lives could not be connected. There was an irony in this: My own methodology reproduced the contradiction between sexuality and intellectuality/professionalism—the personal/private and the political/public—thus preventing a complete analysis of their interpenetration. One cannot tell, for example, in the final version if it was the secondary teacher who secretly gave birth to a baby in her teens or the primary teacher who was a closet lesbian.

After the thesis was completed and my degree had been conferred, I did what most academics do: wrote academic papers for publication. Each time I used a woman's story, I asked her permission; I described the journal and the audience and showed her the paper. Most of the women remain in my life—some as close friends. I began to feel voyeuristic. For this reason, there are no long case studies in this book. It was this feeling of voyeurism that made me decide to give myself back to the 12 women in my study. I did this by writing an autobiographical account of how I had become a feminist teacher (Middleton, 1992a). I put myself into the theoretical perspective developed in the dissertation and closed the circle.

Notes

[1]In New Zealand, doctoral degrees do not involve coursework. They are usually taken after a master's degree (1 year of coursework and a 1-year thesis). A Ph.D. or D.Phil. degree requires a dissertation only. The ideal is supposed to be 2 years full-time or 4 years part-time.

[2]More details of streaming (tracking) are given in chapter 4. All students studied a common core curriculum (English, math, science, social studies, physical education, arts and crafts). However, in most schools, students were placed in classes according to the optional subjects they chose (over and above the common core)—like foreign languages, agriculture, home craft, commercial subjects, etc.

[3]This was adapted from parts of an autobiographical account I wrote for a book edited by Ivor Goodson (Middleton, 1992a). This narrative was also written for the 12 women who took part in my study. It was my way of writing myself into the analysis and giving my story to the 12 women I interviewed.

four

Becoming a Feminist Teacher

*U*ntil the late 1980s, there was very little published research on the educational experiences of those who had become, as adults, activists working for social change through the schools. Rarely within the sociology of education—focused as it was on reproduction—was education conceptualized as "a process of futuring, of releasing persons to become different, of provoking persons to repair lacks and to take action to create themselves" (Greene, 1988, p. 22). By the later 1980s, an international literature on feminist teachers had begun to develop (Casey, 1988; Miller, 1990; Weiler, 1988). In this chapter, I will summarize my doctoral dissertation. This exemplifies the kind of material I use with my students in early sessions in my "Women and Education" course. I use it to explain to my students about my own experiences and perspectives. I also use this material as narratives against which to contextualize the accounts they are constructing in their oral history projects.[1]

This chapter is divided into three sections. The first draws on the analysis developed in chapter 2 as a basis for discussion of some of the ways students' lives were monitored and regulated in secondary schools of the time. It explores the contradictory ways in which women were constituted in such discursive practices. The second section is a collective life history of the 12 feminist teachers studied. Its focus is on the historical and biographical circumstances in which the women came to work in education and the processes by which they began to identify themselves as feminists. The third section consists of four brief case studies of teachers who positioned themselves differently within the feminist discourses available to them at the time.

Contradictions in the Education of Postwar Women

In chapter 2, I discussed some of the ways women were construed within the sociological and educational policy discourses of the 1950s and 1960s. I argued that expectations for women were contradictory. The postwar woman's education was to be based on the assumptions of both equality of opportunity (as in the liberal discourse of the rationally autonomous individual) and of feminine domesticity. As discussed with respect to the Thomas report, women's domesticity was seen as essential for the economic, psychological, and political well-being of society. By means of the life histories, I shall show how these women's experiences of such contradictions, together with their access to discourses that offered alternative possibilities, produced their feminism.

New Zealand's secondary schools were streamed on the basis of optional subjects that pupils took in addition to the subjects of the common core. The streaming of individual pupils was often determined by their scores on intelligence tests, such as the OTIS (Harker, 1975; Olssen, 1988). However, as discussed in chapter 2, criteria such as the gender appropriateness of certain subjects were also influential in decisions about individual students' curricula.

To understand how students' subjectivities were constituted within such regulatory practices, a case study is useful. Hine was a Maori girl who had grown up in a rural community among her *whanau* (extended family) group. At primary school, one of her teachers had told Hine's parents that she was very bright and should aim to become a teacher. Hine's family did not have a history of academic success or professional study. Because at the time—the 1960s—students were paid a salary to attend teachers' colleges, such an ambition was possible for girls like Hine. In her last year of primary school, Hine took the OTIS test, which was used by her local secondary school as the basis for its classification of students into streams. Hine's low score shocked the teachers, who had been told to expect high achievement from her.

> I remember before I went from primary school to secondary school, the test we had to sit there—the OTIS . . . and I failed that miserably. They all had high expectations of me passing through that with flying colours and I didn't. And I remember having to sit it again. They just couldn't understand why I failed that test. When I first went to high school—there was streaming at the time—I was streamed into the academic level, even though I failed the OTIS test. They just put

me into that one. And I refused to go there, because all my cousins, who were my mates, were put into the commercial stream or even lower—which I guess was the home science course. So I went into that for the first day and then they came and got me out of there. And I remember crying the next day, because I didn't want to be in there— I was the only Maori in the class. . . . For several years I was the only Maori, so it was a very lonely existence. I could see the gradual drifting with my cousins at this stage.

As a "bright" student, Hine was seen—despite her low test score—as academic or professional material. At school, she was, as an intellectual, designated a competitive individual. Her desire to be with her cousins—to feel secure in the collectivism of her tribal group—was seen as incompatible with this. Her cousins belonged in the lower streams, where subjects such as typing and home craft were taught. Although feminine domesticity was seen as essential for the maintenance of the social order, within the hierarchies of school knowledge, home craft was seen as a "dumb girl's" option. Home craft streams were where the Maori girls—the menial or domestic workers in the wider society—were concentrated. To become an intellectual or professional, Hine would have to alienate herself from her Maoriness. She would then become a "brown Pakeha." The discursive positionings available to her as bright, as Maori, and as female were multiple, simultaneous, and contradictory.

Students were constituted by science as gendered, raced, and classed subjects. Designed from within the relations of ruling, technologies such as intelligence tests offered a scientific basis for the monitoring, regulation, and classification of the population (Walkerdine, 1984). An idiosyncratic event in Hine's biography—the intervention of a supportive teacher—led to her being seen as an exception. It was, however, her performance rather than the practice of testing that was thrown into question at the time (Olssen, 1988).

During the 1950s and 1960s, girls like Hine in the academic streams received strong encouragement to take up teaching as a career. The postwar baby boom and the raising of the school leaving age meant that there was a severe shortage of teachers. During the 1960s, there was an active teacher recruitment campaign. In 1962, a Department of Education (1962) commission recommended a recruitment target of "one sixth form girl in two" (p. 585)[2] to programs of teacher training. Teaching (like nursing) was seen as an appropriately feminine occupation (Arnold, 1987; Grumet, 1988). The chance to attend universities and/or teachers' colleges on salaries opened up access to higher education for many students whose families had not previously had such opportunities. The teacher shortage was, for many, a time of enhanced possibilities. Girls' career ambitions were, however, to be secondary to their domesticity if they married. The dominant view of the teaching careers of girl school leavers at the time was described by John Watson (1966) as "a short adventure between school and marriage" (p. 159).

The young women of the postwar baby boom, then, were experiencing contradictory expectations in their schooling. This was particularly pronounced for girls in academic streams. Although ideals of liberalism and meritocracy offered equality of educational and vocational opportunity, limited only by merit, we were socialized as women to choose occupations that were seen as feminine—such as teaching, nursing, or secretarial work. Although both men and women were expected to marry and raise children, men were expected to have both family and career, but women were expected to choose one or the other or, if we continued to teach (as many were encouraged to do during the teacher shortage), our careers would be subordinate to those of our husbands.

With respect to our sexuality, we were taught (as discussed in chapter 2) that we must not give in to men's sexual advances. There were strong prohibitions against girls having sexual intercourse before marriage; such activities were seen as signs of "juvenile delinquency" (May, 1992b). Those who trained for teaching or nursing were expected to delay such activities until after they had completed their training. In New Zealand, women who married during their teacher training lost their student cost-of-living allowances, but men who married during training were awarded additional financial support: marriage allowances. As Sari Biklen (1991) has expressed it in the case of the United States, single women teachers were seen as "a-sexual caretakers of other people's children."

Within the discourse of liberal meritocratic individualism, we were construed as intellectually, professionally, and emotionally autonomous; within the discourse of patriarchal femininity, we were ideally financially and emotionally dependent on men. Although domesticity was seen as women's highest vocation, within the hierarchies of school curricula, home economics—the province of the less rational—was accorded the lowest status. The expectations of liberalism and femininity were contradictory.

How, then, did so many of the women who attended schools at this time develop feminist analyses of the social world? How and why did we come to work as activists in education? And how did our feminism influence our teaching and our political activities in education?

Becoming Feminist: A Collective Life History

This section summarizes the life histories of 12 feminist teachers. Its focus is on how these 12 women developed their liberal, radical, Marxist, bicultural, socialist, and so on, feminist analyses of the social world and how they came to interpret their experiences of contradictions and/or marginality as outcomes of social inequalities rather than as signs of personal inadequacy. In C. Wright Mills' (1959) terms, "personal troubles" were seen as social issues or, as feminists have expressed it, the personal became political.

Contradictions of Femininity: From Childhood to Adolescence

Childhood and adolescence were characterized by a sense of ambivalence about the process of being brought up to be feminine. For example: "I was getting into trouble with my parents for not wanting to do feminine things. . . . I kept being pressured to be inside and help my mother. I wanted to be outside . . . doing active things."

Activities associated with males and masculinity were perceived as having higher status and as being more physically and intellectually satisfying than feminine things. During the primary school years, girls' tomboyishness was tolerated.

However, around puberty and in the secondary school years, girls were expected to conform to a more feminine image. For example, one woman, brought up on a farm, discussed her experience at puberty of sudden constraints on her freedom—of getting a hiding from her father for coming home late. She felt as if she was suddenly expected to change her body image from that of a strong farm laborer to that of a feminine young lady: "My father started saying things like, 'You'll have to watch your nails' and things like that . . . those pressures are conflicting. You're out doing things on the farm—and then, you're supposed to be 'looking nice.'"

During later adolescence, girls came under increasing pressure to become sexually interested in boys. Some resisted this pressure, preferring to delay or avoid altogether adult female heterosexuality (Rich, 1978): "If you talked to a boy, there were sexual connotations. To me boys weren't like that at all." To be popular with boys—to accept the dominant construction of femininity—meant for some girls acceptance of intellectual inferiority.

I didn't like being a girl. I hated girls utterly and completely, and that only changed recently when I became a feminist. I took on the beliefs of the society around me and identified with the men. . . . When I got to secondary school . . . I got friendly with some boys and wanted to be accepted by them, to be liked by them, and discovered extremely quickly that if you're bright with boys, and brighter than them, they don't like you. I immediately became "dumb."

Sexuality and intellectuality were experienced as being contradictory. The women's experiences at adolescence of becoming physically and sexually mature had been unpleasant. Coming to terms at this time with the biological process of becoming a woman was made difficult by the reticence in the women's families on sexual matters, which were seldom discussed openly. Female biological sexuality, such as menstruation, was socially construed as a dirty and somewhat shameful secret (Thompson, 1971). "I think it was the times. People just didn't talk about it." They felt ambivalent, then, about the process of becoming feminine, heterosexual, adult women.

A further source of this ambivalence was the women's feelings about and perceptions of their own mothers' lives. All of the women studied perceived their mothers as having been in some sense unhappy, unfulfilled, or frustrated, attributing this to the general lack of educational or vocational opportunities for women before the war, setbacks in the 1930s depression, the effects of the war, and the individual circumstances of their mothers' families. For example, one woman mentioned the effects of her "mother never being able to achieve the ambitions she probably felt she had. I never ever heard her complain about it. She's never, in any sense, held it over my head saying, 'You've got to do better than me' . . . but I always felt she wanted me to."

Mothers were perceived as having unfulfilled intellectual, artistic, and vocational talents and ambitions. In some cases, these had alienated them from communities they had married into—for example, they were seen as too educated for a farming district or, as in the following example, too arty: "When I was a kid I used to be really ashamed that she did things like she danced in the operatic society and she used to practice dancing in the kitchen when we had kids visiting . . . when I was a kid, she was 'different' . . . she used to wear 'fashionable clothes.'"

Childhood and adolescence were described as having been characterized by feelings of ambivalence about being brought up to conform to the dominant image of the feminine woman, which demanded their intellectual, sexual, and personal subordination.

Reconciling the demands of femininity with those of training for a professional career was difficult. Some women attempted this by regarding their higher education as a means of increasing their value to professional men as potential, cultivated wives. For these women, university was a site for realizing personal and/or family marital strategies (Bourdieu & Boltanski, 1971; Tilly, 1979): "I would have a career. . . which would make me more 'interesting.' . . . I would make some brilliant professional man an exciting wife."

All of the women had also encountered—through the personal examples of women known to them, through stories of their ancestors, and through their reading, schools, and churches—strong, politically aware, intellectual and/or artistic women. Such women had provided them with female life histories that were alternative to the more conforming feminine examples in their immediate nuclear families: "My grandmother was always held up to me . . . she was very bright and had got a degree . . . and she'd had a big struggle to get it."

Teachers were also cited as examples of strong intellectual and/or artistic women who had inspired them to seek higher education.

> If I liked the teacher, I did well. I came top of science in the third form because we had this neat teacher, a "doctor." She was one of the old school—she was very maternal and lovely, she wore an academic gown. She had this aura of "European, successful, independent woman." I knew she was a "doctor" and she'd been to an overseas university.

Some teachers had provided the women with strong female images through the curriculum. For example, stories of Catholic women saints, who were "political in that they stood up for what they believed" and heroines of World War II—spies and members of the French Resistance—were cited as sources of visions of change and of women's power to effect it.

> We were told things like the story of Violet Szabo . . . and how she won the Military Cross and how she was a war hero . . . we were read reams about Joan of Arc and how she was a warrior and how that was a really good thing for a woman to be. We were told about the heroines of the French Resistance. We were given amazingly dynamic models of what women could be, as well as men.

It was, then, seen as *possible* for women to transcend the constraints of femininity.

Within their high schools, knowledge was structured and socially organized so as to produce a gendered meritocracy. For example, girls in academic streams were seen as coming from predominantly middle-class or professional parental backgrounds, described by one woman as "the doctors' kids, the lawyers' kids, the boss of the supermarkets' kids, the research scientists' kids." They wore, when not in school uniform (which are still worn today in most high schools), "twin sets and pearls and beautifully cut skirts and neat shoes with discreet heels . . . carbon copies of their mothers."

Studious girls in the top academic streams were described by the women as either swots (probably what Americans call a "nerd"—a person who studies excessively) or intellectuals. The term "swot" was one of derogation; some saw these girls as destined for an asexual spinsterhood. Commercial-stream girls in the study described a curriculum that included dress and grooming as part of the requirements for secretarial training (Taylor, 1984). They saw themselves and their teachers as more glamorous than the swots. Some women described dressing too sexily or too "dykishly" as strategies of resistance to the imposition of feminine styles of dress and manners in adolescence (Connell, Ashendon, Kessler, & Dowsett, 1982).

The academic girls in my study described the girls in commercial and lower streams as being more sexually active—or as appearing to be so—as a group. Although there is little if any empirical evidence that such differences in levels of sexual activity did in fact exist, the women's typifications of the lower-stream girls as being more sexually active supported their ambitions to train for a career. "We were in the top streams and there was no one that I can think of in our group who got pregnant. . . . You were always hearing about someone in the lowest type of classes getting pregnant."

The women who had clear professional and educational ambitions at school regarded becoming sexually active as something that should be delayed at least until their higher education and training were completed. To get pregnant would have damaged both their career and their marriage prospects. One girl had begun to sleep with her boyfriend out of a fear of losing him. Others, as shown in chapter 3, had been victims of rape and incest—events that threw them into involuntary heterosexual activity during their school years. This led them to drop out of education temporarily.

All 12 women had been aware of the stigma against unmarried mothers and mentioned this as a major deterrent against their having sex. Some had felt themselves pressured by this into marriage. Girls who were seen as "easy" were subjected to the harsh judgments of the sexual double standard. Those who got pregnant sometimes felt compelled to hide their condition from their parents and other family members. One woman thus found herself pregnant and "on my own, in a strange place, broke, at the age of nineteen and a half."

Some academic girls reconciled the contradiction between their sexuality and their intellectuality by constructing a subculture of virginal, feminine intellectuality. For example, one woman described her teenage bohemian fantasy of life as the girlfriend of an intellectual and artistic male in the early 1960s in a provincial town:

> The boys . . . would lie around with candles and read Eliot to each other. They were quite amazing guys. I remember reading Eliot ad infinitum in the seventh form—we had to read the complete works. I grew to hate T. S. Eliot. Well, I don't think I ever understood a word of it, but I did know that it was a frightfully amazing, intellectual thing to understand.

Intellectuals strove to gain knowledge of bourgeois arts and tastes through such activities as "going to all the right concerts and listening to the tone of the violins and reading all the right books."

A sense of marginality with respect to their positionings in the dominant and contradictory discourses of patriarchal femininity was evident throughout the women's schooling. For example, becoming heterosexually active could lead to pregnancy, while becoming "too intellectual" was to be an unattractive swot. They knew, however, of examples of strong, intellectual, artistic and/or politically active women in their families, whakapapa (genealogies), religions, and schools. These examples provided them with alternative female life histories to those in their immediate families. They came to believe that changes in women's lives were both desirable and possible.

The experiences of educated postwar women were contradictory— their education promising both equality and subordination. As Juliet Mitchell (1973) observed, educated middle-class women who attended universities in the 1960s were offered "a mystifying emancipation" and participated "in an ideology of equality" (p. 28). However, their experience was one of contradictions and inequality—a situation that "enabled them to feel 'cheated' and hence has acted as a precondition of their initial protest" (p. 28). It was in this sense of something wrong that such women's feminist perspectives were grounded.

Race, Class, and the Experience of Marginality: The Personal Becomes Political

Although some women's families and wider cultural backgrounds had enabled them to feel comfortable as feminine, bourgeois intellectuals, others felt alienated from the culture of the top stream—its curriculum, tastes, fashions, and language—what Pierre Bourdieu (1971a, 1971b) called its "habitus." If one's habitus was that of the top academic stream—for example, the same style of language, literature, music, and taste—one had, to use Bourdieu's metaphor, academic "cultural capital." Those with working-class and/or Maori backgrounds expressed a sense of marginality at school. Some of these women gained access at this time to alternative discursive positionings—radical ideas that articulated these personal experiences as social/political issues.

A sense of marginality in the top academic streams of secondary schools was particularly accentuated for Maori girls. Racism was institutionalized in that Maori culture and language were not considered cultural capital. For example, one Maori woman described how "to get into the Maori language classes you had to be in the general stream, which meant second- or third-class intellect . . . and because I was top stream, I had to be fed a diet of French and Latin." She stated that racism was also overt in the attitudes of some of her Pakeha classmates in the top stream: "Kids have cake stalls [bake sales] . . . and I got up and said, 'I'll bring a rewena bread.' 'Ooh, what's that?' And I said, 'Maori bread.' 'We don't want that on our stall.'"

Feminist ideas were not widely accessible to schoolgirls of the 1950s and 1960s. The impact of the second wave of feminism did not hit the New Zealand news media and bookstores until the early 1970s. Although they may not have had access to specifically feminist ideas in their school years, a number had access to other radical political discourses that articulated their sense of cultural marginality in educational settings. For example, some of those who described themselves as socialist feminists had had access to socialist ideas during their school years through the involvement of their family:

> Very early on I was aware that my father was, that my family were, strongly Labour supporters, that my Dad was a unionist. I got told things about the Depression and the waterfront strike later on—from the side of the workers always. And I'm sure that's where my sympathies for socialism really grew.

Maori politics and the "Irish question" were other sources of political awareness within the family. For example, a Catholic woman explained, "We had the Irish thing going on in our house. The Orange and the Green. So we were made aware that there were political fights in your life."

Some women came from more conservative families. For example, some described fathers who had originally come from working-class backgrounds as holding conservative or instrumentalist views of the value of education, which they saw as useful only insofar as it led to financial security (Sharp, 1980; Willis, 1977):

> My father's family were incredibly right wing; even though they were poor, they bought the capitalist myth—if you work hard, you can make it. . . . The only future . . . for a young man is in the office and that's where you get your pension. You don't want to go working for yourself, because that's the road to ruin.

However, these women found education to be more than a chance to gain a meal ticket—it provided, in addition, access to radical ideas that challenged their parents' beliefs. During their schooling, many of the women became involved in the Left-wing politics of the day. They did this on a very personal level—for example, beginning to question one's father's support for America's and, therefore, New Zealand's involvement in the Vietnam War: "It was an emotional thing. I just couldn't bear the pictures of the starving children and the napalm and the women—that started to get to me in an emotional way."

Experiences of cultural marginality were not pleasant; a sense of not belonging can be fraught with tension, particularly if the group to which one is "the stranger" (Schutz, 1944) is the dominant group. For example, the women who had been in commercial streams left school without higher qualifications and resumed their secondary and higher education as adults. As adult higher education students, they felt disadvantaged by the level of education they had received at school and marginal in their identity as intellectuals. "I'll never catch up. I'll never be able to catch up on those 'booky'-type things in my whole life."

Their personal experiences of marginality led the women to view change as desirable, while access to radical theories such as Marxism and theories about racism helped them to consider such change to be possible. Those who had become aware, during their schooling, of inequalities and injustices of race and/or class reported that they had little difficulty identifying with feminism as adults when experiences specific to them as women were articulated.

Female Sexuality and the Sexual Revolution

As young adults, some of the women experienced heterosexual and/or lesbian sexual relationships outside marriage—behavior that was unacceptable in terms of their parents' and schools' codes of sexual morality.

During the late 1960s, new contraceptive technologies, such as the pill, dramatically changed the discursive field of female sexual morality. According to Mary O'Brien (1982), the invention of the contraceptive pill can be seen as:

> . . . a world-historical event . . . in that men and women are both in the position of being able to mediate the separation of copulation and reproduction. The material and conceptual base of the "double standard" no longer exists and women are now exploring the ramifications of freedom and control. (p. 110)

Indeed, many married women gained considerable freedom. For example, one woman teacher, who had been brought up in a religious denomination with strict prohibitions against extramarital sex, had married young in order to have sex. The pill made it possible for her, unlike the other young women in her church youth group, to delay having children, to further her career, and to travel—to combine sexuality and intellectuality/professionalism.

> I felt I was quite radical. At least I was getting married and going on the pill and not having to have children. Everybody else I knew was saving for their first house . . . we thought we were quite "with it" . . . we didn't even buy furniture when we got married. We got married and then went overseas for a [working] holiday.

The medicalization of sex (Foucault, 1980a) placed decisions about women's access to contraception in the hands of doctors, whose personal moral codes sometimes held them back from prescribing the pill to single women (Fenwick, 1980). Women's reproductive capacities were thereby considered a matter for scientific regulation. "You couldn't get the pill in those days . . . it was just dreadful. If you knew a doctor that would give it to somebody that wasn't married, the word would get around like wildfire."

During the early 1970s—when the feminist teachers in my study were university students or were beginning their teaching careers—the discursive positionings available to them as sexual women were contradictory. Within the discourse of monogamous marriage—the official sexual ideology in schools—overt sexual activities outside marriage were considered sinful and/or delinquent. Within the textual representations and other discursive practices of the so-called sexual revolution, virgins were considered prudes, or as having "psychological hangups" (Firestone, 1979). Magazines such as *Playboy* helped construct the image of the "swinging chick." The sexually liberated woman made no possessive claims on her sexual partners. As feminists of the time pointed out (Firestone, 1979; Mitchell, 1973; Rowbottom, 1973), the permissive discourse of the sexual revolution was based on *male* sexual fantasies (Hollway, 1984). Many of the women studied had tried to position themselves within the discourse of the sexually liberated woman and described this as leading them to severe stress and, in one case, serious illness.

The decision to lose one's virginity outside marriage was, for women whose parents upheld the dominant ideology of feminine domesticity, a stressful one. For such women, becoming a nonvirgin could alienate them from their parents if it became known. Rather than confide in their parents, such women led a double life (Alther, 1976; Glamuzina & Laurie, 1991; Ingham, 1983; Piercy, 1983). For example, girls who were having heterosexual and/or lesbian affairs often concealed the fact from their parents because to be openly sexually active could lead to being regarded as a "slut" by one's parents and, particularly in the case of lesbians, as deviant or abnormal in terms of the official ideology of femininity (Gifford, 1981; Laurie, 1987; Rich, 1980). Some women found the conflict between the demands of studying for a profession and their desire for sexual expression and/or companionship too intense. One adult student commented:

> I very much wanted a steady relationship with one person, and most of my energy, when I was young, was directed at finding that. I don't think I could ever have succeeded at university without that. I feel so much different studying now, because I've got all that sorted out.

Feminism

The various feminist discourses made the contradictions in their lives as *women* visible and comprehensible through naming and offering theoretical tools for analyzing them. The process of coming to adopt a feminist perspective was described as one of coming to articulate their personal experiences of female subordination or marginality as outcomes of broad social inequalities in access to power and to knowledge. This process was described as a dramatic shift in perspective, which challenged their previously taken-for-granted reality:

> I'd see . . . women tottering on their high heels with their hair looking uncomfortable or wearing clothes that didn't look comfortable.

And the men striding along beside them, much more using their bodies, much more in their clothes and using body language, it would seem more comfortable and free and it seemed to me at the time that the women were absolutely captive. It seemed to me that they were less than human, less than the men.

Feminism offered the women substantiation of their experience and the beginnings of an analysis of why they were experiencing contradictions in their intellectual/professional and their sexual lives.

There's this sort of separation between what you read and your theory and practice—it's very hard to get them together. . . . It wasn't until I had children that for the first time I realised what feminism, what all the books were about. . . . It was having to give up my job. . . . I hated being financially dependent.

Many of the women had come into contact with feminist ideas through university study—women's studies and the social sciences.

I've had all these loose ideas floating around from the last 4 or 5 years—from teaching, from [my children's playgroup], from being a "Mum," from being a Mum back in education after all that time. And suddenly there are people talking about things that have happened to me.

Summary

These life histories show that the contradictions that were evident within the policy texts of the time became the basis of regulatory practices in schools that materially shaped the everyday realities of girl students, constituting them as raced, classed, and gendered subjects. From their perspectives as feminist adults, these women described many experiences of such contradictions and the unpleasant feelings of conflict, marginality, alienation, and tension that resulted.

These women did not, however, become merely passive victims of their monitoring and regulation within discourse. They were not, as Maxine Greene (1988) expressed it, "overwhelmed by external circumstances, victimized and powerless" (p. 3). Although their experiences of conflict and contradictions created a sense of the desirability of change, the circumstances of their times and of their personal biographies generated in them visions of alternative possibilities. The teacher shortage gave them access to higher education and to a profession. In their families, their schools, their churches, and their reading, these women encountered the radical ideas of women and men who had devoted their lives to political and revolutionary causes. They developed a "capacity to surpass the given and look at things as if they could be otherwise" (Greene, 1988, p. 3).

How, then, did their feminist visions—their feminist politics—influence their lives as teachers?

Feminists Teaching: Four Case Studies

In chapter 2, I summarized the kinds of typologies of feminist theories that were commonly described as characterizing the academic and grassroots feminist movements of the 1970s and early 1980s. The 12 women in my study were each interviewed several times during the years 1981 to 1983. These women were familiar with terms such as "liberal," "radical," "bicultural," "Marxist," and "socialist feminism" because they were used in the feminist debates of the time—in women's studies and other social science texts, in academic and popular feminist journals, and at women's studies conferences. The following four case studies are presented as examples of the ways the different kinds of feminist theory of the time were practiced in education. My intention is not to label each woman a particular type of feminist or reduce whole persons to abstracted categories. What I have done here is follow through on certain theoretical strands in the women's much more complex and multiple discursive positionings.

Jane: Liberal Feminism

Jane attributed her feminism to her experiences of discrimination, victimization, and marginality as a student and a teacher of home economics. As a student teacher, she had become aware that the pupils and teachers of home economics were regarded by their peers as "dumb" or "thick." During one of her teaching-practice placements at an all-girls' school, Jane attended history and social studies lessons that covered topics such as the women's suffrage movement. These women teachers explained to Jane the connections between this 19th-century issue and the contemporary struggles of women teachers for promotion within the profession. Jane began to make connections between these and the status of home economics.

On completing her training, Jane began teaching in a brand-new coeducational secondary school. She helped arrange a timetable in which pupils of both sexes took all of the technical or manual subjects at some time during their junior year. Many of her students chose to continue home economics in their school certificate year. "Bright" students of both genders were among them. Jane became active in her local home economics teachers' association and began to run workshops on raising the subject's status.

When she was promoted to a senior position within her school, her colleagues in the subject were impressed and surprised that a "home economics person" would get such a position. However, this elicited sexist responses from male colleagues: "Really! Should a home economics person get such a high position of responsibility?"

Jane, a teachers' college graduate, decided to complete her university degree through attending classes in the evenings. In social science courses taught by feminists, she began to read academic feminist theory. Jane's description of her theoretical perspective at that time in her career positioned her very explicitly within liberal feminist discourse. She mentioned Betty Friedan's *Feminine Mystique*—a key text in second-wave liberal feminism—as having influenced her thinking at the time:

> Then I would have been a liberal feminist. Equality of opportunity, those sorts of things. I thought, "That's where it's at, that's what we've got to do, we've got to change things from within the system. We've got to talk to the Department of Education."

At the time she was interviewed, Jane had taken time out of teaching to care for her preschool child and to complete her degree part-time. Her reading of feminist theory in women's studies courses was changing her theoretical position.

> When I wrote an essay for a women's studies course, I kept changing, thinking, "I think I'm a Marxist—no, I'm definitely a radical feminist." I'd have doubts the more reading I did. And people would say to me, "It's good that you're changing." I think that feminism is something that isn't constant.

Aroha: Bicultural Feminism

Aroha saw her feminism as based on an awareness of the strength and history of Maori women and on her exposure to Western feminist theory in a university context. She used liberal feminist strategies as a first step toward a wider goal by encouraging other Maori women teachers to attain senior positions in order to combat racism among teachers and pupils and to promote the teaching of Maori culture and language. A primary school teacher,

Aroha attributed her own success in attaining a senior position to the support and encouragement of other Maori women in education.

Aroha's sense of pride and confidence in being a Maori woman had come about partly through her awareness of the Maoris' importance in history. She had read the writings of Rangimarie Rose Pere (1983) on the status of Maori women in her tribes' traditional modes of learning (see chapters 1 and 2). She described this work as having been highly significant in her appreciation of the different but equal or complementary status of the genders within these traditions.

Aroha had also learned of the power of Maori women through conversations. She described an encounter with a leading male Maori academic, versed in both Maori and Pakeha scholarly traditions, about the symbolic role of women on the marae (tribal meeting place). No formal occasion could begin unless both genders were present. Both were of equal status and importance.

> This scholar discussed with me the importance of Maori women in traditional Maori society and it made me think we were really important. In fact, we had an elevated status in some instances above men. According to the Maori myth, woman was the first being ahead of man; but you look at Christianity—it's Adam, isn't it, before woman? Adam created woman. The scholar said that the Pakeha interpretation of the tangi [funeral] situation is that the men have the most important part because they're doing all the speeches. But he said the most important part is the women when they give that initial call to welcome everybody back to the marae and to bring the dead back to the marae. He was saying it was because of Hine-nui-te-po. Hine-nui-te-po was the offspring of Tane, who was one of the gods. Tane mated with his own daughter. She got whakama [embarrassed or ashamed] and so she went into hiding. He went and tried to get her to come back, and she said, "No, you go, and I'll stay here. You go and you have our children now and I will receive them on death." When these things were written up [by Pakeha anthropologists] Hine-nui-te-po was seen as the personification of death. The Pakeha or Christian interpretation, I suppose, was that woman represented evil, the unknown. Whereas for the Maori, it was just the "other place"— the place to go back to mother. I felt good listening to this scholar explaining that to me. The woman does the initial call on the marae— there's an initial call to Hine-nui-te-po to say "we are bringing back your offspring." So the woman is the giver of life and the taker back of life.

Western liberal feminist demands for the abolition of differentiated sex roles were antithetical to this perspective, which Aroha regarded as enhancing rather than demeaning women's status. As a Maori woman, Aroha was committed to collectivist goals of helping Maori children to be secure in their own tribal epistemologies. Within the teaching profession, she also positioned herself within the discourse of liberal individualism—applying for promotions and encouraging other Maori women to do the same. She believed that from such positions, Maori women would effect more radical change. Her feminism, then, was bicultural.

Marie: Radical Feminism

Marie had been a high school dropout who had lived a hippie lifestyle in the late 1960s and early 1970s. She had reentered formal education after marriage, when her children were young. Her husband had encouraged her to take adult education classes, and her teachers there had urged her to go on to the university. At the time she was interviewed, Marie had graduated from the university and was at teachers' college gaining her teaching credentials.

Marie had encountered feminist ideas at university and had synthesized these with her anarchistic, hippie view of the world. Like radical feminists, she did not believe that emulating men's careers would liberate women and felt that women's mothering activities gave them a certain moral superiority over men, whose career patterns and socialization for masculinity deprived them of the opportunity for sustained reflection on questions of personal relationships or morality. Like many radical feminists, whose theories are grounded in the valuing of women as carers and nurturers, Marie favored child-centered pedagogies (Grumet, 1988).

She described the curriculum of her teachers' college as a kind of technocratic behaviorism with a strong emphasis on intelligence tests. College for her "epitomized the high school environment, and I hated high school. The teachers and the students have got a sort of wall between them." Her outspoken criticisms were bringing her into conflict with the staff and with fellow students. "They see me as something rather vile and low." She was particularly worried by the large numbers of fundamentalist Christian students in the college: "They have tunnel vision. They see the natural role of women as in the home. When they go out to teach they will encourage little girls to 'be little girls.' They are actually putting the boundaries up."

Similar conflicts had emerged during her teaching-practice placement in a primary school class of 5- and 6-year-olds.

> I did [a unit] on ballet, and I took along tutus and pointed shoes. . . .
> I let them put on the costumes, and I said to them, "You can put on a
> ballet." Well, that went on all day. . . . They were so engrossed. . . .
> That's very threatening to a teacher who sticks to a rigid program,
> because she can't see where it applies to everyday life. I felt I was pro-
> viding those children with a living experience that they would
> remember for the rest of their lives. You know—"the day I wore the
> tutu—danced."

In educational settings that were dominated by technocratic discourse, Marie's radical feminism and her child-centered pedagogy ensured her continuing marginalization. She was experiencing severe stress and felt as if she would be working against the system in her teaching.

Terry: Socialist Feminism

At the time of her interviews, Terry was teaching adults in an institution of higher education. Her sophisticated knowledge of Marxist and feminist theory had been put into practice in her teaching, and she had become well known in feminist circles for her innovative, nonhierarchical approach. Terry said that she had developed these skills during her early teaching days in primary schools. From a working-class background, she had struggled during her early teaching days to articulate the sense of inferiority she had felt in the top academic stream of an urban girls' secondary school. "My schooling was just so influential in what I've ended up espousing as a phi-losophy, my experience as an individual."

Like many Marxist feminists of her generation, Terry, one of the older postwar women in the study (born in 1945), had had access to Marxism before she had encountered feminism (Mitchell, 1973). At primary teach-ers' college in a large city in the 1960s, she had encountered "people who were incredibly involved in race issues and Vietnam, Black consciousness— we were always having people in to talk to us in assembly about those issues. It was the 'red' teachers' college." Although school had failed to make con-nections between her personal experiences of oppression as female and working class, the red teachers' college helped her to make those connec-tions through exposing her to the radical theories of the time. While at teachers' college, Terry became active as a folksinger in local coffee bars and regarded this experience as an important part of her political awakening.

> I seemed to identify instantly with the class-based songs of my ances-
> tors, my Scottish and Irish ancestors. . . . That whole working-class

experience was opened up to me there and I loved it from the start. It was really important, and I still identify with a lot of that.

Terry drew on her own experiences of marginality in educational settings to devise teaching strategies that would help students to come to terms with these experiences in their own lives. Like Marie, Terry favored a child-centered pedagogy. She also, however, supported the liberal strategies of getting members of oppressed groups into positions of power. She saw this as a means to the wider end of "breaking down inequitable structures." Her personal feelings of marginality were grounding her political activism: "My feminism influences me at the personal, methodological level, like trying to break down the structures that are there. I feel alienated from them naturally."

Her feminist consciousness raising had come about when she had enrolled in university social science courses as a mature student. Her feminism was grounded in an awareness of the multiplicities of women's oppression. "The system is not just patriarchal, but it's also a class system, and, of course, it's also a race system. What is created is a whole hierarchy of winners and losers."

Conclusion

In this chapter, I have constructed a collective life history of 12 New Zealand feminist teachers of my own age group—the post–World War II generation. Our feminist ideas were influenced by the overseas theories of academic women's studies, by local feminist and wider political debates, and by people known to us. Differing—and at times contradictory—discursive positionings have become available to us during our lifetimes. Individual women's access to and degree of affinity with the various discourses of our times vary according to geographical location, class and cultural background, and idiosyncrasies of biographical circumstances and events (such as the kinds of school attended and the influence of specific individuals or groups). Ideas become attractive if they are encountered at a time and in a form that make sense of personal experience. A woman's sense of relevance and grasp of possibilities influences her choices of theoretical and political positionings from those perceived as available.

As radical teachers, we experience in our workplaces continuing marginalization. This marginalization is experienced as both a personal and a group, or collective, phenomenon. The women in my study described their feminism, their socialism, their lesbianism, their Maoriness, and so on, as theoretical and political articulations of their personal experiences of discrimination, victimization, or oppression—as expressing solidarity with others of their kind. Within the educational institutions in which they worked, some experienced not only personal prejudices but also incompatibilities between their feminist and other radical philosophies of teaching and the authoritarianism and technocratic rationality that dominated their institutions. They experienced the marginalization and denigration of their pedagogies—a phenomenon that is now well documented in the literature on feminist and other radical teachers (Bowles & Klein, 1983; Culley & Portuges, 1985; Grumet, 1988; Miller, 1990; Weiler, 1988).

As Bourdieu (1971a) has argued with respect to universities, such continuing marginalization in educational settings can be productive of further radicalism. "The attacks against academic orthodoxy come from the intellectuals situated on the fringes . . . who are prone to dispute its legitimacy, thereby proving that they acknowledge its jurisdiction sufficiently to reproach it for not approving them" (p. 179).

Notes

[1]As a brief summary of a 411-page document, this chapter reviews only the main arguments and records the main flavor of the case studies. I have not quantified the data. The form of this chapter is based on that of the conclusion to the thesis (Middleton, 1985b). For a more detailed example of how individual case studies were theorized, see Middleton (1987b).

[2]The sixth form was the senior year at high school, the year in which students could take the University Entrance examination. The Department of Education was aiming to attract one half of all girl seniors into teaching. At that time, only a small proportion of high school students would have remained at school until the sixth form. It was common for students to leave school after the School Certificate examination at the end of the fifth form. New Zealand high schools do not have graduates in the American sense. At this time, the majority of students would have left school without formal qualifications. The sixth form was only for those students who intended to go on to higher education of an academic or professional nature.

five

Academic Feminism: Living the Contradictions

*A*cademic feminists are multiply marginal. As women, we are a minority among male academics; as women academics, we are anomalous among women and are seen as elitist by some grassroots feminist activists. As feminists, we are "other" to some women academics. As feminist academics teaching women's studies, we are associated with a vulnerable field of marginal status. The multiple positionings of academic feminists have been usefully framed by Nancy Fraser (1989):

> In relation to our academic disciplines, we function as the academic wing of an expert public. In relation to extra-academic social movements . . . we function as the expert wing of an oppositional public. In addition, many of us relate to still other publics. As teachers, we try to foster an emergent pedagogical counterculture. As faculty advisors, we try to provide guidance and lend legitimacy to radical student groups on our campusses. Finally, as critical public intellectuals, we try to inject our perspectives into whatever cultural or political public spheres we have access to. (p. xii)

This chapter explores the everyday working lives of feminist university teachers—the ways in which, in the various dimensions of our lives, "oppositional discourses and expert discourses intersect" (Fraser, 1989, p. xii). I use my own experiences as a teacher of "Women and Education" courses within a university as a case study of the politics of feminist knowledge in an educational institution.

Like many feminist courses, my "Women and Education" course is positioned in two undergraduate university programs:

education and women's studies. This dual location brings women's studies students into a course that would otherwise contain only education students. As a teacher of and contributor to courses in both programs, I take my educational knowledge into classes in women's studies and bring my feminism into those in the education department. My feminism and my educational theories inform my public and private life outside the university, and my feminist community activities influence my curricula.

> Blurred boundaries; intersections; fluidities—ebbs and flows in time and space; harsh interruptions . . . these will not "write themselves" in tidy arguments. They will not follow linear paths, or submit to the ordered hierarchies of headings. The sociological voice is interrupted by "internal talk" (Noddings, 1991, p. 164). The logic of argument is disturbed by anger, laughter, pain. Across the screens of my reasoning drift the faces of students, the words of colleagues, reflections of the greening trees by the lake I pass on my walk from kitchen to classroom. . . . My typing fingers follow the driftings of consciousness, transfix in print scores of their tunes and cacophonies. Refusing to remain in the "sensible emptiness" (Pagano, 1991, p. 193) of theory, they compose narratives, "tell stories" about my experience of "being a feminist academic."
>
> "Telling stories" becomes a basis for educational theorizing. Life histories, biographies, autobiographies now form the basis for a growing literature in educational theory (Casey, 1988; Goodson, 1988; Goodson, 1992; Schaafsma, 1990; Witherell & Noddings, 1991).
>
> I am composing a polyphonic score; a counterpoint of many voices. I speak as a teacher, a feminist activist, a sociologist, a politician, a "public intellectual," a citizen. You will hear "the ghosts of students past"[1] and the loud arias of sociologists. Sometimes the voices are solos; sometimes they sing in harmonies; sometimes they shout—a rebellious rabble. While some sing the scores of previous composers, others indulge in free improvisations.

An Encounter

It is a still morning—the birds are strangely silent. I try to think abstractly of the structuring of educational knowledge but find myself thinking of Joe—a student past, who will not stay out of sight in the shelved pages of my doctoral thesis. He takes over my thoughts. As Janet Miller (1990) has argued, "curriculum is centred within students' and teachers' biographies, histories, and social relationships" (p. 2).

Joe was Maori, of about my age, of working-class rural origins, and a primary school teacher. He was taking my multicultural course, a course I convened in the mid-1980s. The course was called "Teaching in Multicultural Settings." As a Pakeha, I felt competent to teach about the ethnocentrism and colonial power relations in which school knowledges are inscribed. However, I refused to teach about the experiences and perspectives of Maori and other cultural minorities. Consequently, I relied heavily on visiting Maori and other ethnic minority speakers. When I organized the course, I focused it on issues of racism and class oppression. I believed that as Pakeha and middle class, I was positioned within the oppressor class rather than the oppressed class in New Zealand society.

As a feminist, I was particularly concerned that Maori women's voices be heard among the visiting speakers and in the set readings, for Maori academic scholarship, like its Pakeha counterpart, has been seen as male dominated (Irwin, 1992b; Te Awekotuku, 1984). Within the Waikato region where I work, there were at that time many prominent Maori women educators. My educational and feminist networks gave me access to such women. Accordingly, my course included more women than men speakers. One student wrote in her end-of-course evaluation that "the high proportion of women speakers was unnecessary."

Apart from that, I was unaware that my feminism was showing in this course to any significant degree. However, no doubt, some students would have seen me as having a reputation as a feminist on campus. For example, for part of 1983, I was acting convenor of the women's studies program.

> Jo Anne Pagano says (1991), "I think we all have a tendency to fictionalize ourselves when we write about ourselves. Force is added to the impulse when autobiographical work will function in some judgmental scheme" (p. 194). These narratives, the stories I construct about my feminist university work, are brought into being by and within the academic power relations that are their object of inquiry. As "an academic book," this will be positioned in various "judgmental schemes." I choose carefully which feelings, thoughts, and information are to enter such public domains. My accounts are positioned and partial.

After several weeks of absence from class, Joe came to see me in my office. He had stayed away, he said, because my feminism had put him off at first. He had found it incomprehensible that I, as a Pakeha academic, could consider myself oppressed.[2]

> I wasn't talking about women in general. I mean I'm not uncomfortable with Maori women, and if they are more eloquent and more forceful and higher ranking in terms of society, that doesn't worry

me at all. But what it was, what I was trying to tell you was, that being Pakeha as you were, and being in charge of the place, and the rangatira [leader] of the course. . . . What it did was remind me of certain things I learned in school. And the fact was that then, you know, there were girls who were white, pretty from the Pakeha point of view, dressed nicely, they ate nice lunches, and they were successful in school. And the thing that I always remembered was that they would giggle at my, and my relations', and my friends' clumsiness in using the English language. And they would laugh at us when we were strapped because we didn't do our spelling or our maths or we didn't get enough right. We were walloped in front of them. This kind of an attitude, this kind of a feeling within me towards women, white women especially, has always been there. And when I hear feminists going on about how tough their lives are and being oppressed by men, I understand that, I agree. But they've got bloody higher chances than I had, and I'm a Maori man. Now, relate that to Maori culture, where a man is pretty well assured of a place or a dominant position, you know. And a woman too, but there are different criteria for measuring it. . . . I find it difficult to side with the radical elements. You know, it was sort of hard. I was thinking, "Goddamn it, here she is, she's running this thing and she is saying that women are being oppressed." And I'm thinking, "Goddamn it, she ought to have lived some of my life and see what it's like." That's what I was sort of trying to get at. I think, a bit of resentment on my part. Then I thought, "How stupid. I've just got to get along—why the hell—I've just got to get along there and learn what there is to learn." And so that's what I did. It was getting to the stage when I was having dreams about those days, and I knew it was coming from this course . . . you know, school days, getting the strap . . . and those girls giggling and laughing. And us boys ganging together and beating up some other poor person, or going and playing football and pumping the hell out of anyone we could get hold of. But you know, in that way I'm also very pleased to have confronted that problem and come to terms with it.

Without realizing it, I had taken my feminism into an education course. While I had tried to bring to the foreground issues of class and race, Joe had read me as a radical feminist who prioritized my own oppression as a woman. My presence as a Pakeha woman in a position of power in education had surfaced in his consciousness the taunts and pains inflicted in his school days by middle-class Pakeha girls.

As Patti Lather (1991) has argued, "rather than dismiss student resistance to our classroom practices as false consciousness," we should "explore what these resistances have to teach us about our own impositional tendencies" (p. 76). From Joe, I learned about some of the ways my teaching and my personality could be read. I had not wanted my Pakeha academic feminism to overshadow the horrors of racism. I decided that I would in the future position myself much more overtly with respect to issues of race and class at the beginning of all my courses so that students could deconstruct my teaching if they needed to. The autobiographical account—the archaeology of my pedagogy outlined in chapter 1 of this book—had its origins in such encounters.

The Politics of Academic Women's Studies

Pedagogies are created in institutions: preschools, schools, universities, and colleges. The institutional structures within which they come to form are influenced by the historical and political events, the material conditions, and the cultural contexts of their time and place. Pedagogies are rendered desirable and conceived of as possible within the political configurations of an institutional culture. Much of our work as academics involves analyzing and participating in the power relations of the institutions within which we write and teach. To explore this, I shall move beyond the personal by positioning myself within the disembodied conversations—the discourses—of curriculum theory. I speak for a while with my sociological voice.

To understand the positioning of women's studies within university structures, the work of the British sociologist Basil Bernstein is useful. Bernstein saw the organization of educational knowledge as patterned on two major "knowledge codes": "collection codes" and "integrated codes." He used the term "collection code" to refer to patterns of curriculum organization in which the contents of various academic subjects are insulated from one another through such organizational devices as compartmentalized timetabling, hierarchical subject-based departments, and subject specialization among teachers. Conversely, the term "integrated code" refers to curricula in which boundaries between contents or disciplines are blurred. The teaching is often done by staff from a number of different departments. Many university women's studies programs share the characteristics of an integrated code.

According to Bernstein (1971), the dominant knowledge code in modern secondary schools and universities is the collection code, in which "knowledge . . . is private property with its own power structure and market situation" (p. 56). Collection codes structure collegial relationships—within and between disciplines and departments—in hierarchical, encapsulated, and competitive ways.

> Where knowledge is regulated through a collection code, the knowledge is organised and distributed through a series of well-insulated subject hierarchies. Such a structure points to oligarchic control of the institution, through formal and informal meetings of heads of department with the head or principal of the institution. Thus, senior staff will have strong horizontal work relationships (that is, with their peers in other subject hierarchies) and strong vertical work relationships within their own department. However, junior staff are likely to have only vertical (within the subject hierarchy) allegiances and work relationships. (p. 61)

Sociologists and historians of the curriculum have argued that the existing collection code classification of educational knowledge into subjects in universities reflects the power struggles of groups of male academics as much as any epistemological categorization of academic knowledge (Arnot, 1982; Bernstein, 1971; Coyner, 1983; Goodson, 1988; Spender, 1981; Spender, 1982a). Due to historical circumstances, some fields of study have constructed a power base and, because they are represented at the higher levels of decision making, can arrest the development of new subjects that might compete with them for scarce resources.

In contrast, integrated code subjects such as women's studies are administered by "a committee system of staff . . . which will perform monitoring functions" (Bernstein, 1971, p. 65). In contrast to subjects structured according to the hierarchies of a collection-coded discipline, integrated code subjects such as women's studies are often not represented directly at the most senior levels of decision making. As Bernstein described it, the administrative anomaly of an integrated code within an institution structured according to a collection code creates "a type of organizational system that encourages gossip, intrigue, and a conspiracy theory about the workings of the organization, as both the administration and the acts of teaching are invisible to the majority of the staff" (p. 61). I shall use this model as a framework for a brief discussion of the changing institutional structures and political dynamics in which my teaching of "Women and Education" takes place.

The women's studies program to which my course contributes began as one course in 1974 (Ritchie, 1982; Seymour, 1976). By 1981, the year I began to contribute to the program, it had grown to a total of six undergraduate courses. Four of these, including "Women and Education," were subject based and taught from their host departments. Two were interdisciplinary and team-taught by women from several departments. Cross-listing meant that students could take departmental courses such as "Women and Education" as part of their women's studies package (at that time not a major, but only a minor for a social science degree).

Women's studies was administered and coordinated by a voluntary committee on women's studies, which included students and other interested members of the university feminist community, as well as those who taught the various courses. The majority of the teachers were untenured, and during one financial crisis in the institution, 46% of the women academics, including the majority of the feminists on the faculty, were threatened with termination of their contracts.[3] With no departmental structure or staffing of its own, the program was continually at risk. It was not formally represented at the higher levels of decision making and survived largely through the lobbying of senior staff by junior staff. At this time, the information networks among the program's feminist staff and students were riddled with the gossip, intrigue, and conspiracy theories identified by Bernstein as characteristic of the politics of integrated codes within hierarchical collection-coded institutions.

These institutional fragmentations were superimposed on a feminist movement whose boundaries were not confined within the academy. Like its counterparts elsewhere, Waikato's women's studies program was organic to various feminist communities outside the university gates. Although individuals were positioned unequally within the university as teachers and students, outside the university in various feminist organizations, networks, and activities, we were positioned differently in relation to one another—as coworkers, as activists, and as friends.

In Hamilton, New Zealand, as in many university cities elsewhere, academic women's studies was cultivated in the soils of wider feminist movements and debates. For example, the evolution of our program took place in an environment of local and international debates about the place of feminist knowledge in the academy. Many liberal feminists supported the development of university programs in women's studies as a way of encouraging women into academic scholarship and of combating sexism within other disciplines (Bernard, 1973; Tobias, 1978.) Some radical feminists, however, criticized the institutionalization of women's studies courses in an academic context, arguing that the setting up of an elite hierarchy of feminist "experts" defeated one of the objects of feminism, which was to challenge the hierarchical structuring of academic knowledge (Rich, 1976). As Dale Spender (1982a) argued:

> . . . feminists . . . seek an end to hierarchies and standards, as they have been constructed, on the grounds that they are *not* an inherent part of learning, but of a stratified society . . . in the current context where a body of knowledge is rapidly becoming available, and where the possibility of "transmission" exists—with all its concomitant attributes of hierarchies and competition—it may be very important for feminism to focus on past achievements and to keep the cooperative model in mind, for it could begin to get "lost" as feminism enters institutions. (p. 169)

The 1970s and early 1980s saw heated debates among feminists on this question. While liberal feminists pressured women to succeed in terms of the institution, separatists accused those who did so of becoming coopted agents of the male power elite. Academic feminists were accused of exploiting the movement to gain privileges.

As feminist university teachers, we were positioned inside the feminist educational theories and debates that were the objects of our curriculum. It became impossible to separate content from form. The traditional divisions identified in curriculum theory—the binary oppositions between the overt and covert and between intentional and hidden dimensions of curricula—collapsed.

Feminists in a Classroom

When I started "Women and Education" in 1981, it was the only university course of its type in the country. As I explained in chapter 2, to gain credibility for the course and to have it accepted as a part of the degree requirements, I structured it as a conventional academic discipline. The first half of the course consisted of an introduction to the typologies of feminist educational theories and was taught as a guided reading program. Classes took the form of prepared discussions of the set material and corresponding exercises in the study guide. The guided reading section of the course was assessed by an essay and an open book test. Although much of the content of this part of the course was radical, the format was in the liberal mode of initiation into a body of theory and did not in itself challenge the dominant style of university teaching (Hirst, 1975; Peters, 1966). Students were required to read and critique examples of writings that exemplified conservative (e.g., biologically determinist) perspectives, liberal perspectives, Marxist, radical feminist, Maori, and socialist-feminist perspectives on women's education.

This approach, I believed, would allow students of all backgrounds and persuasions to work on developing, stating, refining, and critiquing their own theoretical positions. The majority were education students—either teachers in training or experienced teachers. These students had a knowledge of schools, some familiarity with educational theory, and maybe little knowledge of or interest in feminism. Some were suspicious of or opposed to feminist ideas. Conversely, some of the women's studies students who were coming in from other disciplines may have previously given little thought to educational theory or processes but had some prior knowledge of feminist history and ideas and had become very interested in women's issues. Several of the women's studies students had strong radical feminist theoretical beliefs and political agendas. Within the class, conflicts developed between the nonfeminist/liberal students and those who were passionately converted to radical and separatist feminism. Such students became impatient with what they saw as retracing their steps by being required to work through liberal and Marxist concepts, which they had long ago rejected.

The second part of the "Women and Education" course was designed to encourage students to state their own theoretical positions and to use these to analyze an aspect of women's education that was of particular relevance to them: their own or their children's educational experiences, a political project with which they were involved, and an aspect of education policy. Radical students who were members of feminist collectives could then include theoretical analyses and documentation of their own political activities on and off campus. Several feminist students used this opportunity to challenge the course and my teaching of it as hierarchical and antifeminist.

I quote from the essay of one such student—I shall call her Diane:

> The very act of writing this essay involves me, as a radical feminist, in a series of contradictions. Firstly, I am required to present a critique of my university education by presenting a piece of work in what I see as a patriarchal academic mode—that is, an essay which requires that I legitimize my own experience by providing "adequate referencing." I am obliged to validate my experience by quoting the writing of those who have "succeeded" in the very institutions that I am attacking, and therefore have enough academic "clout" to earn credibility and the privilege of access to publishing resources. Furthermore, I had a limited choice of topic for presentation and the end product is subject to assessment by a person placed above me in a hierarchical system, who will "grade" it and rank me on a success/failure scale using "standards" which I had no hand in setting. Paradoxically, in order to challenge the structure, value systems, and operation of the university, I

am forced to use those very forms which I find distasteful and alien—
result: academic schizophrenia.

As a student and an intellectual, Diane was positioned inside the
academy. As a radical feminist, she positioned herself outside it. Because I
was a power figure—the designer, selector, and assessor of her knowledge—
Diane positioned herself in relation to me as an antagonist.

Within the class that year, debates took place between the liberal and
radical feminist students. These are exemplified in the following excerpt
from a tape-recorded class evaluation at the end of the course:

CATHERINE: Assessment implies that there is a standard, that you either fail
or you win.

TANYA: I agree, but the university just won't allow a course without assessment.

JOANNE: Well, then, it's not a feminist course, and women's studies is just
part of the status quo and women's studies is no challenge to the establishment.

BETTY: Are you saying that the course is mere tokenism then?

JOANNE: I'm saying that it's maintaining the status quo.

BETTY: What do you suggest?

JOANNE: What do I suggest? Well I don't think that real feminist women's
studies can happen in the university.

BETTY: Where do you think it could happen?

JOANNE: I think it happens "out there" in consciousness-raising groups, in
informal groups.

AMY: Can I come in? Even though I largely agree with you that things can be
done better, and differently, and more feminist-oriented outside the
university, don't you think it's also good that there's something here
within the institution?

SANDRA: There's a lot of people here that probably wouldn't have been
exposed to it otherwise.

MARY: I think that the course is important and I think that it should be
within the university. What goes on outside, and this comes down again
to the thing about what we mean by being educated . . . I hope that it
doesn't stop here, that it's something that goes on all the time. All Sue is
doing is passing on what she has learned, what she has gathered, to us,
and we can go further. But for me Sue has got the know-how, because
she's been in contact with more of the research, etcetera, etcetera, that's
been done than you and I have. I know that we could go to the library

and we could look up "feminism" and we could look up the various sub-
sections and we could read them, but I think that with a course, we're all
different I know, but with a course we're forced to look at certain readings which we mightn't do otherwise on our own. I'm only pointing out
why I think it's important that we have a leader.
JOANNE: That you have a leader.
BETTY: Yes, that I need a leader.

Like the feminist students who were criticizing academic women's
studies, I was positioned both inside and outside the dominant discourses
of my discipline. At the time, I, too, was struggling for legitimacy in order
to survive in the academy. The legitimacy, status, and continuation of the
"Women and Education" course was by no means assured. These were the
years in which I was drawing my map of feminist educational theories—
struggling to make a discipline that would be sufficiently acceptable to gain
legitimacy within the degree structure. I was also designing a feminist doctoral thesis under two male supervisors. I was a very recent recruit to university teaching—a person who, in younger days, would never have
dreamed that an academic career was possible. Like many women academics, I felt shaky, insecure in my role as an expert, disbelieving in my
right to teach and my authority (Aisenberg & Harrington, 1988). I was
working in a small city; I needed the personal and professional support of
local feminist networks.

The conflict I have described was a minor incident. But there were
many other much more painful conflicts among campus feminists. Feminist writings and feminist folklore record numerous examples of the ways
in which, in the early 1980s, feminists who were teaching and studying in
universities were torn apart during institutional conflicts. Women were
pulled by divided loyalties and found themselves positioned on opposite
sides during struggles over assessment (Fletcher, 1991), appointments and
tenure, and sexual harassment. We had believed in the solidarity of sisterhood (Jones & Guy, 1992). Sisterhood shattered into jagged splinters.

Feminism and Pedagogy

I was then, as I do now, designing my curriculum with two pedagogical
principles in mind: the importance of teaching about existing feminist
educational theories and research and the importance of students' personal knowledge and experiences as a grounding for their own educational
theories and strategies. I wanted my students to have available to them

some theoretical tools with which to craft their understandings of experiences—to focus also, as Maxine Greene (1988) has expressed it, "on the range of human intelligences, the multiple layers of language and symbol systems available for ordering experience and making sense of the lived world" (p. 125).

As discussed previously, many feminist writers, especially those of radical feminist persuasions, have argued that a feminist pedagogy is a student-centered pedagogy that emphasizes the educational worthwhileness of using students' personal experiences as a basis for learning. As received knowledge, theories—even feminist theories—can become "conceptual imperialism" (Stanley & Wise, 1983). Some have argued that certain formal teaching techniques, such as imparting knowledge through top-down methods such as formal lecturing, is inherently unfeminist. Previous discussions of such questions can be usefully grouped into three major sets of arguments: political, empirical, and psychological.

Political rationales are derived from various versions of the consciousness-raising model, which developed in the early phases of the second wave of feminism. Consciousness raising originated in grassroots settings and has been adapted for more academic situations. It was a technique of finding words for what Betty Friedan (1963) described as "problems with no names," as women met in informal groups to share their "sense of something wrong" (Mitchell, 1973) with their experiences as women in particular (usually middle-class, white, Western, and urban) settings. It was a way of making knowledge where no prior written records remained (Spender, 1978, 1981). Ann Foreman (1977) described consciousness raising as a process in which women learn

> to look at themselves through their own eyes rather than through those of men . . . it is the . . . often painful process of breaking through the experience of femininity. By discussing and comparing their individual experiences women develop an understanding of the emotional structures of their dependency (p. 151).

Critics argued that within this framework, experience was conceptualized as unproblematic: It was assumed that pure experience could be described and was in and of itself valid knowledge. A politics grounded in consciousness raising rested on women's experiences to provide a basis for an oppositional women's knowledge and feminist culture. Such assumptions, said socialist feminists, rendered invisible the material conditions and power relations of the wider capitalist/patriarchal society that structured such experiences. For example, Sheila Rowbotham (1973) wrote that "the problem created by simply rejecting everything that is, and inverting male values to make a female culture out of everything not male is that the distortions of oppression are perpetuated" (p. ix). Juliet Mitchell (1973) commented that "the rise of the oppressed should not be a glorification of oppressed characteristics" (p. 178). What was needed, they argued, were historical and materialist analyses that would contextualize women's experiences within the wider power dynamics in which they had come to form. The teaching of theory within this perspective was an aid to liberation.

Although some have grounded feminists' preferences for student-centered pedagogies in political imperatives, others have seen these primarily as a historical fact. Empirical research supports the claim that women teachers—to a greater degree than men teachers—prefer the pedagogies that are based on students' personal knowledge. For example, in a study of academic women in Massachusetts, Nadya Aisenberg and Mona Harrington (1988) noted a tendency for women's scholarship in their various disciplines to focus "on the relation of actual daily experience to larger social or moral patterns" (p. 94). Similarly, all of the feminist school teachers in Kathleen Weiler's (1988) study "mentioned the value of nurturance and caring in themselves and their work-values that are emphasized as positive aspects of women's experience. . . ." (p. 78). The Catholic religious and Jewish women in Kathleen Casey's thesis on feminist teachers spoke of "a genuine care of children" as their major motivation for becoming teachers; a "kind of attachment," argues Casey, that "has enormous potential for progressive action" (1988, p. 225). The New Zealand feminist teachers in my own study (see chapter 4) expressed similar concerns.

Marxists, sociologists, and socialist feminists have sought explanations in the historical and material conditions of women's work (Bernstein, 1975; May, 1992a). Women teachers have worked disproportionately with infants and younger children, but men have worked disproportionately with adolescents closer to the public world of work. Various forms of progressivism in which students make choices and express themselves freely have taken root more readily in the lower-status feminine world of early childhood education than they have in the higher-status masculine domain of formal secondary and higher education levels.

A third set of writers have drawn on psychological theories, such as object relations (Chodorow, 1978; Gilligan, 1982), to argue that student-centered pedagogies are grounded in an inherently feminine epistemology (Grumet, 1988). Such writers have argued that in Western cultures, from infancy, masculine identities are defined through separation from the mother and that adult men are often threatened by intimacy and have difficulty with personal relationships. In contrast, from infancy, female gender identity is defined through attachment (identification with the mother); many adult women feel threatened by separation and have problems with individuation. According to Carol Gilligan (1982), these distinctive developmental patterns, which result from the fact that it is women who are the primary care givers of infants, predispose men toward abstraction ("a morality of rights or fairness") and women toward connectedness ("an ethic of responsibility based on equity, the recognition of differences in need" (p. 164).

Drawing on such object relations theories, radical feminist curriculum theorists such as Madeleine Grumet see feminists' espousal of student-centered pedagogies as expressions of women's essential femininity. As teachers, women draw their "experiences of reproduction and nurturance into the epistemological systems and curricular forms that constitute the discourse and practice of public education" (Grumet, 1988, p. 3). Concerns with what Nel Noddings (1991) calls "caring and interpersonal reasoning" structure such feminist, or women-centered, curricula.

If we leave aside some major criticisms that have been made of the essentialism of these positions (Grosz, 1990; Sayers, 1986), these positions do lend support to the previous arguments that, for a variety of reasons, many women teachers place great emphasis in their classes on students' personal experiences and knowledge. This preference for student-centered pedagogies has been made prescriptive in much feminist educational writing (Bowles & Klein, 1983; Culley & Portuges, 1985). Such approaches are in contradiction to the dominant and accepted teaching styles in a university, and as many feminist writers have observed, feminists' emphasis on the personal in teaching and research has brought about accusations of unscholarliness (see chapters 1 and 2). My own pedagogy, as outlined in this book, has been an attempt to weave together the personal, the theoretical, and the political.

The various student-centered pedagogies in which personal experiences can be shared are difficult in introductory courses, which may contain hundreds of students. Furthermore, continuity and intimacy between teachers and students are particularly difficult in a team-teaching situation. Many introductory women's studies courses take the form of a formal lecture with a succession of different lecturers followed by small tutorial discussion groups. Somewhat ironically, such a structure is imposed by the collective/cooperative/cross-departmental structures that are characteristic of an integrated knowledge code. As Bernstein has explained (1971):

> Integrated codes will, at the level of the teachers, probably create homogeneity in teaching practice . . . integrated codes will reduce the discre-

tion of the teacher in direct relation to the strength of the integrated code (number of teachers coordinated by the code). (p. 60)

Two Lectures

My "Women and Education" course (department based within the dominant collection knowledge code) permits me great autonomy as a teacher. However, my occasional contributions to the large, core women's studies courses (interdepartmental within the subordinate integrated knowledge code) take the form of formal lectures. On the podium, facing the serried rows of students, I am positioned as an expert.

> When I was a student in the 1960s, lecturing seemed such a tidy activity. Lecturers read books, summarized their contents, wrote neat notes, and read them to the students. . . . Feminist knowledge resists such tidiness. It will not stay encapsulated between the covers of books, it will not follow the neat meanderings of rationally argued lecture notes. The waters of "women's everyday lives" leak onto the pages. "Writing a women's studies lecture" is to confluence the streams in our experience that are diverted and dammed by conventional academic practices.

On August 7, 1987, I was to give a lecture on "Marxism and feminism" to the first-year-level introductory feminist theory class taught within the Centre for Women's Studies. I was invited to give this lecture because of my background in Marxist theory and my espoused socialist feminist perspective.

The night before this lecture, I had been distracted from its preparation by an item on the television. Some months previously, feminist women had published an article in an upmarket Auckland magazine in which they had argued that at a major Auckland public hospital, women diagnosed as having carcinoma in situ had been given unconventional treatments as part of their doctors' medical research (Coney & Bunkle, 1987). The women had not been told that they were in research or that their treatments were unconventional or controversial. Several of the women had developed full-blown uterine cancers and subsequently died. The television report that night concerned the outcomes of an official inquiry into the matter.

> On the night of August 6, 1987—the night of the television report, and the night before my lecture on Marxism and feminism—I dreamed I was standing at an inquiry desk in a large, busy hospital. I had been running and was out of breath. I was struggling to hold onto a huge

pile of "dangerous information," which kept growing larger and larger. I felt anxious that it not get into the wrong hands—it was dangerous to women and must only be given to those who recognised this and who were sufficiently concerned about it to try and stop it. As I stood there, pleading with the chaotically indifferent people behind the desk, the pile kept growing, engulfing me—bits began blowing away in a sudden crescendoing wind. . . . Then I found myself in a university lecture theatre about to give the lecture on Marxism and feminism. On the overhead projector I placed a transparency. But it was not the one I had prepared, with its typed quotations from *Capital* and *The German Ideology*. Instead, it was a line drawing—an outline—of the body of a naked woman. Where her breasts should have been was a gaping hole, emerging from which was a giant parrot's beak. I woke suddenly—fearful, anxious. . . .

Like any account of a remembered dream, this one is open to multiple readings. At the time, I analyzed it as follows.[4] I saw it as signifying my experiencing of deep contradictions: a blurring of conventional boundaries between sexuality and intellectuality, between good and bad images of female sexuality, and between feminist sexual politics and the fundamental liberal freedom of access to knowledge and information. I had gone to sleep thinking about and feeling several things: anxiety about my unprepared lecture and joy and grief at the outcome of the inquiry into the unfortunate experiment at National Women's Hospital. Like my dream, this inquiry had concerned issues of sexuality, power, and knowledge. The inquiry had shown that women had died as a result of being denied information about their own bodies; knowledge about their disease (carcinoma in situ) had been alienated from them, appropriated by doctors as *their* intellectual property as data for experimental purposes.

A few days before having this dream, I had returned from what was my second sitting of the Indecent Publications Tribunal in Wellington. In preparation, I had read 4 books and 117 pornographic magazines. In the dream, pornographic images had intruded into my intellectual discourse—in this instance, Marxist theory. The woman's body on the screen was mutilated—as in pornography, women's bodies are symbolically mutilated and distorted.

As a member of the Indecent Publications Tribunal, I act as what Nancy Fraser (1989) described as a "critical public intellectual" (p. xii). My expertise—my professional knowledge as an educator who had specialized in women's issues—was a reason for my nomination by my local member of Parliament and my subsequent selection by the minister of justice during the now-displaced Labour government's administration.

The Indecent Publications Tribunal consists of four members of the public plus a barrister of at least 7 years' standing as chair. We work within the Ministry of Justice. Our statutory role is to categorize sexually explicit and/or violent printed materials according to legal criteria as specified in the Indecent Publications Act of 1963. Indecent, as defined in the act (section 2), "includes describing, depicting, expressing, or otherwise dealing with matters of sex, horror, crime, cruelty, or violence in a manner that is injurious to the public good."

Printed materials that come within the terms of the act are regulated and monitored through banning or classifying in ways designed to limit their availability to certain classes of persons—for example, persons aged 18 and over. The tribunal, then, is an ideological state apparatus backed by the coercive powers of the justice system (Althusser, 1971). Like a court, it often makes decisions on grounds of precedent—former decisions often reached by former tribunal members.

Having official, public responsibility for deciding what constitutes injury to the public good has been work that has embodied profound contradictions in both the professional and the personal dimensions of my life. It has affected me intellectually and emotionally at both conscious and unconscious levels. The problems it poses—intellectual, emotional, and political—have seeped into the content of my teaching.

Shortly after I was appointed,[5] I was invited to give a lecture to a second-year education course: "Education and the Individual." The students had been studying Freud under the guidance of two of my male colleagues—one a philosopher, the other a psychologist. The topic they had invited me in to speak about was "Psychoanalysis, Sexuality, and Feminism." My reading in this field had been stimulated by my struggle with issues pertaining to pornography. I thought that psychoanalytic theories would be a useful aid to understanding this because the object of psychoanalysis as a mode of inquiry is the understanding of human sexuality and the ways its repression generates dreams, fantasies, wishes and desires—as well as neuroses and more severe mental disorders. Feminist readings of psychoanalytic materials—such as Juliet Mitchell's (1974) reading—offered ways of understanding male sexual fantasies as they have been constituted within patriarchal/capitalist cultures. Pornography depicts selected male sexual fantasies.

In my lecture, I discussed Lacan's view that Freud had intended the phenomena of penis envy and castration anxiety—central to the Oedipal drama—to be read in symbolic rather than literally biological terms (Grosz, 1989; Mitchell & Rose, 1982; Sayers, 1986). For Lacanians, the phallus is the privileged signifier of patriarchal cultures. To illustrate the phallic symbol, I screened slides made from photographs in so-called soft-porn magazines—magazines that I had supported some weeks previously in gaining R18 classifications and that could as a result be purchased at news stands throughout the country. In the clinical sterility of a university lecture theater, what had appeared to me in the context of hundreds of other pornographic images as relatively harmless now appeared as symbolic rape.

> Two of the slides were taken from a series of colour photos—a striptease sequence, which was a common format in some of the magazines. The model is called "Ruth." She is a scientist, in her laboratory, wearing a white coat. Beside her, on the bench, is a microscope and a flask. Frame by frame, she removes her clothes, until she is lying naked on the hard wooden bench. In one shot, the cold steel shaft of the microscope points parallel to her vagina—a symbolic erection. In the final shot, she lies prostrate, clasping over her belly a round glass flask full of liquid.
>
> There in the lecture room, the image was horrific. As a scientist, "Ruth" was a power-figure, clad in the white coat of authority. An intellectual. The striptease reduces her to "just another fuck." A receptacle for sperm. A toilet.
>
> The phallic symbol of the microscope and the uterine symbol of the filled flask remind me of Marion Cotton—a New Zealand woman who was raped with broken bottles until she died.
>
> But certain male colleagues would tell me this is "all in my head." What's wrong with showing a scientist as sexy? At one tribunal hearing, a feminist member of the tribunal questioned a witness about a striptease sequence photographed in a rubbish tip—"the garbage man's daughter." Did this not imply that women were rubbish? He argued that the photographs did not imply this to him. Rather, they embodied a contradiction: how could anything so beautiful be found in a place like this?

The Rational Individual: Living the Contradictions

Within the feminist classroom—even in the context of a formal lecture— the public domains of theory collide with the personal worlds of experience. Such collisions also occur in other spaces in the institution: in institutional relations outside the classroom setting. I have found myself and my censoring activities becoming objects of prurient interest for some male colleagues and associates. There's a covert sniggering from some of the men. I get lots of "Can I help you read the books?" nudge, wink. On one such occasion, I answered that I would very much appreciate the man's assistance in advising me how to categorize a huge pile of gay men's magazines and then proceeded to describe the penises in these pictures. He did not pursue the matter. There is a feeling of being contaminated, polluted, or unclean as a result of being on this tribunal. Some people have commented to me that I should not have accepted this job. It's not a nice thing to do. Nice girls don't. The materials become a secret—I become furtive, anxious about violations of my private spaces. I have had to develop strategies for dealing with such invasions.

The magazines arrive in the early mornings by courier—flung onto the front porch with a loud thud around 6.00 AM, which is one of my favorite times of the day. I am usually reading or writing. The arrival of the material at this hour violates my privacy, my intellectual morning calm. I groan when I hear the pack arrive. Twenty volumes devoted, for example, to rubber or vinyl fetish, sodomy, "big tits," or spanking hold the promise only of monotony, subterfuge, and the suspension of intellectual engagement in the act of reading.

When and where to read the magazines became a problem. My daughter has been told that the courier packs contain pornography, why I read it, and what I feel about it. I have told her that it mainly presents images of women as objects, not as people. I used to but no longer read at work in my office behind locked doors. It would be awkward to be caught in the act by students and some of my more conservative colleagues. Once opened, the packs become a problem. It's as if they emit a foul gas. I hide the opened packs. I don't want children coming across them. Nor do I want my office at work or my study at home—my spaces—becoming arenas of prurient interest. I feel unclean after reading some of this material. I need to bathe.

As an intellectual, I am expected to make rational judgments about pornography. But it is a genre designed to cater to the irrational—the sexual fantasies, desires, and fetishes that lie deep in the mysteries of the unconscious. As such, they affect the intellectual reader as well as the prurient consumer for whom they are designed.

As a feminist and a censor, I straddle the contradictions within Western constructions of the individual: between the rational and the sexual dimensions of experience. Such contradictions have been usefully explored by some postmodernist feminists (Fraser, 1989; Lather, 1991; Nicholson, 1990a; Weedon, 1987). Drawing on Derrida and other deconstructionists, these writers have argued that the theoretical apparatuses available to Western scholars bifurcate consciousness (D. Smith, 1987) and create splits between reason and passion, logic and emotion, the intellectual and the sensual/sexual dimensions of human existence. Such binary oppositions, they argue, are hierarchical: The first term in the dualisms I have listed here is privileged over the second. Within modern conceptualizations of the individual, reason must rule over emotion. From my positioning as a censor—from within the apparatus of ruling—I must make rational judgments about the permissibility of certain forms of erotic discourse.

Generations of feminist philosophers have studied the Western liberal ideal of the rationally autonomous individual as a male construction (Eisenstein, 1981; Fraser, 1989; Martin, 1987; Vetterling-Braggin et al., 1977). For example, in 1792, Mary Wollstonecraft (1792/1978) criticized the male Enlightenment social philosophers of her time—in particular, Rousseau—for having a model of reason that was socially constructed by them as unattainable by women. Women, these philosophies argued, were intellectually inferior by nature and could therefore justifiably be denied full citizenship. They were creatures of passion whose education must teach them purity and ways of making themselves pleasing to men. But, like the male liberals of their day, first-wave liberal feminists believed that civilization rested on the rule of reason over passion. Women, they argued, lacked equal reasoning power only because they had been denied adequate education. Only this would enable them to play an equal part with men in public life (Mill, 1869/1983).

Liberal, including liberal feminist, theories have had difficulty accommodating human sexuality. As Engels (1891/1971) argued in the 19th century, under capitalism, men could live by a double standard. Their wives, through monogamous fidelity, would ensure the reproduction of the family and the rightful inheritance of property. A sexual underclass of women—hidden from public recognition—could service their sexual pleasures. Women were thereby divided into classes of good women and bad women—a bifurcation that structures women's lives today. Intellectual (rational) women were faced with several options: to deny their sexuality (an asexual spinsterhood), to become respectable wives and mothers (abandoning careers or subordinating these to the demands and desires of family members), or to become bohemian (unrespectable) members of an intellectual/artistic demimonde.

Contemporary liberal discourses such as those of the New Right (see chapters 1 and 6) constitute the individual—the citizen in modern states—as primarily rational, competitive, and engaged in the pursuit of self-interest. Like previous liberal theories, these cannot accommodate female sexuality. Bad sex is to be controlled through censorship (the imposition of rational criteria). However, even good sex for women—reproductive heterosexuality within a stable relationship—falls outside modern liberal constructions of the individual (Martin, 1982, 1987).

In 1987—when I was writing the lectures discussed earlier—I was, like many of my academic colleagues, reading the vast number of government and departmental reports that were being produced with alarming rapidity as part of the restructuring of education. As critical public intellectuals, we wrote academic critiques, submissions to select committees, and letters to ministers and officials. As part of a collaborative project, I undertook a feminist reading of the New Zealand Treasury's briefing papers on education (Lauder, Middleton, Boston, & Wylie, 1988). In the Treasury's (1987) 400-page report—a New Right analysis of education as a private commodity—I found the following statement:

> The question of equitable access to child-care for working mothers is essentially one of public policy—whether affirmative action is required to assist the life-chances of women. The assumption is not just that the benefits of child-rearing do not compensate for the disadvantages from what would be (without the compensation) the result of *an irrational desire to have children*. Or, in the case of unplanned children, that the public should compensate parents for the unexpected net loss. The validity of these assumptions will not be self-evident to all, and depends largely on conclusions reached about the degree of community responsibility for having children. (p. 57) (Emphasis mine)

   Within this and other market-liberal (New Right economic) texts, motherhood—legitimate female reproductive heterosexuality—is construed as contradictory to the idea of the citizen—the rationally autonomous individual. According to the Treasury papers, the rational individual competes in the marketplace, and having children is an irrational decision because it prevents this. At the same time, women's unpaid work in the family is viewed as an essential part of their children's education. Women who wish to work outside the home are seen as endangering their children's well-being. As individuals competing in self-interest, mothers and children are locked in conflict (Middleton, 1990a). As in pornography, women are considered in opposition to the masculine ideal of individualized, competitive, and autonomous rationality. Only men—and asexual women—can be the rationally autonomous subjects that such versions of liberalism demand.

Conclusion

As a woman, as a public intellectual, as a university teacher/researcher/writer, and as a feminist, I am positioned inside the contradictions in liberal constructions of the individual. In my teaching about women and education, I seek to deconstruct the androcentrism of major educational theories, including those that have informed recent educational restructuring policy. I also aim to show students how we are positioned inside what we are studying. The positionings of my students within the various nonfeminist and feminist discourses of women's education will be addressed in the following chapters.

Notes

[1]With apologies to Charles Dickens, *A Christmas Carol.*

[2]After this conversation, I asked Joe if he would be willing to be interviewed as part of my ongoing research into feminist and antiracist teaching. He agreed and came to my office on another occasion to make the tape from which this quotation has been extracted.

[3]Details of this event, and of a fuller sociological analysis of the Waikato University women's studies program, are in Middleton (1987a). The original analysis of untenured staff was done in collaboration with Logan Moss and other members of the untenured staff support group.

[4]This analysis was brought into being by a request from Allanah Ryan of Massey University. As editor of *Sites,* an interdisciplinary journal, she asked me to write about my experiences on the Indecent Publications Tribunal for a special issue on the role of critical intellectuals in New Zealand society. The paper appeared in the summer 1988 issue of *Sites* (Middleton, 1988a).

[5]My appointment is for 5 years; at the time of writing, I have completed 4 years of service. I am now the longest-serving member on the tribunal. I have seen changes not only in personnel but also in the criteria on which decisions are made. I have therefore played a part in changing the precedents for legal decision-making. This will be a topic for a future analysis.

six

Equity Issues in the 1990s: School Administrators Speak

S ince the mid-1980s, the institutions in which we and our students study and teach have been subjected to restructuring. This restructuring has dramatically affected the lives and work of academics in university education departments. As "critical public intellectuals" (Fraser, 1989), we have read the relevant reports, written submissions to the various policymakers and committees, and developed academic critiques of the new policies. As researchers, we have engaged in empirical investigations of the processes and effects of restructuring. As teacher educators, we have included analysis of restructuring in our course content. At the same time, we have been living through the restructuring of the institutions in which we work and the schools that our children attend. This chapter results from my own attempts to make sense of the restructuring processes and activities in which I have been involved.

The maintenance or introduction of provisions for equal opportunities and affirmative action within the new structures have been of great concern to feminists. Such concerns have generated feminist critiques of restructuring policies in various countries—for example, in Australia (Yates, 1990, 1991); in Britain (Arnot, 1991b; Deem, 1989), in Canada (Gaskell, McLaren, & Novogrodski, 1989); in New Zealand (Jones, 1990; May, 1990; G. McDonald, 1992; Middleton, 1990a, 1992c); and in the United States (Secada, 1989).

This chapter begins with a feminist reading of the various discourses concerning equal opportunities for women and girls and gender equity that were evident in the key texts in New Zealand's recent restructuring of schools. I then draw on life-history interviews with parents and teachers who were elected to their schools' boards of trustees immediately after the new system of school administration was put into place at the end of 1989.[1] My object in this is to gain an understanding of the ways that gender equity is being conceptualized in the schools in which my students teach. As a researcher, I hope to provide information that will help my students to untangle the strands of the debates that are taking place both at the government level and in the community and to position the various opinions and arguments within the larger philosophical, historical, and political traditions of which they are a part. In other words, I aim to help students to position themselves inside what they are studying—to see theory not as disembodied intellectualism but as lived, as structuring their own and others' lives in schools.

Feminist Sociological Theories in Educational Restructuring

In chapter 2, I showed how prefeminist theories about women's education were inscribed in the educational policies and the sociology of the 1950s and 1960s—when my generation of feminist teachers were at school. In chapter 4, I argued that at that time, expectations for educated women were contradictory and that our experiences of such contradictions were in part generative of our feminism. Not only are we productive of educational sociology, but we ourselves—our perspectives, our choices, and our identities—are produced by and within it. In this chapter, I move the analysis forward in time and explore the extent to which *feminist* theories in the sociology of women's education have become articulated to the ruling apparatus.

My generation of feminists was educated in schools designed by New Zealand's first Labour government (1935 to 1949). Our schooling was planned according to a liberal philosophy based on a belief in the equal rights of individuals to compete for positions in social and educational hierarchies. Opportunities would be limited only by lack of ability or effort: a meritocratic view. However, these policies were not feminist in that they were also based on assumptions about the naturalness of gendered curricula and the sexual division of paid and unpaid labor.

As young adults during the second wave of feminism of the 1970s and 1980s, we made such assumptions a focus for our feminist activism. We fought for equal access to the various curriculum subjects and to nontraditional occupations, equal representation in senior positions in educational hierarchies, and increased visibility of women in curriculum content. In New Zealand, the presence of several older feminist women in senior positions in educational research and policy-making gave the mass movement—composed largely of the postwar baby boom generation—role models, strategies, and access to decision makers (Neville, 1988). Details of the incorporation and rejection of the various feminist agendas in the 1970s and 1980s by successive National and Labour governments have been analyzed by Geraldine McDonald (1980) and Helen Watson (1988).

Feminists were also active in the political parties. Some worked within the National Party to bring about legislation designed to achieve equal opportunity. Feminists rose to senior positions within the Labour Party and, after Labour's victory in the 1984 election, several prominent feminists were elected as members of parliament.

The fourth Labour government required every school board to write a charter in which were stated their school's general objectives and specific goals. These were to become the criteria against which state educational review officers (formerly called school inspectors) would make their assessments and evaluations of schools. Although parts of the charters were left to the schools to design, the equity clauses were nonnegotiable. With respect to gender issues (see chapter 1), all schools were required to develop policies designed to bring about equal opportunities for both sexes, to provide role models of females and males in a broad range of occupations and levels of seniority, to develop nonsexist and nonracist curricula, and to develop procedures for the prevention and redress of sexual harassment (Ministry of Education, 1989). Feminist agendas, then, in Foucault's terms, had become inscribed in an apparatus for the monitoring and regulation of populations.

The fourth Labour government's gender equity policies in education, as outlined in the official framework for charter writing (Ministry of Education, 1989),[2] were theoretically pluralist: They wove together liberal, liberal feminist, and radical feminist assumptions. As Chris Weedon (1987) has expressed it, these various feminisms offer "competing ways of giving meaning to the world and of organizing social institutions and processes" (p. 35). Many feminist writers have argued that liberal feminism is the perspective that most speaks "the language of the fathers" (Lather, 1991) and therefore has most readily been incorporated into mainstream educational policy-making. Although various forms of liberal feminism have become "articulated to the ruling apparatus" (D. Smith, 1987), more radical forms of feminism have been less influential. As Weedon (1987) has expressed it, "not all discourses . . . carry equal weight or power" (p. 35). Labour's restructuring policies—which incorporated both liberalism and radical feminism—provide an interesting case study of the unequal weights and powers of the various feminist discourses.

Liberalism and Liberal Feminism

The differences between liberal and liberal feminist ideas can be usefully illustrated by comparing the equity objectives of New Zealand's first Labour government (as stated in 1939) with those of the fourth Labour government (as outlined in the school charter framework of May 1989). In 1939, as discussed previously, the government emphasized the rights of a citizen "whether he be rich or poor, whether he live in town or country . . . to a free education of the kind for which he is best fitted and to the fullest extent of his powers" (Beeby, 1986, p. xxxii). Socioeconomic status and the geographical location of students were at that time seen as matters that an equal opportunities policy should address. In 1989, as described in chapter 1, issues of culture and of gender had been added. Schools were to "include programs that redress existing inequities and address the current and future needs of students, particularly: Maori, Pacific Islanders, other ethnic groups, women and girls, students with disabilities, students with other special needs" (Ministry of Education, 1989, p. 4). Within this framework, about 75% of the school population—everyone except white, middle-class males—were seen as having special needs and as in need of compensatory provision. The normal individual human subject of liberal individualism was white, middle class, and male: Women, ethnic/cultural minorities, and working-class men were constituted as "other."

Equal opportunities for the two genders has usually been interpreted as meaning that women should be encouraged to enter nontraditional courses and occupations and should aspire to senior positions (G. McDonald, 1980; Novitz, 1982; H. Watson, 1988). Although postwar policymakers had accepted—even encouraged—curricular provisions that reinforced the gendered division of labor, policymakers of the late 1980s regarded this as a matter for state intervention. Merely following tradition could not ensure equality. Labour's 1989 gender equity policy conceptualized equal opportunities for women and girls as meaning that both sexes should make informed choices on the basis of having experienced the full spectrum of curricular activities. The charter guidelines stated: "The aim will be to ensure equal opportunity for all students to participate and succeed in the full range of school activities" (Ministry of Education, 1989, p. 4). Measures of affirmative action were seen as necessary. In the popular jargon of our times, this is an interventionist liberal and feminist position. The school charter guidelines defined equity as "the application of principles of fairness and natural justice. In schools it involves the provision of unequal resources to students so that fair outcomes can be achieved" (Ministry of Education, 1989, p. 3).

Liberal feminist strategies—designed to effect the enhancement of individuals' life chances within the system—have often incorporated the language of the policymakers. In the following example, New Zealand's Women's Advisory Committee on Education (WACE) used the technocratic language characteristic of the New Right to convince a Labour minister of education that measures of affirmative action were necessary for women and girls:

> The National Policy for the Education of Girls and Women is urgently needed because the current system is failing to meet the educational objectives of efficiency; and the social objective of equity. . . . By changing our current inefficient, inequitable practices which prevent women from reaching their individual levels of excellence we will be improving over 80% of the country's population. (WACE, 1988, pp. 7, 41)

Similarly, feminist-inspired research carried out in or on behalf of government agencies has usually rested on the assumptions and employed the kinds of methodologies that have been acceptable to policymakers. For example, one prominent New Zealand feminist sociologist described the theoretical assumptions behind a Department of Education (1982b) research project in which she was involved—a comparative study of male and female teachers' career and promotion patterns:

> The taken-for-granted is the existing hierarchical promotion structure and the data are oriented towards testing how well women and men match up to the "model" career and investigating the reasons for any deviations . . . . the hierarchical structure of the promotion system is not challenged by the research. (Fenwick, 1983, p. 24)

Within such a liberal feminist framework, the male is constituted as norm. Such a feminism becomes inscribed within the ruling apparatus (D. Smith, 1987).

Radical Feminism

Under the 1984–1990 Labour government, educational policies also incorporated objectives that were derivative of the perspectives and strategies of more radical feminists. For example, in requiring school boards to work for the prevention of sexual harassment and to set up grievance procedures to deal with any such occurrences, the government was admitting that even the white, middle-class male was in need of remedial attention! Male sexual violence against women and girls in education was seen as a problem—as behavior that should be an object of monitoring and regulation.

A second significant and potentially radical feminist Labour policy was the requirement of boards "to ensure that the curriculum is nonsexist and nonracist." Curriculum was defined broadly as including

> all the intended activities, events and experiences that take place in the school and includes provision for the personal welfare of students. This also includes all activities arranged by the school out of class and/or out of school time. (Ministry of Education, 1989, p. 23)

Among other things, such a policy required a fundamental questioning of the nature of school knowledge and the rewriting of curricula. For, as Jane Roland Martin (1982) has expressed it, "The disciplines exclude women from their subject matter; they distort the female according to the male image of her; and they deny the feminine by forcing women into a masculine mould" (p. 133).

In addition to questioning the content of instruction, the idea of a nonsexist curriculum also requires attention to its form, or pedagogy. For example, as discussed in chapter 5, radical feminists of the object-relations tradition in psychoanalysis have generated a large literature on women's epistemology or ways of knowing and on gender differences in styles of reasoning (Belenky, Clinchy, Goldberger, & Tarrule, 1986; Chodorow, 1978; Fox-Keller, 1985; Gilligan, 1982; Grumet, 1988). These writers argue that many women may approach academic activities differently from many men and that such differences should be equally valued. Such arguments are controversial; many see them as essentialist (Grosz, 1990; Sayers, 1986). They can, if misinterpreted, be used to support the reintroduction of stereotyping. However, if female students are to receive the best possible education, such theories must be critically explored. They could imply fundamental changes in some teaching practices.

The National government was elected in October 1990. In chapter 1, I noted that immediately after its landslide victory, the National government announced its intention to reverse Labour's more radical equity policies on the grounds that they were social engineering and therefore incompatible with National's free market philosophy. First, Lockwood Smith, the incoming minister of education, announced that the equity clauses in the school charters were to become optional. Second, National repealed Labour's pay equity legislation. In 1972, it was a National government that passed the Equal Pay Act, which gave women equal pay for doing the same work as men—a liberal, equal opportunities policy. Pay equity—equal pay for work of equal value—is premised on the more radical feminist assumption that the work women do should be valued equally as the work men do. Such a perspective is compatible with radical feminist arguments about different epistemologies, styles of reasoning, and moral judgments between the genders. Such a perspective is incompatible with National's agenda of letting the market decide. National's commitment to equal opportunities is minimalist with respect to women: freedom of individual choice within the inequitable hierarchies of laissez-faire capitalism.

Summary

As Donna Haraway (1990b) has argued, feminism is

> characterized by its tensions, oppositions, exclusions, complicities with the structures it seeks to deconstruct, as well as by its shared conversations, unexpected alliances, and transformative convergences . . . feminist discourse [is] a field structured by shared, yet power-differentiated and often contentious conversations, but not by agreements and, unhappily, not by equality. (p. 151)

Within the ruling apparatus, liberal and radical feminist discourses are power differentiated and unequal. A noninterventionist liberal equal opportunities position—one of allowing both sexes freedom of choice of available options—is compatible with the free market model espoused by conservative or libertarian-right governments (Arnot, 1991b; Klatch, 1987; Yates, 1991).[3] A more interventionist model of affirmative action and compensation may become—and has been in New Zealand—a site of struggle between conservatives and those who espouse more liberal or left-wing positions (e.g., Labour Party politicians). A radical feminist approach, which challenges both the sexual power and the epistemological authority of men, is less likely to enter the discursive practices of governing and, if it does (as in New Zealand), it is particularly vulnerable to a conservative backlash.

Board Members Speak: Background to the Research

To date, like other academic studies, many feminist critiques of the recent restructuring have been based on the analysis of policy documents. The theoretical assumptions of the policymakers have been the object of such analyses. However, studies that rely too heavily on academics' reading of texts can bracket out—render invisible—the everyday conversations, experiences, and perspectives of people in the schools. It is possible to assume from reading some academic critiques of policy texts that teachers and school administrators are passively socialized puppets of the New Right and that schools are merely sites where populations are governed through techniques of monitoring, surveillance, and regulation. Policy research that is grounded purely in the analysis of texts makes, as Dorothy Smith (1987) has expressed it, "a continual transcription of the local and particular activities of our lives into . . . abstracted and generalized forms" (p. 3).

If we are to gain a wider understanding of educational restructuring, it is important that we study processes of administrative reform—such as the introduction of equity policies—through the eyes of and in interaction with key protagonists in the various restructuring dramas as they are lived (Ramsay & CRRISP Team, 1990). We need studies that explore relationships between the theoretical assumptions of the policymakers and the ideas and actions of the people who are, within the schools, involved in the everyday implementation of the new policies. For, as John Codd (1990) has observed, policy texts are "decoded in different ways depending upon the contexts in which they are read" (p. 133).

In the remainder of this chapter, I use a life-history method to explore the ways in which gender equity was conceptualized by members of New Zealand school boards when they assumed their new positions and were required by the Labour government to formulate policies on the issue in their school charters. I offer this analysis as content that can help us to prepare student teachers for the world out there in schools with respect to their future and, in some cases, their present employers' versions of equal opportunities for women and girls.

The research on which I draw was carried out as an initial phase of a wider study designed to monitor the impact of New Zealand's educational restructuring within schools.[4] The larger project, Monitoring Today's Schools, has been funded by New Zealand's Ministry of Education for a 3-year period. Coordinated by David Mitchell, 16 researchers are each monitoring one school's experiences of educational restructuring. An objective of the project is to give voice to those who have initially been most directly affected by the administrative changes: board members and teachers. A variety of methods are being used: interviews, observations of meetings, quantitative postal surveys sent to a larger number of schools, the reading of policy documents issued by the ministry of education, and descriptions of texts written in schools (minutes and agendas, memoranda, and official forms).

In the initial phase of the study, which is here under consideration, we explored with board members, by means of life-history interviews, their reasons for being on a board of trustees, their opinions of their own schooling in comparison with that of their children, their opinions of the restructured system, and their priorities as board members.[5] We asked them for their opinions on the social policies (equity issues) that they were required to address in their school charters. Board members were invited to comment on each of the equity issues that were constituted in school charter frameworks as requiring special treatment in education: equity in general, biculturalism and multiculturalism, the place of Maori language and culture in the curriculum, the educational significance of the Treaty of Waitangi, equal opportunities for women and girls, the education of pupils with handicaps and disabilities, the role of teachers' unions, and religion in state schools.

A total of 111 board members were interviewed: 85 parents, 24 teachers and principals, and 2 student representatives.[6] There were 65 males (49 parents, 15 teachers, and 1 student) and 46 females (36 parents, 9 teachers, and 1 student). When asked to describe their ethnic/cultural identity, the 111 board members chose the following categories: 20 Maori, 3 part Maori, 25 Pakeha, 38 European, 12 New Zealanders, 13 other. With few exceptions, the board members were aged between 35 and 45. Like the feminist teachers discussed in chapter 4, the majority had attended school from the 1950s to the early 1970s. The majority of the board members were Pakeha and middle class. Sixty one (44 parents and 17 teachers) had had fathers with occupations in the top three categories of the six-point Elley and Irving socioeconomic scales (Elley & Irving, 1985; Irving & Elley, 1977).[7] Of the 85 parent representatives, 57 worked in occupations that placed them in the top three socioeconomic categories. Although 49 (38 parents and 11 teachers) described their mothers' occupation as housewife or homemaker, only 4 of the 36 female and none of the male board members defined their own occupation in this way. Those who worked part-time in paid work chose to define their occupation as part-time teacher and the like.

> As I write, I hear myself speaking with a "contract researcher's voice."
> As a member of a "research team" whose activities are funded by government, I do not "own" my data. I must use a language and a methodology that are acceptable to those who "own" the knowledge. Although I was the principal designer of the life-history project I am describing here, the analysis of the data has passed through the filters of the research team. The report from which this data have been extracted (Middleton & Oliver, 1990) has been subjected to Ministry of Education scrutiny. My writing is shaped and constrained within these power-relations. . . .

Equal Opportunities for Women and Girls: A Discourse Analysis

The kinds of narratives that interviewees construct in the course of a life-history interview are informed by the setting in which the interview takes place (see chapter 3). Our interviews took place when certain equity issues were at the forefront of public debate: between October 1989 and February 1990. February 6, 1990, was the date on which the sesquicentenary of the signing of the Treaty of Waitangi was commemorated (see chapter 1). Accordingly, our interviewees expressed strong opinions, and many spoke at length on this issue. In contrast, gender and women's issues had received little media coverage at that time. When we interviewed the board members, most were preoccupied with coping with the early stages of setting up the new system of administration, such as establishing the amount and allocations of their schools' budgets. They had not, at the time of interview, written the equity policies in their charters.

Only one topical issue concerning gender was mentioned. Hagley High School, a Christchurch coeducational school, had received nationwide publicity when it set up single-sex classes for girls in science and in mathematics as an affirmative-action measure. This had been very controversial. Single-sex secondary schools have a long tradition in New Zealand; the older state high schools and most of the private schools are single sex. The majority of high schools—those established since World War II—are coeducational. Single-sex classes in core subjects in such schools had not been common. Board members who mentioned Hagley High School's experiment were divided in their views.

All of the 111 board members said that they agreed with the requirement to have equal opportunities for women and girls as an objective in their school charter. However, interpretations of exactly what this meant and what its implications were for everyday school practice varied widely.

Liberal and Liberal Feminist Perspectives

Since the mid-1940s, educational policies have been based on the liberal assumption that equality of educational opportunity means that individuals should have equal formal rights of access to fair competition within schools and in employment. Within this discourse, equal means the same in the sense that all students should be given the same range of choices. Further intervention is not seen as necessary.

When we asked our 111 school board members to comment on equal opportunities for women and girls, they were almost unanimous in their support for the idea. Fifty seven commented that it was particularly important to include equity in a general sense in school charters, and 33 emphasized the importance of including equal opportunities for women and girls. However, many—particularly those on the boards of primary schools— were unaware of any gender discrimination or unequal opportunities in their schools. Forty of the board members made comments similar to the following: "They're basically there now at school level. The opportunities are there in schools." Twenty spoke of the existence of such equality in their schools. "I don't feel particularly that such issues will come up at our school. The children are encouraged to be children working and playing together—both boys and girls."

Twenty-two of the board members supported the need for stronger action rather than the provision of the same opportunities. "I feel it's important. Kids seem to be getting equal opportunity to take the initiative. Something needs to be done to 'over-provide' in some areas to get girls into them." Some gave specific examples of such targeting:

> I have strong views. I have two daughters. We need affirmative action.
> I support single-sex education for girls, but not for boys. I like Hagley
> High School's option of single-sex classes in some subjects. Schools
> need a policy to address the imbalance. A firm policy is to support
> women and Maori in senior positions till equity is addressed.

Although all board members expressed support for the idea of equal— the same—opportunities, they were not all convinced of the need for targeted funding or for special measures of affirmative action. "Everybody has the same opportunity if they wish to take it up. There shouldn't be different payments because of people's socioeconomic status or culture."

Eight board members offered the opinion that the issue was being pushed or given too much emphasis. Those who opposed measures of intervention or affirmative action—and the targeted funding that was to make them possible—saw them as incompatible with the liberal presumption of an individual's right of entry to fair competition in the marketplace. They questioned whether the compensation of groups through targeting threatened or contradicted traditional criteria of individual merit. As one board member expressed it, "Equity has to be achieved in the treatment of pupils and staff, but it mustn't go overboard. In the case of staff appointments it still has to come down to the best applicant for the job, but females should be given every chance to apply."

One board member emphasized the importance of equal opportunities as a goal and supported setting up positions for women but warned that such encouragement must not lower standards for job incumbents: "I think the school charter needs a statement on equality. Staff should be selected on merit, not whether or not they're male or female. Opportunities should be created for women, but in the end the best person should be selected."

Another board member felt that with some encouragement and the passing of time, more women would work their way up into senior positions:

> The opportunities are there for women but they need encouragement. . . . Time will see many more women as educational leaders. At present, though, the majority of women teachers do not seem to be aspirational here, and those who are, are very hardworking concerning promotion.

Several used the example of pay equity—equal pay for work of equal value—as an example of their reasons for opposing affirmative-action measures. "They [women] have equal opportunity. They want equal pay but a lot of women can't do some jobs. I agree with equal pay for the same job."

Eight of the board members argued that existing inequalities were due to lack of ability and/or effort on the part of women and girls: "Equity is up to the woman. Women don't need to go all feminist lib! Some are as equal as they want to be." "Everybody has equal rights . . . a lot of people use race or sex to blame their failings." "Children should all have the same education."

Although both primary and secondary school board members mentioned questions of equal employment opportunities for women teachers, the board members of secondary schools tended to see equal opportunities between their girl and boy pupils as presenting more of a problem than did those in the primary or intermediate schools. "I feel there should be equal opportunity. I feel the school is catering to it. It will show up more at high school than at intermediate."

Some of the secondary school board members mentioned sex differences in subject choice as a matter of concern. Several of the secondary schools in our study had been making efforts—before the new system of administration had been introduced—to encourage girls to choose subjects that were nontraditional for women. Board members in these schools gave a variety of reasons for supporting such measures of affirmative action. For example, Bill, a teacher of male technical subjects, described the recent phenomenon of female participation as benefiting not only the girls as individuals but society, the economy, and the male sex as well: "It's a pleasure to have the girls in the workshops. They excel in drawing (especially the more academic ones) and have a settling effect on the boys." Another teacher, who had been elected a parent representative at his children's high school, emphasized the economic importance of preventing a "wastage of talent." "It's important . . . there's a way to go yet. We must consider females as well as males, otherwise we're cutting off half the brainpower. There are not enough women in senior roles yet. It will take a long time."

A secondary school principal—a supporter of affirmative action—resented the fact that schools rather than society as a whole were being seen as the cause of inequality.

> A consciousness is needed here. Sometimes unequal provisions may be needed to achieve a just outcome. We need to raise the sights of girls to see that something is possible. I resent the emphasis being on schools—we're only part of the problem. Employers are just as important. Many of them went to single-sex boys' schools and have hardened attitudes. It will involve educating the community which we're part of.

Radical Feminism

Although the majority of the board members positioned themselves within the discourses of liberalism (equal means the same) or liberal feminism (recognition of the need for targeting or affirmative action to compensate for inequality), a minority expressed more radical opinions. Of those who expressed such opinions with respect to gender, many were school staff representatives on their boards, teachers on the school's staff who also had their own children attending the school and who had been elected parent representatives, and parent representatives who were teachers in other schools or who had taught or received teacher training in the past. Taken as a group, such individuals were also more likely—at least in the interview situation—to express strong support for Maori parents in their quest for a more bicultural approach in schools.[8] As I shall explain in the concluding section of this chapter, this is significant.

Five of the board members made comments that rested on the radical feminist assumption that gender inequalities result from patriarchal power. These board members made comments to the effect that if boards were to bring about equal opportunities or equity for women and girls, men would also have to change. For example, one feminist teacher described sexual harassment and other forms of male violence as serious problems among pupils and in the wider society.

The board of trustees need to address violence and stereotyped attitudes amongst the students. The senior girls accept their sexual role. We had a bus trip and the girls were having to tolerate taunts and abuse. There was "slicing"—boys putting their hands between the girls' legs. There are boys who believe that sexual relationships involve hitting.

Others commented more generally on the problem of sexism among boys. For example, a secondary school staff representative commented that the removal of discriminatory barriers to women's achievements was not enough. Males had to change. "There's no discrimination as far as courses and subjects go and staff—we have women in positions of responsibility. . . . We have strong female staff at the school. . . . Among the pupils the chauvinistic boys will need educating."

Several male teachers on boards were aware of specific situations in which sexism was a problem in their classrooms. "In physics, teachers must make sure the boys don't always take a lead role." And in another example,

I'm aware that there are disadvantages at times . . . teachers need to be sensitive. I don't like separatist approaches to the problem [e.g., the recent setting up of single-sex classes for girls at Hagley High School in Christchurch] but action should be taken in the classrooms.

A woman who had taught in boys' private schools expressed concern at the narrow and pressured education received by such boys.

I'm also keen for boys to have equal opportunity. I don't think they have it. At [a private boys' school] the boys had dreadful expectations by parents. They were pushed into moulds. Now concerns are raised about girls, but ignoring boys, who are equally pushed. I felt sorry for those boys. Although more doors are open to them in some ways, doors to full-time fatherhood are closed.

Bicultural Perspectives

As discussed in previous chapters, Maori women have challenged Pakeha feminist notions of equal opportunities. For example, although many Maori women have strongly supported women seeking positions of power and influence within state education, they have questioned the relevance to Maori settings of the liberal feminist idea that equal means the same (Irwin,

1992b; L. Smith, 1992). Several of the Maori women board members we interviewed discussed such questions.

One argued that a school modeled on traditional Maori whanau (extended family) structures and values would, in and of itself, be a sufficient basis for an equal opportunities policy for women and girls. "A whanau basis would address this problem. Men have their role and women have theirs, but one can't do without the other. A tradition we can't break away from."

Others took a more bicultural view. They stressed both Pakeha/Western opportunities and Maori traditions. For example, Julia, a business-woman with higher education qualifications, emphasized both her own access to and achievements in education and the importance of women in marae protocol, for example, in formal welcoming or funeral ceremonies.

> I find the idea of equal opportunities for women and girls hard to relate to because I always felt I had equal opportunities. My parents encouraged both of us. We encourage our children. We need to know the things we women do better than men and men do better than woman. It's not a threat. In Maoridom the women are the first that you see. A man would never question that. I've never seen a Maori woman question a man about mihi [a formal welcome at a tribal or family marae] and whai-korero [formal speeches made by senior men on the open ground in front of the meeting house (Irwin, 1992b)]. . . . Neither is any good without the other.

Maori women in our study frequently mentioned the importance of their children receiving both equal opportunities—the same opportunities—in the Pakeha sense and an education in Maori knowledge, language, values, and perspectives, which could include, for example, a knowledge and understanding of men's and women's different traditional roles on the marae (Irwin, 1992b). This was seen as giving the children both a clear sense of cultural identity and the knowledge and skills to survive comfortably in the world of work. For example, one Maori woman, a university graduate whose daughter was in a total immersion Maori language class, said:

> My daughter's education is much better than mine was. I've got lots of confidence in theirs. Preschool—I don't remember having any formal preschool as such. Their kohanga reo [Maori language preschool designed and run by Maori people and funded by the state (Irwin, 1990)] experience has been good for them. They're more prepared for the school system when they move into it. There's a strong emphasis

on things Maori, Maori language. It's better in that way. I want them to have very good bilingual educations and be able to speak well in English and in Maori, do well at school—academically, in sports, in music—have access to as many things as possible at the end so they can make choices—go home to the marae or be a doctor.

Points of Tension and Conflict

Responses to open-ended questions such as those asked in the course of our life-history interviews tend to underreport the extent and distribution of certain opinions and experiences. However, our data suggest that liberal perspectives with varying degrees of interventionism were the dominant equity discourses among those we interviewed. As in government policies since World War II, liberalism was the dominant ideology of board members.

Other than those who mentioned Maori traditions, few mentioned any theory or belief system as having shaped their educational ideas. Only 10 identified a religion as a major influence, and those few who belonged to churches that were socially conservative (Klatch, 1987; Ryan, 1988) with respect to gender relations said that they did not believe that their personal religious philosophy should influence educational provisions in state schools. The conservative takeover of school boards—predicted by some— did not happen in the schools we studied.

The report from which the examples in this chapter were drawn (Middleton & Oliver, 1990) was structured as a series of case studies of the variety and distribution of equity discourses within each school board. This case-study methodology highlighted the possibility of conflict between some members of certain boards with respect to gender and other equity issues.

As noted previously, on some boards there were differences between the opinions of the teachers and the parents. For example, one staff member of a rural primary school explained that the Treaty of Waitangi was a particularly sensitive matter for his board: "Many parents are negative and are making the school's job difficult. Issues must be interpreted in the light of the district one is in. In our community, for example, we should move cautiously—rushing could unleash potential conflict." A principal of a rural school commented that staff and parents disagreed over the need for targeted equity policies: "There shouldn't be a question mark over this [equity]. In our school they can't see that all children don't have all opportunities. . . . The board doesn't see it as an issue."

A small number of board members—while supporting offering the same range of choice to all—believed that females were different by nature from males and would therefore never achieve actual equality: "Women have maternal instincts. They're made for the home." Another commented: "They are equal—with males—that's it! Same as there shouldn't be any racial prejudice. Yet let's face it—boys and girls seem to be made to be boys and girls." And a third said:

> There's too fast a push, too much emphasis on this area. In both the gender and the ethnic area they're not meeting halfway. . . . Women are biologically different and, whatever happens, women will always have a disadvantage. They should still have equal opportunity.

These biologically determinist views were at odds with the more liberal ideas of the other members of their boards. Several women members of one primary school board commented that gender equality of opportunities already existed and was unlikely to become a problem in their school. However, a male member of their board argued in his interview:

> I agree with this [equal opportunities for women and girls]. Male domination has existed. At the same time, this male domination has helped to make women boring. Buying them all these work-saving things, so they're not satisfied with ordinary things like sewing, baking, etcetera. Somebody's got to be in the home. There's so much dissatisfaction among women today. They're more materialistic than men! Got to have the best fridge, washing machine, car, TV, etcetera—necessarily, rather than as a requirement. I'm amazed at how many young women I know are unhappy with their husbands because they're not successful enough. As good as the Jones's isn't enough. You've got to beat the Jones. There's a place in society for the home.

Although on one hand he believed in offering the same chances and choices to both sexes, he also believed that women were suited by nature (instincts) for domesticity.

Summary

The dominant ideologies of the board members with respect to equality between the sexes were liberal and often noninterventionist. Many of those with experience as secondary school teachers or as employers had come to adopt a more interventionist or liberal feminist view that affirmative action was necessary. Radical feminist analyses of patriarchy (male power and violence) as a problem were a small minority and were more likely to be expressed by board members with high educational qualifications—in many cases, practicing or former teachers. Some of the Maori women argued for both equal opportunities in the Pakeha/Western sense and the teaching of gender-differentiated marae rituals. Although a few boards had a more conservative member who believed in innate differences and female subordination, such board members also believed in equal offering of formal opportunities. Within each board, then, members positioned themselves in discourses of "unequal weight and power" (Weedon, 1987, p. 35).

As teachers, my students are likely to find themselves involved in struggles over the equity clauses in their school charters. As Alison Jones has argued (1990):

> While some see the . . . charters as an example of the government interference they thought they could escape with local administrative control, others recognize that the charters' egalitarian thrust is necessary to guard against the entrenchment of conservative influences in education. (p. 102)

Experiences of Schooling: Intergenerational Comparisons

Our life-history interviews with board members took place several months before the 1990 parliamentary election. As discussed in chapter 1, in the election campaign, the National Party had characterized New Zealand education as failing by international standards and as providing inadequate preparation for life in the competitive global economy (New Zealand National Party, 1990a, 1990b). With very few exceptions, the board members in our study expressed high opinions of their children's schooling, preferring it greatly to their own. They did not describe education's core aim as competitiveness but wanted their children to become well-rounded individuals.

During the interviews, many offered specific examples of ways in which schooling had improved since their own childhoods. To illustrate such contrasts, I offer a brief case study. Mary was a 38-year-old Pakeha intermediate school teacher. She was single and active in several sports, which gave her "a knowledge of the community which will help my role on the board." When describing her childhood, she spoke at length of the significance of gender. She described her mother as the source of her academic cultural capital.

> My father was a farmer. My mother helped on the farm. I went to
> a small country school, then to a larger town school. My mother was

more encouraging than my father, who was busy all the time. She checked my homework and showed interest, which was impor-tant. . . . I was influenced by being the only girl amongst three boys.

Mary attended a large town coeducational secondary school. Her expe-riences of subject choice at secondary school provide useful insights into the ways knowledge was classified and stratified according to ability and gender (see chapters 2 and 4). "There was an academic course with two lan-guages, and a commercial course. I didn't want to do them. I had to do the general course." The general course, as Mary and her mother had probably not understood at the time her choice was made, was perceived as a low-ability course. This meant that Mary was prevented from taking full math-ematics: General-stream students took core mathematics (simple arith-metic only). According to Mary, in her school, it was only the girls who had a forced choice in this respect: "I liked maths, but was not able to take full maths because girls didn't do it. I was told to take history." Mary's gender, combined with her perceived low ability, made it impossible to take the combination of subjects she wanted. In contrast, Mary saw today's chil-dren's choices as not so limited.

Language, reading, maths are all stronger. There's more opportunity for kids to diversify. My experience was straight and narrow. The rou-tine never varied. Today there's more opportunity for them to be indi-viduals. You're not necessarily wrong because you're different.

She believes that equal opportunities for women and girls today "are there, but not always taken." She is grappling with the reasons why girls continue to opt for traditional areas and sees this as a wider social issue with a basis outside the school. "Girls are not pushed into traditional areas, but the boys are showing more interest in computers. I'm looking at it in my class to see why. It may be the result of years of conditioning in the family."

A small number of the board members described their own negative experiences at school as a reason for working as adults for educational change and wider social change. Four described their own marginal sta-tus—their identification with educationally subordinate groups—as their major reason for seeking election. As one Maori woman explained:

I believed I had something to offer. It's about time the *tangata whenua*[9] had someone in the school. . . . I bring representation of a group of people who would not approach the others—a lot with a Maori background. . . . I knew my people would support me. There were not enough women or Maori voices and I felt I could represent two viewpoints.

A Pakeha working-class woman described a similar motivation: "I thought of myself as a not highly educated person. There were a lot of people in the same boat as myself who would be happy with someone like me on the board, someone of the same kind who could be approached." She said that she hoped that her presence would give confidence to others with similar background. "If I succeeded, other people like me will feel they can do it, too."

Conclusion

Although at the time of the interviews, most boards had not yet developed equity policies for their schools, the vast majority of board members in our study expressed support for some form of equal opportunities or equity policy in their schools.

There is, however, evidence from other sources that some boards are prepared to abandon equity policies. For example, Adrienne Alton-Lee and Prue Densem (1992) have quoted the following passage that appeared in a South Island newspaper (*Christchurch Press)* 5 days after Lockwood Smith's postelection announcement that the equity clauses in the charters were to be made optional:

> Government plans to make equal opportunity and Treaty of Waitangi sections of school charters optional have drawn a strong but mixed reaction from Canterbury schools. . . . Of 19 schools contacted by The Press yesterday three said they were likely to take out those sections of their charter. (p. 197)

Alton-Lee and Densem (1992) commented, "We and our daughters belong to a gender whose wellbeing is negatively affected by these social policies and for whom fair treatment in the education system is openly and publicly optional" (p. 197).

As I revise this chapter for publication—in April 1992—the National government is about to pass an education reform bill. Among other measures, this has altered the criteria for membership of school boards of trustees. Labour had required elected members to be parents of students currently enrolled at the school. Under the impending legislation, school board members will no longer have to be parents of students at the school.

As noted earlier, some of those who were elected as parent representatives were also on the teaching staff of their children's schools. These people—teachers at the school who are also parents of current students—are now formally disqualified from seeking election as parent representatives. As exemplified in this chapter, some of these parents—trained as teachers and sensitive to inequities within the schools—had expressed strong feminist and pro-Maori views. These recent government measures could result in the further marginalization of feminist and antiracist discourses and an increasing business or New Right managerialism on some boards (Deem, 1989).

In his recent edited collection of papers, *Equity in Education,* Walter Secada (1989) stated: "Equity in education seems to be uniquely an American notion. Most writers who write about equity and equality of education come from the United States" (p. 68). As the earlier examples illustrate, issues of equity have been central in New Zealand education—not only in its official policies but in the everyday discussions and activities of parents, teachers, and school administrators. As elsewhere in the Western world, the restructuring of New Zealand's schools by successive governments has served as "an incitement to discourse" (Dreyfus & Rabinow, 1986). Those beginning teaching in these schools need an understanding of the broader theories and politics in which such debates are inscribed.

Notes

[1]Under the previous, centralized system of school administration, elected school boards had much more limited powers. The elected school committees for primary schools had employed school cleaners and grounds staff, made decisions about religious instruction in their school, and raised funds for and looked after facilities such as swimming pools and sports equipment. Major decisions about curriculum and the hiring and firing of teachers were made by the central Department of Education. Secondary school boards of governors had some powers over the hiring and firing of teachers: They selected their staff, but decisions over the conditions of employment (e.g., salary) were made centrally. The new system is a much more radical change for primary than it is for secondary schools.

[2]The Labour government issued several modified versions of the charter frameworks during the 1989 to 1990 restructuring process. Details of these modifications—a source of intense controversy at the time—can be found in Codd and Gordon, 1991. The clauses on gender equity, however, remained unchanged throughout.

[3]The philosophical blend of New Right administrations varies within and between countries. For example, in the United States, especially during the Reagan years, social conservatism influenced by fundamentalist Christian sects has gained greater influence within government than in other Western countries (Eisenstein,

1982; Klatch, 1987). Although fundamentalists have at times influenced policy in New Zealand, their influence has been less effective than in the United States (Jesson, Ryan, & Spoonley, 1988; Ryan, 1988) or in Queensland, Australia (Knight, 1985). Religious fundamentalism does not seem to be a major political force in Britain (Arnot, 1991a).

[4]Although the central arguments and methodology developed for this chapter are my own, the life-history data in it were gathered as part of the wider research project, Monitoring Today's Schools. The case studies are drawn from a 35,000-word report of which I was the principal author and for which I was the principal research designer (Middleton & Oliver, 1990). Data for the original report were gathered or critical comments were made by the following: David Mitchell (coordinator of the project and editor of the report), John Barrington, Ian Calder, Alan Hall, Barbara Harold, Mike Hollings, Richard Jeffries, Bob Katterns, Paul Keown, Robin McConnell, Clive McGee, Angela Main, Ruth Mansell, Kath Mason, Roger Moltzen, Debbie Oliver, Peter Ramsay, and Cathy Wylie. Some of the material in the present paper—especially that pertaining to the New Right—has not been discussed with the research team. I have theorized the gender issues further in Middleton (1990a, 1992c, 1992d) and the bicultural issues further in Middleton (1992b).

[5]In this early phase of our study, 14 schools were participating; there are now 16. Because there were 14 interviewers, we designed a questionnaire to give form to the life-history narratives. Interviewers used their discretion in deciding in which order to ask the questions. Some interviewers and interviewees preferred to begin with their own schooling and proceed chronologically; others preferred to begin with their present work on the board and then to move back in time. Because of the lack of time and resources, we were unable to tape and transcribe the interviews (although one interviewer did this himself). The majority kept detailed notes. These were verified by the interviewees before being written up. Respondents also had the opportunity to comment on the draft of the report before it was finalized.

[6]The quantitative data were obtained from tables drawn up from the questionnaires. This work was done by the team's research assistant, Deb Oliver, and I would like to thank her for this.

[7]These were developed for New Zealand. Like such numerical scales elsewhere, they are based on the average incomes and education levels of members of occupation categories. The Elley and Irving scale (1985) measures male occupations, and the Irving and Elley scale (1977) is for females. We used the former to classify the socioeconomic status of the male board members and the latter to classify the female board members.

[8]This interpretation of the data is impressionistic rather than quantifiable because of the open-ended nature of the questionnaire and the large number of interviewers. It may be that teachers know what to say to university researchers and that parents are more reticent and less confident. It seems likely, however, that trained teachers have thought in greater depth about the issues, which they confront on the job. Such questions are new to many parents.

[9]*Tangata whenua* (people of the land) refers to the local people with claims to

land rights in that area. Sometimes the term is used to refer to Maori people as the indigenous inhabitants of Aotearoa and sometimes to the rights of local tribes or whanau (extended families) within a more specific geographical location. For example, the local tribe would be expected to be represented on the board of its local school.

seven

Students' Voices: Intergenerational Conversations

*I*t is mid-December, 1991. In pale morning sun, I have walked the five kilometers from home to the university. Classes have finished. Students have departed; their learning, their writing, and their thoughts now abstracted, inscribed in the records as grades, as data (D. Smith, 1987). I return to the question with which I started this book: How can we middle-aged and older teacher educators develop feminist courses that are appropriate for the lives and times of today's students? In this chapter, I view my course from the vantage points of students. Has my course—has my teaching—been appropriate for their lives and times?

Learning is an essentially private process. Most of what students experience in a class is invisible to teachers. I have only fragments from which to piece together this account. The "Chapter 7" file on my disk contains paragraphs I extracted while marking the students' learning diaries handed in 6 weeks into the 12-week course. The file contains excerpts from their course evaluations—written in haste after the final test. I have the various official documents through which I structured students' learning: course outlines, study guides, assignment sheets, and set readings. I have my memories, my feelings, and my impressions.

As I type, I think about my colleagues overseas. I wonder how you have engaged with this text. I try to hear through your ears. The "formally organized interchanges" (D. Smith,

1979, p. 146)—the international discourses—of feminist educational theory unite us. But I do not want to lapse into jargon. I write also for the New Zealand undergraduate students who agreed to be "in" this chapter. I would like this text to be a meeting point, an engagement, a conversation between us all.

I have transcripts of two tapes that I recorded earlier this year in the United States: discussions with American doctoral students who had heard my life history, watched my slides (see chapter 1), and read papers that were later to be merged and transformed into these chapters. But their voices are dim and blurred—the tapes unclear, the many voices disembodied, unnamed, at times a babble. I will use what I can. You will hear the occasional American voice in these conversations.

My computer takes me from file to file; it splices transcript to diary, teacher's course outlines, to students' course evaluations, and cuts and pastes a collage-like text. Computers make possible—encourage—such "intertextuality" (Grumet, 1988). As author and as composer, I select quotations and juxtapose texts. As I decide what to include and what to make public from what students have written and said about my teaching and writing, I am conscious of my positioning within the ruling apparatus with power to record and to inscribe (D. Smith, 1987). In making my selections from the data, I have not attempted to convey the relative weightings and distributions of student experiences, opinions, and perspectives. Rather, I have tried to make each voice equally audible. As Kathleen Casey (1988) has argued, it is useful to present "alternatives on an equal status with the dominant version" (p. 30) of events. I have tried to resist the temptation to interrupt my students; I have tried to let them speak for themselves. But there are times when I reflect on and raise questions about what they have said, and struggle to articulate some implications of their comments for my future teaching. Such reflections appear in a different typeface, interspersed among students' comments.

Loud male voices in the corridor—something about equivalent full-time students. Shortly, I have to attend a departmental meeting. It is the meeting season. I become aware of my surroundings. This office is seldom my space for academic writing. It is the place where I compose memoranda, file minutes of meetings, and write letters in response to the contents of brown envelopes. It is also the space where I meet with students. It is appropriate that I reflect on them here.

I have made this office as safe and as much like home as possible. The bureaucratic flooring is covered with a large rug in earth colors: ocher red, gold, beige, black. There is an old armchair in one corner. The cream walls are hidden behind shelves of books. Above the smaller bookcases are pictures: a poster from Queensland and a batik from Kenya. In front of my computer is a Picasso print: a sketch of two hands, one presenting and the other receiving a bouquet. It is mounted on red—signed by colleagues—"Congratulations on publishing *Women and Education in Aotearoa,*" my first book. Near the door is Kate's sketch of a 1960s protest march. Hippies—black, white, and brown faces—beads, flowers, and slogans. Facing me is my feminist bookshelf. On the top shelves are Australian, British, and American books about feminism and postmodernism. I search my files and locate my course outline.

I begin with the following official document—the first two pages of a handout my students receive at the beginning of the course—my list of aims, my public statement of intention.

31.331 Women and Education Study Guide
Introduction
Welcome to 31.331, Women and Education. This is an interdisciplinary course which brings together theories and methodologies from the sociology, history, philosophy, and psychology of education as well as from other interdisciplinary fields such as educational administration, policy analysis, curriculum theory and women's studies. [My reasons for beginning this document with a reference to disciplines will be addressed in the Epilogue.]

Although the course focusses on women and schooling in New Zealand, some comparisons are made with women's education in Australia, Britain, and the United States.

The course is designed with a dual focus—on women's personal experiences of education and on the historical and structural contexts which make such experiences possible. "Biography, history, and social structure" are studied simultaneously. In this I hope to help you to understand how educational theories, policies and provisions shape our everyday experiences and help construct our "gendered identities" as women or men; how such "gendering" has changed over time; how it varies between cultures and social classes.

The pedagogy (teaching style) of the course is designed to help you to achieve the following [these categories were later to be used as a framework for the students' end-of-course evaluation forms]:

1. An increased understanding of the educational processes that have made you what you are today.
2. A knowledge of some of the major social theories which have

informed educational policy and research in the field of gender and education.

3. An ability to identify "genderedness" in what you read, what you see on television and other mass media, in the curricula of schools, and in your other academic studies in education.

4. Some experience in doing qualitative research.

5. Ideas of your own about current issues and debates concerning gender and education and a willingness and confidence to enter such debates.

Pedagogy

I have been developing this course for ten years. It changes every year as a result of changes in my own thinking, changes in the field of study, and as a result of student feedback. This year I am researching the course as I teach it, so you will be helping to determine its outcomes for next year's students.

I am aware of the heavy work loads most of you are carrying. Accordingly, I have devised a mode of assessment which gives you credit for having done the reading each week. I shall briefly summarise how this is to be done. Full details of assessment and assignments are given on the separate sheet headed "Assessment and assignments 1991."

Briefly, the course requires of you *three tasks:* a learning diary, a life-history study, and an open-book test. These are each of *equal weighting* (i.e., each is worth 1/3 of the course's total grade).

1. *Learning Diary.* This is to be kept weekly during the first six weeks of the course. . . . Weekly requirements are listed as "diary entries" in the study guide. [Tasks included open-ended responses to the slide presentation, as described in chapter 1 of this book; critiques of and responses to films and excerpts from films of the lives of Sylvia Ashton-Warner and Janet Frame; and questions requiring responses to specific set readings.]

2. *Life-History Project.* A comparison of the educational experiences of two adult women (of different ages). [Details were given in chapter 1.]

3. *Open-Book Test.* [A wide range of topics was given on students' popular culture, on recent educational restructuring policy, and so on.] This is designed to help you bring together what you have studied in the set readings and the assignments. It will also help you to evaluate your own learning in this course and will build on

the writing you have done in your diaries and in the life-history assignment.

[Students negotiated their test questions with me. I will not discuss the test in this chapter.]

Generative Themes

You, my readers and my students, have all been through the first session in the "Women and Education" course: the slide presentation of my educational autobiography that was included in chapter 1. In the first entry in their learning diaries, the "Women and Education" students were asked to write a response to this presentation. Many chose to describe personal experiences with respect to the generative themes I had identified: racism and colonialism, the sexual division of labor, and the contradiction between feminine heterosexuality and rationality/intellectuality.

Racism and Colonialism

Liza (36): My first reaction to the readings and pictures was that in many ways it was similar to my own schooling in the 1960s and early 1970s. I remember with clarity studying "the Maori Wars" (as they were known then) and the savagery of Maori as epitomized by the acts of war, Hone Heke and the flagpole, when the Pakeha were trying to give to the Maori a better (and superior it was inferred) lifestyle, raids by Te Rauparaha [a 19th-century leader] on his own people, etc. Colonialism and racism were rampant in my own schooling—all while I was trying to be a "good brown-skinned Pakeha."

Jan (mid-30s): My experience is of similar concepts being taught at school. My first experience of schooling in New Zealand was at Intermediate School. I arrived from England in 1968. I fitted right into school here because it was so much a white European education system.

Carol (early 20s): I experienced culture shock when I changed schools within New Zealand. My primary years were in a small town. With most of the population being Maori, I was unaware of my difference. We all mixed in well—not separate groups. I felt very secure in this environment. Then I moved to [a provincial city] where there was a

clear distinction between race groups and the haves and the have-
nots. I found this hard to adjust to. I was used to the warm friendships of the Maori—here they distanced themselves.

Maureen (mid-20s): I found it most interesting that Sue Middleton
read, understood, and was attracted to the image of Sylvia Ashton-
Warner at the age of 13, having just read *Spinster*. I assume also from
statements made in her autobiographical account that this attraction
and understanding were based on the recognition of likeness of mind.
I was exposed at teachers' college to some of Sylvia's ideas and their
subsequent development and application in child-centred education.
My initial reactions to her were feelings of suspicion of her intentions
and integrity of her work with, and theories about, Maori children. I
thought how very weird this woman must have been. I believe my initial reaction of suspicion had been fed by my then awakening awareness and reaction to my Maori heritage.

Gender, Work, and Sexuality

Shelly (21): Sue's theory that rural women might be more likely to
become feminists[1] interested me. . . . I grew up on a farm until I
went to boarding school for my sixth and seventh form [senior] years.
I am also a feminist, but I think for different reasons from those Sue
mentioned. I really detested the fact that my father was the "head of
the household" for no other reason than that he was a male. When he
married my mother, she had to give up working (paid work, that is).
She works very hard—in the house, on the farm, on various committees, in charity work. It just did not equate that my father automatically had the ultimate say in all the family decisions. I always tried to
encourage a more democratic system of decision making, but I think
Dad was offended. Perhaps it meant taking away some of his manli-
ness? In my experience, farm life has been a very traditional "stereo-
typical role-model" life-style. I knew from an early age that I wanted
to break free from tradition. I don't condemn my parents for choosing
their life-style—it works well for them and they are happy. But I'm
glad options have opened up for women.

Wiha (30): My experiences of rural life were similar to yours, Shelly.[2]
As in Sue's slide, our local garage had all male attendants. It was usually a family business. Women worked only in the office and as tea
ladies. My uncle had a garage. . . . He worked the garage, taking on

extra men when required. His wife did simple bookkeeping and petrol serving. He later allowed his daughter control over the accounts and the office side as a way of keeping her from going to the closest town for work. My own experience with machinery as a male dominated area, was with the opportunities given to my brother but denied me. Learning to ride a motor bike—my brother was given special lessons. I had to demand that I be allowed the opportunity to learn as well. This never extended to other machinery.

Myra (30s): I too was brought up in the country—on a plant nursery. Boys and girls worked on the farm, though the boys got much more credit for their work. And after the daylight hours girls were expected to work in the house—cooking, cleaning—while the boys had leisure time.

Kirsty (21): I grew up in a conservative small town. Sport played a role in keeping society gender-segregated. In our town it was very clear that the "cool" boys played rugby and the "in" girls played netball. Hockey and soccer were for the "not so in" people. . . . In my school days there was still a conflict between being popular with boys and being an intellectual. The popular girls were the ones that were "pretty" and the ones that had boyfriends in the first fifteen rugby teams—there was no criteria that you had to be intellectual.

Jan (34): By the time I reached high school, the lines between male roles and female roles were becoming blurred. Still, we had the school dances and it was considered wise for a girl not to let her date know how clever she was—males were scared off by brainy girls. Thus, even in the "enlightened 70s" it was still important to be popular (particularly with the boys) rather than a swot. . . .

Vicky (21): I had always enjoyed working with wood and would have loved to become a carpenter. However, I just knew that it was not an appropriate profession for girls. I took woodwork to the fourth form. It was always a "hobby subject," but the boys in my class saw it as a "career subject." I took it, because it was a subject I had always been good at and enjoyed. However, I got an E. I couldn't understand it at the time, but now can see exactly why, suddenly, at 14, I stopped achieving. I was one of two girls in the class, and we both "lived down" to the expectations of our peers and teacher. I remember purposefully getting things wrong and mixing the wrong solutions together so the boys would come to my aid and help me. I got the attention I wanted, but I also reinforced the notion that girls were clumsy, needed help and aid when attempting male subjects. I regret it severely.

When I first became aware of feminist issues, encouraging girls into nontraditional subjects and occupations seemed relatively unproblematic. But for this young woman, a nontraditional activity became a site for the reproduction of the contradiction between being an autonomous individual and being feminine. Women's education remains contradictory. Feminist-inspired policy changes (such as the opportunity to take formerly male subjects) have merely created new arenas for the reproduction of this contradiction.

Sylvia (21): I wonder whether such a conflict between "sexuality and intellectuality" has encouraged my career direction. The seventh form [senior year] was a year when I decided to socialise rather than work. Placed in a scholarship class, I struggled with why I had been placed with such an intelligent bunch. I didn't get a scholarship or even an A bursary.[3] I had to contend with a B. While in the class there were only two females, it only annoyed me because I didn't have other girls, my girlfriends, to talk to. The reason why the class was dominated by males, in my eyes, was because it was a year when the so-called "intelligent" were (somehow) nearly all males. . . . Four years later, I met up with a number of my former school mates. They all were shocked to hear I had almost completed my teaching diploma, as they'd all considered I'd move towards accountancy. At school I had never considered being an accountant, even though I surpassed two such friends in the bursary exam. Both guys have almost completed management/finance and a law degree. . . . My mother would have liked me to take a degree in accounting. I have felt pressure to succeed. I wonder whether I moved towards teaching so as not to fear failure—more likely to succeed in a teaching profession perhaps?!

Vicky (21): I applied for teachers' college because I heard they took sixth formers with lower grades if they had a "good character." I was accepted and I am now completing my B.Ed. degree and very much looking forward to teaching next year. I still have to pinch myself sometimes, as I never ever in my wildest dreams thought I'd be a university student. University was for "wax-heads" and "geeks." I remember dreaming about being a lawyer, but never saw it within my reach. I used to tease and punch the "bright girls" at school because they had what I hadn't—intelligence. It all changed when my parents moved and I was supposed to go into the bottom stream. However, my father's cousin was head of the English department and somehow put me in the top stream. I hated every minute of it, but I knuckled down and started to achieve in the subjects I enjoyed.

These comments shocked me. For these young women, training for teaching was a lesser option than accountancy, law, or in the following example, medicine—the high-status male professions. Has feminism contributed to the devaluation of the traditionally female occupations? For women of my generation and social class, to become a teacher was seen as the pinnacle of success[4]—as academically demanding and as a vocation contributing to the public good. These young women saw their choice of teaching as a sign of their lesser intelligence.

Jan (34): I'm ten years older than you, Vicky, and ten years younger than Sue. By the time I got to high school, girls were schooled for careers, but these were still to fit around the time when you got married and gave up work to have babies. I had originally thought of becoming a doctor. Although I don't ever remember having this said to me or being encouraged away from the career path, the concept of work as "a short adventure between school and marriage" (J. Watson, 1966) still existed in the 1970s. As I had always wanted to have a family, I couldn't see how long years of career training would fit into my future. To a certain extent, once I got married, I believed that any well-paid job was OK so long as it paid the bills. . . . I have worked hard to support my husband in his career—not because his career is more important, but mainly because I knew that he would one day be the sole provider for our family. In addition, it had always been agreed that he would support and help me during my studies and in establishing my own career—once the children are both at school. I am comfortable with this arrangement—it works well for us and my husband has always acknowledged that *we* built his career—as a unit.

My generation of women were taught that paid work would be a short adventure between school and marriage. However, by the time we reached adulthood, most worked at least until they began to have children. It was our generation that lobbied for child-care centers to enable us to continue to work by choice. Jan and her husband—somewhat younger—had a well-reasoned long-term strategy for working out how they would accommodate two careers and a family.

Sylvia (21): The pressure for us younger women has moved from wifedom and motherhood (after a number of years working before marriage) towards succeeding within a career. How frowned upon is it today to want a home, husband and children, to be a "professional" housewife/mother? There are those who feel pressure not to marry, as they are only in their early 20s: "Too young! Use your independence, intelligence and 'plentiful' (?) opportunity in other ways beside marriage!" A conflict between career and wife/motherhood is common amongst myself and friends. Marriage is acceptable in your early thirties. Remaining single or childless is seen as a bit "iffie" throughout your entire life.

When I was young, my parents emphasized the importance of finishing one's training before marriage—delaying marriage until one's early 20s. This would mean that as a trained teacher, I would always have something to fall back on in times of need. My parents' generation had survived the 1930s depression, and it was seen as essential for a woman to be able to support herself if she "had to." There was always work for teachers, nurses, and secretaries. However, this young woman is describing a prolonged pressure to delay marriage and child rearing until her 30s. She feels pressured to establish herself in a career first. Is this a result of feminist pressure? Or a response to the scarcity of employment—the need to be competitive in hard times? Or both?

Myra (30s): When I was at high school in the 1970s, many female peers encouraged sexuality. If you were also intelligent, female friends attempted to tone your brain down. Fears of being different, i.e., more intelligent than others, were evident especially when in competition with males over exam marks, especially in maths/science—females were not encouraged to do well. If you got a better mark than a boy, you were teased and shunned by the guys and often also by the girls.

Ailsa (20s): My experience was completely different. I found there was all the options open to me. Taking physics and technical drawing was seen as nothing out of the ordinary.

Lyn (mid-20s): I have so many confusing memories of high school . . . having to explain, yet again, that I wasn't going to ballroom dancing because I had no intention of going to the ball . . . getting good marks and trying to do even better . . . not wanting to end up like my mother . . . having a feminist teacher who introduced me to Katherine Mansfield, Jane Austen, Sylvia Plath, Doris

Lessing, Patricia Grace, and Keri Hulme . . . hating school . . . reading Simone de Beauvoir and Betty Friedan . . . having friends who weren't sure what to think of me but were friends anyway . . . being told by a teacher that I'd "better watch out" for wearing a pro-lesbian badge . . . spending lunchtimes in the library reading *New Internationalist* magazine and anything vaguely radical or sociological . . . wishing my friends would stop talking about what they were wearing to the ball . . . having a feminist revue group perform at school . . . refusing to go and wave my flag at the queen . . . doing better than I thought I would in Sixth Form certificate (but wishing I'd done better). . . .

First American Voice:[5] When I saw the slides and read this document [material similar to that in chapter 4] I just kept being struck by the fact that I had similar reactions and experiences in a very different environment.

Second American Voice: Me, too.

Third American Voice: And it's like—not to say that there are universals. . . . You think your own experiences are so individual, and then, in reading it, you realize that, well, it's only individual because our education forces us to "become individual." We can exchange stories and our understanding of theory becomes entirely different.

Doing Life-History Research

Students did two life-history exercises during the course. The first, an archaeology of our schooling, discussed in chapter 1, was an in-class exercise. Students brought to class artifacts from their own school days and discussed these in age groups. Each group reported back to the whole class so that intergenerational profiles were constructed. The second exercise was the life-history interview project, which also involved cross-generational comparisons.

Claire: The group I was in for the "Archaeology of our Schooling" consisted of two 26-year-olds and four 34-year-olds. Despite the eight-year difference in our ages, it was surprising to see the similarities in our schooling. There were differences as well but a lot of our experiences were the same.

Kirsty (21): Looking over one of my old school reports which Mum sent for me to look at sparked off many memories of my convent days. The reaction I got from sharing my report with others was a little unexpected. They were amazed at the format of the report—the large section on Christian attitudes and the cross on the front. These things were all so "normal" to me. Even more amazed were my friends as I told them about our religious studies and our daily greetings—"good morning Sister Catherine and may God bless you." It was a small school in a country town. When I first arrived it was still being run by the nuns, but by the time I had reached standard two, the nuns had all left. Although the school promoted Christian attitudes, and a regular part of our week was to attend church, at a young age I never thought my schooling was any different to the "regular" kids at the primary school across the road. This was until about Standard two, when the dental nurse[6] became situated across the road at this [state] primary school. It was a harrowing event for most of us at the convent school. This served as great amusement to the "regular" kids, who had much delight in throwing acorns and chanting "convent dogs, stink like hogs, in their mother's bathing togs." Of course I was far too timid to pick up an acorn and throw it back, so often I arrived at the dental nurse close to tears.

There has been little if any research on Catholic schools in New Zealand or of relationships between Catholics and Protestants. I have only my own case studies to offer my students. We need ethnographies of Catholic schools, such as Nancy Lesko's (1988) study in the United States. Kirsty's discovery of her "otherness" as a convent girl among the public school majority threw into question her own and other class members' taken-for-granted realities.

Marjorie (early 40s): The "Archaeology of our Schooling"—I came away from the class group exercise with a feeling of depression. I felt very old. I was reminded of the narrow scope of my childhood and my schooling. The practice of streaming students according to perceived ability (narrowly defined) provided me with an "academic education" which left me with the "choice" of nursing, teaching, or office administration/clerical training (on the job). My own experience is confirmation of the ways that women's choices are limited by social conditions. At age 17 I chose teaching and was accepted for training (with the small allowance available at the time). However, I could earn 20% more in the Public Service, which my widowed mother could claim as board to meet the rental on our state home. I was "locked out" of higher education because of family needs. I was trapped by class structures and lack of cultural capital. In 1982 I spent one year teacher training (and obtained a few university papers) which was interrupted by a second marriage breakdown, full-time employment, and several years of saving to obtain a secure home. Now in the 1990s I am still trying to complete what I should have had the opportunity to do in the 1960s. Hence the feelings of depression.

Melanie (21): It can be quite depressing to realise that I didn't have as much choice as I first thought I had. But I have learned a lot. Before I didn't think about what was actually happening.

Fiona (21): I always thought all my decisions were made by me—pure and simple—but examining my past (school and family life) I found some strong influences there. It was very valuable; I found it very interesting and got lots of learning done.

These comments on structure and agency are pleasing to me. One of my objectives has been to challenge the assumptions expressed by many women student teachers that their major decisions have been purely a result of free choice. At the same time, I did not wish to imply that we are mere passive victims of our socialization and situation. The tensions between biography, history, and social structure were the intended focus of the course.

Cheryl (22): Well, I've become more aware that one *personally* can affect life outcomes—women are not passive but actively take part in society and their own life. I've thought about the interrelatedness between biography, history, and social structure, as well as more general educational processes and developments in New Zealand.

Sally (26): I especially liked the archaeology of our schooling. Just going home and finding all my old school things. Writing the diary also made me more aware of things which I experienced at school, i.e., sexual harassment by boys and teachers.

Myra (36): I found the "Life-History Interviews" research project extremely interesting. I learned techniques of interviewing and also it was good to weave the historical, social, and biographical details together so that the interviewees' schooling took shape and meaning. The younger woman in my assignment—I had seen her grow up from the age of eight, and even taught her. It was interesting to compare my interpretation of her schooling and life to hers.

Fiona (24): It was wonderful in terms of getting in touch with the history of my family and seeing how educational experiences affected "ordinary" women (as opposed to published feminists).

Cheryl (22): I had the opportunity to learn the life histories of my mother and grandmother. With their biographies and the historical events of the times I understood where they were coming from, the similarities and differences in our lives, and can now understand the pressures they place on me.

Ngaire (22): Doing the life-histories has inspired me to look at my whakapapa [genealogy]—especially the women in the whanau [extended family]—and to research this further. I learned heaps about Mum and myself and our educations—similar and different.

Melanie (21): It was really good going and talking to older women about their educational experiences.

Helen (21): I did this on myself and found it immensely helpful. I learned a lot about my actions and how education shaped me.

Sarah (26): It was my first interview ever. I was quite nervous about this, but everything went great.

Stella (21): The life history method was a useful experience for both the researcher and the person being interviewed.

Joy (36): I enjoy researching in an interview type situation and picking out the interesting parts but hate relating it back to research and what somebody else has already found.

American voices: When you get down to it, academic assignments are set up as an individual thing . . . the researcher is, like, the pivotal point. . . . I could go into a community, and it doesn't matter, you know, I'm still "from the university." I still have that position. Whether I position myself as the pivotal point or as part of the collective group, I'm still—it would still be my study. I'm still getting something out of it that these people are not. There are still motivations for me that don't exist for them. It's really problematic.

Barbara (44): I liked the interviewing experiences, as did the subjects, but I wasn't comfortable with incorporating references to social settings and theories into the final offering.

Relating Theory to Everyday Life

The course required students to cover several set readings per week. These covered the history of New Zealand women's education and introduced local and overseas research that was representative of the major disciplinary and theoretical traditions in feminist scholarship on women's education. The readings provided background for the weekly whole-class sessions (slide presentations, lectures, and so on) and were discussed in detail in the smaller-group tutorials.[7] Several of the required diary entry tasks addressed specific readings, and many students chose in these to use the readings to theorize on their own educational experiences.

For example, in the following examples, students are reflecting on some socialist-feminist ethnographic readings and thinking about class and gender relations in their own schooling. The first comments concern a paper by New Zealand sociologist Alison Jones (1988). Jones's paper was concerned with the class-cultural locatedness of curriculum processes. She used cultural capital theory (Bourdieu, 1971a) as a basis for a neo-Marxist analysis of classroom dynamics in an inner-city all-girls public high school and developed a critique of radical feminist assumptions about the egalitarianism of single-sex schooling for girls.

> The same sort of power dynamic which Spender and others indicate disadvantages girls in the classroom also happens among groups of girls, and with the same effect: knowledge is "differentially distributed" on the basis of race and class to different groups of girls in the classroom. Girls as members of race and class groups receive quite different knowledge about learning and teaching and about their own ability. (p. 144)

Kit (23): I was particularly interested in the chapter in the text by Alison Jones (1988) on class and cultural differences in a girls' school. It made me think about one of my teachers. She was a white (middle-class presumably) woman of a lovely, caring nature. I thought she was absolutely wonderful, in fact all my girlfriends did, as she paid us a lot of attention and hence we interacted with her frequently within the classroom. However after reading Jones' chapter, I now recall that most of the teacher's attention would focus upon my group of friends and that the pattern of interaction she initiated was primarily orientated toward the Pakeha children. I remember the Maori and Pacific

Island children being really quiet within the classroom (almost nonexistent) and hearing them say they hated the teacher once out of the classroom setting. . . .

Jan (34): I thought, while reading Jones' chapter, that the Pacific Island girls' background of respect for the teachers—all elders with knowledge—would not be conducive to aggressive classroom interaction. Even when teachers were aware of this, it made no difference to the way they ran their classes. This made me go back and analyse my classroom experience. I came from England. When I started school here, I had been in New Zealand about two or three months. I was worldly from my adventure on the high seas and I was a novelty to my classmates. I was brought up to be assertive and had none of the self-effacing tendency which I think characterised the New Zealand temperament in the 1960s. . . . Thus, I was eager to speak and they (my classmates) let me. A lot of the boys in that class were lazy—why bother to speak when "that Pommie [slang term sometimes used derogatorily for an English person] girl" will do it for you. Teachers encouraged me because I was prepared to answer and because I had different views to express (which is the novelty value). This pattern continued. As Alison Jones suggests—it is self-perpetuating. . . .

Miranda (25 to 35): I went to a private boarding school, so I was really interested in Sue Kedgley's (1987) and Jane Kenway's (1990) articles on private girls' schools. Boarding school is more than secondary schooling. It was my life for four years and I have some good and bad feelings about it. Bad feelings are memories of the snobby attitudes, "you don't wear cardigans" for example. . . . I could identify with many of the things in Sue Kedgley's article. Manners and speech, for example, were very important in our school also. . . . The "social status" hierarchies within the school were also similar to those described in Sue Kedgley's article—whether one's parents had been to private schools and if so, which ones, was quite important.

The diary was handed in during the 6th week of the 12-week course. By then, we had worked through the history of New Zealand women's education and discussed readings that emphasized the different kinds of feminist research in education. We had not yet covered feminist theory in any explicit sense, although some students had read ahead and covered some of this themselves. In the final diary entry, I asked the question, What is feminism?

Imogen (30s): When I was a teenager during the 1970s, women's liberation was emerging. I remember the women's liberation movement being quite vocal and the protest marches they organized. I was not familiar with the word "feminism," only "women's liberation." But there is one thing that I remember vividly, and that was the women's libbers' slogan of "burn your bra." So if I saw any women who were not wearing a bra, I would automatically associate them as being a women's libber. I was only a naive 13-year-old. There was a song that came out in 1971 to support the women's liberation (or to make fun of it) called "come on ma, burn your bra." During the seventies I did not pay much attention to the issues of women's liberation until I came to teachers' college and university. I have never really classified myself as a feminist but a friend of mine who tutors in women's studies says I am. Feminism to me is a question of equality and equity for women in society. Women should have the same opportunities as men in the work force and education as well as in the area of decision making on important issues.

Vicky (21): Had this question been posed to me seven years ago, I would have said that feminism was "some strange type of religion which only women belong to. Some of their characteristics are hairy bodies, wearing lots of purple and necklaces with 'the symbol.' They enjoy hating men and do body building." I now see feminism as very much part of my life and thinking. I see it as a movement which strives for equality, true equality. . . .

Myra (21): I wrote an essay on radical feminism when I was at high school. My mother, who had broken up with her husband a year previously, influenced the essay, with such ideas as "underdogs," "matrimonial properties act." Her idea that femininity was more important than feminism influenced my idea that women were not out to dominate the sexes but to find equality. . . . In my essay, I wrote that in the past women did not have equal opportunities and there was a real need for feminism. I went on to say: "Radical feminism produced women who did not want to stay at home and rear children or to be made to be a housewife or a mother. Their sense of values was to hold a good job and to prove their equality with men, sometimes to prove their superiority. Females ignored that they were made to be different to men, e.g., more compassionate, more emotional, and even more cautious to 'jump into things.' So they did not take into account that

females are made differently inside and outside for a purpose. . . .
Ann Hercus [a senior Labour politician] is a feminist. She was trying
to weaken the authority of parents and family, e.g., a young teenage
girl could have an abortion without parental consent—or knowledge.
Six years later, I feel that there ought to be some recompense for this
patriarchal society—not that we overrun it but that as a female I
should be entitled to have my say and have a go at whatever I desire.

Jan (34): I was a teenager during the "second wave" and I saw male
confusion and over-the-top feminism as a bad thing. I did not want to
be identified as a feminist because there was, by then, an unflattering
stereotype attached to the label. Besides which, I felt no need for liberation as I had been brought up to believe that I was equal—to my
brothers and to all people. I have never felt oppressed by gender, but
that does not mean that I do not recognize that such oppression
exists. . . . In my past three years of study at Waikato University, and
particularly in this course, I have been forced to face up to the fact of
my own feminism. I have not undergone any great process of "radicalisation." I am more an "accidental feminist"—I was born and
socialised into it. My belief has always been that women are equal to
men and as such deserve the same rights and opportunities. I do not
believe that one race, one class, one gender has the right to oppress
any other group which it perceives to be inferior. . . . And, therefore, it must be stated, although my teenage self would die a thousand
deaths, that I am a feminist.

As in the United States, there have been in New Zealand a strong
antifeminist backlash and distorted depictions of feminists—and of
women's studies—in the mass media. The kinds of feminist stereotype
that these women are describing are characteristic of such media
depictions (e.g., du Chateau, 1990; Fahrdi, 1992). Feminism is equated
with masculinity; femaleness with a more conventional femininity. To
be a feminist within such a discourse is to be abnormal.

Penny (37): I find the whole feminism issue quite controversial and
provocative, as far as the general public go, which I think is a worry.
How can young girls say there's no need for feminism when there are
so *many* primary teachers who are women, and so *few* female principals? Can't they see such an obvious bias?

A similar range of attitudes to feminism was expressed in several students' end-of-year course evaluations in response to the questions, Why did
you take this course? What were your expectations of it?

Patricia (35): I took this course because another course was not available. I thought it would probably be very feminist. It was interesting, relevant, thought provoking, up to date, not too strongly feminist.

Dorothy (20): I dropped a course at the start of the year and had to take another in the second semester—timetable allocation. But I must admit it seemed interesting, as we had taken courses like this at teachers' college. I just hoped it wouldn't be too over the top in feminism.

Sarah (26): I thought it would be pretty radical, men-bashing maybe (that's with the experience of not having done any women's studies before).

Melanie (21): I thought I wouldn't like it as my meaning of feminism wasn't too positive. After the first lecture I thought I'd enjoy it.

Stella (21): I'd enjoyed my other women's studies papers [courses].

Fiona (24): I took it to develop an awareness of influences on women and education and learn about women in the history of education. I also wanted to become aware in my own teaching of discrepancies between girls' and boys' experiences in the classroom. As a teacher and a woman I felt that it would be good to know more about women's role in educational processes, influences on us, etc., that may help me in my teaching.

Barbara (44): I took this course as preparation for teaching. I need to be conversant with actual equity issues.

In the anonymous, end-of-course written evaluation, I asked: Has the course helped you to identify genderedness in what you read, what you see on television and other mass media, in the curricula of schools, and in your other academic studies in education?

Jane (36): This was already developed in me, but has been heightened. This has increased my frustration with the gender-blindness of psychology.

Julie (21): I was already familiar with recognizing gender in toys, images in advertising, in magazines. However, the section on pornography[8] and discussion on genderedness in literature [teenage romances] were really interesting.

Pauline (33): I am far more discerning than I used to be and frequently get told off for abusing TV ads (at home) for their sexist content/portrayals.

Tracy (21): It made me very aware of sexist language and how to effectively use nonsexist language. I'm concerned about being involved in gender issues that my sons and daughters will face.

Claire: I found the lecture on the equity clauses in the charters really practical and aimed towards achieving the desired goals. Children as well as parents should be aware of them. One of the charter goals addressed sexual harassment. This brought back a few memories about my school experiences that were definitely sexual harassment. At Intermediate we had an art teacher who used to rub his hand up and down the backs of the girls! I knew of some girls who went to the principal (a woman!) and complained, but I don't know what happened. He was still teaching there when I left high school six years later! And then there were incidents of boys "feeling" girls up and giving them "grundies"! So disgusting when I think about it now.

I also asked my students in the evaluation: Has the course helped you to develop ideas of your own about current issues and debates concerning gender and education and a willingness to enter such debates?

Elizabeth (21): I've always felt confident in debates but now I've got more material to back them up.

Leanne (21): I'm unsure about this. I might be willing to enter discussions, but debates—I don't think so. It's not that I won't know what the issues are, but more that I don't like debating.

Sarah (26): I think I have a way to go in sociology and women's studies before I was "confident" but I'd probably have a go in a quite smallish group. I could imagine myself arguing with a brother, boyfriend, or father over this stuff.

Jane (36): I have always enjoyed debating in this area and do not lack confidence when with women. I find it harder to share my views in a group with a majority of males though. It has been excellent hearing the variety of views of the other women.

Sharon (21): I feel more confident in presenting my thoughts and argument but I still get shot down by the males in my circle and still need to be more forceful and back up what I say and believe in.

Ngaire (22): I am sick of being shot down by men who don't know about gender and education. And constantly having to validate my argument. But I will live, and keep on trying!

> The presence of men, no matter how sympathetic, constructs dynamics in women's studies classes that are different from those in classes that are all women (Spender, 1980). These students' comments confirm my impressions.

Noeline (34): My debate is whether I shall send my daughters to single-sex or co-ed secondary schools. Research suggests that single-sex schools are more beneficial to girls. I think bright kids do well wherever they go if they have the right home environment. I have one extremely bright one and one average and my feeling is that the average one will do better in a single sex. I am extremely happy with their school presently on issues of gender.

Beverley (33): We are withdrawing our two girls from school and will finish the year at home. On a recent visit—one of many, and after continuing concerns—school seems to be a place to fool around, to take others for granted. Yes, they are being socialized, but to fit a society I don't like the shape of. My partner and I will endeavour to educate, and shape, and provide for them, in order for them to be intelligent, sensible, caring, sharing people. The gender issues in the classroom are of great concern to me. There are a lot of double-standards.

Power Relations in a Feminist Classroom

Feminist academics have recently begun to write about the problems of power relations in their feminist classrooms (Ellsworth, 1989; Lather, 1991; Lewis, 1990; Miller, 1990; Snow, 1991). When I asked students to comment on any aspects of the course that needed improvement, they came up with several examples of ways in which my classroom continued to reproduce the kinds of power relations that such writers had identified in their classes.

Margaret (44): I know it's very hard to structure a course to take account of the different stages people are at—age, life-experiences, work experience. And when you have mature students with a lot of young ones—generational differences are heightened. Perhaps more opportunities for older students to confer would have helped me as a mature student. Tutorials were excellent though for that sometimes.

Fay (22): It is important to recognize that we all come into the course with views and experiences we can all learn from. I felt as a younger student uncomfortable at times.

Jeannette (20): I found that after the first tutorial I didn't want to say any more, as I felt it was regarded as not important and the older women's experiences were.

Julie (21): Some outspoken people kept interrupting discussion before one had finished. Sometimes others needed to be encouraged to speak. It was often the same people. Having a class of all women made this easier. I felt more confident because of this factor.

Leanne (21): It's a pity that the Pacific Islander women in our class didn't talk very often, because I would be really interested in their schooling experiences. Perhaps more encouragement of students to talk could be attempted.

Myra (36): You need a more prominent focus on Maori feminists and their writings—their interpretations of how gender, education, and social policies affected them and their schooling. I also do appreciate how difficult this may be and I am not entirely clear how this could be done. I felt the first session focussed only on Janet Frame and Sylvia Ashton-Warner—both interesting women, but both Pakcha. Could you focus in on a Maori woman for one session?

Despite my conscious attempts to be inclusive—of students' diverse ages, cultures, social classes, and perspectives—my teaching continued for some to exhibit what Patti Lather (1991) called "impositional tendencies" (p. 67).

Conclusion

Throughout this book, I have explored my experience of being a feminist teacher educator. I have analyzed the processes of feminist educating as "located." I have made visible—brought into the foreground—the situation or vantage point from which my analysis has been produced. As Magda Lewis (1990) has argued:

> Pedagogical moments arise in specific contexts: the social location of the teacher and students; the geographic and historical location of the institution in which they come together; the political climate in which they work; the personalities and personal profiles of the individuals in the classroom; the readings selected for the course; and the academic backgrounds of the students all come together in ways that create the specifics of the moment. (p. 487)

Educational theories must take into account all these ingredients.

. . . . A loud knock on my door. It is time for my staff meeting. The demands of the institution—administrative and political—intrude upon any time that one tries to claim for reflection. It is hard to create spaces for thinking about educational questions. Frantically I shuffle through the cascade of papers that litters my desk. Underneath my students' course evaluations—the texts that concern me most at present—I locate the papers I require for the staff meeting. But I keep thinking about what my students have said. How can my teaching be improved? I shall think in the luxurious solitude of my evening walk home. What is a feminist education? How can feminism be of value to students in developing their own educational theories? How can feminism help them to create pedagogies that will tap their "native imagery" (Ashton-Warner, 1973) and be organic to their lives and times?

Notes

[1] I had commented during the slide presentation that in the feminist movement, I had come across a very large number of women who had grown up in rural areas, although I had not seen any research evidence on this issue. I suggested that those who moved away from home at a young age may have felt freer to experiment with dangerous ideas.

[2] These statements were brought into being in students' diary assignments; they were written for me as teacher/assessor. Accordingly, as atomized individuals, the students did not address one another. I have taken some literary liberties in turning these statements into conversations. All students have been given false names. Precise ages were not given by some students.

[3] In the seventh form (senior year) of high school, students may take the bur-

saries examination. An "A" bursary pass gave students a higher living allowance from the government than did a "B" bursary. At the time this student was at university, scholarship examinations provided the opportunity for students of exceptional ability to compete for additional funding. Students who lived away from home were entitled to an accomodation allowance. From 1992, students whose parents earn a total of NZ$30,000 (US$17,400) or more per annum will no longer have rights to the accomodation allowance.

4See Chapters 2 and 4. Academic girls of my generation were offered few other choices. However, upper-middle-class girls (those who did not "have to work") would probably not have shared my view of teaching. Recent ethnographies by Jones (1988) and Kenway (1990) suggest that teachers are regarded by such girls as paid servants. I do not think, however, that the young women speaking here were from such a high-class background.

5Several people are talking, interrupting one another. Because it is impossible to identify the number and sequence of speakers, I have run these voices together in continuous paragraphs. When it is possible to hear one speaker at a time, I have formatted the text as dialogue with one speaker per line. However, I have avoided giving names because I cannot tell if or when the same person speaks more than once.

6Since the late 1930s, primary school–aged children have received free dental care in school dental clinics. As I write this, the National government is in the process of sacking large numbers of dental nurses as a cost-cutting measure. Dental nursing, like teaching, has been a popular career path for New Zealand women.

7The course ran for one semester (12 weeks); each student attended the class sessions (2 hours) and a small-group tutorial for 1 hour per week. Students were required to read between two and four readings per week.

8During one of the tutorials, I used some of the material on pornography (slides) discussed in chapter 6. We compared pornographic with romantic images of women. Students had read some of the literature on teenage romantic fiction, and many had chosen this as a topic for their end-of-course test (Christian-Smith, 1991).

Epilogue

*I*t is time to leave the office for Christmas break. I will spend a few days with relatives near a summer beach. Then there will be space—not for rest this year, but for writing. I slip a floppy disk into my handbag and walk through the empty corridors and then out into the leafy light. The grey rectangularities of campus buildings are brightened by flowers and masked by trees. As I pass the little lakes, I feel a soaring release. For 6 weeks, there will be no departmental or faculty meetings, torrents of memoranda, administrative minutiae. I will be in control of my diurnal rhythms, freed from the segmentations of bureaucracy.

My body, cramped and sore from hours of seated stiffness, stretches into the sunlight. Walking is my space for thinking. Even at boarding school, I was a peripatetic. Confined by iron fences, I swotted for exams on foot—I read history notes and recited French verbs while pacing the peripheries of tangled gardens. Like other writers, I have a great need for personal space. The solitude of windswept beaches, the impersonality of crowded cities, or these long walks serve me equally well. Sentences from memoranda and comments from the staff meeting intrude upon my reflections. Equivalent full-time students, programs, courses, majors, minors. . . .

Billy Holiday mourns from Contact FM student radio as I pass the hut known on campus as the cow shed. It *was* a cow shed once. Until the 1960s, the magnificent parklands that are now this campus were a swamp. I glance across the wide playing fields towards what was until very recently the teachers' college.[1] A few weeks ago, it and the university amalgamated. The resulting restructuring—the topic of the staff meeting I have just attended—is changing the shape and dynamics of the institutional configurations in which my teaching takes place.

I used to teach in courses over there in the college. Although the teachers' college and the university were separate institutions, they had, since their foundation in the 1960s, developed a closer working relationship than had similar institutions in other cities. Together, we taught a B.Ed. (Bachelor of Education) degree. Most teachers' college students were simultaneously enrolled in the Diploma of Teaching (the professional credential) and the B.Ed. degree. Degree courses in professional training and curriculum were taught by teachers' college staff. My department—the university's education department—taught or contributed to most of the courses in the education major, in which the various education disciplines were compulsory components. In our department, we were continually restructuring the major. But each version rested on the assumptions that all students were to have some exposure to the history, philosophy, psychology, and sociology of education and that each staff member was, in essence, a specialist in one of these disciplines. Whole courses about women and education, gender and education, feminist theory, and biculturalism or multiculturalism were seen as optional extras. As someone who describes her professional and academic identity as a feminist educational theorist, I tried to resist being categorized as in essence a sociologist.[2]

I could never fit my ideas about educational theory into the disciplinary categories that formed its institutionalized basis. I think back to my own graduate studies in education. When I left school teaching and came back to university in the mid-1970s, education degrees were like smorgasbords. A balanced diet consisted of small helpings of each educational subdiscipline, and students were exposed to the various master narratives within these. Somehow, it was reasoned, we would make our theories as educators from these ingredients. Making an educational theory was a matter of rational choice. I could never think in these categories. My thinking drifted with the currents that flowed across, between, and around them. The disciplinary boundaries leaked. I saw making a personal educational theory as a "worthwhile activity" (Peters, 1966) in and of itself.

Amalgamation has meant that our department has been swallowed by the much larger teachers' college. Ours is now one of five university departments in the new School of Education. Some of these departments are offering majors that compete with ours. The number of compulsory courses we can offer in the degree is being cut back. Disciplinary categories harden as individuals and interest groups defend their territories. Groups look inwards. Many academics feel the pressure to vocationalize, and some teachers' college staff fear that vocational and practical knowledge is undervalued.

Across these divisions, some of the feminist women meet. We gather to drink wine and laugh in restaurants. We tell stories. But the walls between departments are growing higher, insulating us from one another. How can we create spaces to come together (Greene, 1988), to address with the students, and with one another our kinds of issues and our kinds of questions in our kinds of ways? The hierarchies of academic and professional knowledge—the fences around territories—fragment and divide us. Bernstein (1971) was right about the boundaries that collection knowledge codes create (chapter 5).

I hear the mooing of cows. Friesians graze as I walk down Old Farm Road through the green paddocks of the Ruakura Agricultural Research Station. Sensations from a rural childhood flicker into consciousness. The smell of mown hay, the gentle warmth of ponies, the sense of "otherness" of being a town girl living in the country. The pull toward cities—reading my mother's copies of *The New Yorker;* listening to the children's session on big-city National Radio[3] with its stories about the great European composers, painters, and artists; dreaming of being an artist who lived in a garret in Paris and frequented smoky, jazz-filled cafes.

Many of my students come here to university from farms and little towns. They come from Ngaruawahia—its carved marae a testament to Tainui people's resistances to colonial invasions[4] (King, 1982). They come from Thames with its long verandahed main street like a set from a "wld west" movie—a legacy from gold-rush days. They come from Cambridge— with its huge elms, polo players, and cricket on the green. They come from Raglan—by the sea, a fishing village. These students share much of my native imagery. They know that so much knowledge comes in ships (see chapter 1). They cannot see themselves in much of what we, as academics, require them to read.

As Madeleine Grumet (1988) has argued, "Theory is cultivated in the public world. . . . Theory grows where it is planted, soaking up the nutrients in the local soil, turning to the local light. A theory of education that is cultivated in the academy, the library, or the laboratory, accommodates to its environment" (p. 14). In teaching theory as somehow external to students—as consisting of selections from the intellectual property of remote academics—we alienate. Students are "initiated" (Hirst, 1975; Peter, 1966) into someone else's knowledge. They learn to write essays by stringing together items from someone else's lists of references from other people's sets of relevances.

The references we choose for our students to read are works that *we* consider to be the most interesting or important. They are signposts in *our* intellectual journeys, significances from *our* academic biographies. The reading lists we compile contain the submerged narratives of the academic life histories that brought them into being. And although it is important that we tell our students about our favorite writings and make visible to them our feminist and educational heroes, we should not expect that these lives and works will necessarily be the ones that most light up our students' worlds. Our feminist theories will not necessarily name what for them is most intolerable in their lives or give form to their visions of what Maxine Greene (1988) has called "a better state of things" (p. 16). They need spaces to develop theories that tap their own native imagery—that are indigenous or organic to their own biographical, generational, cultural, historical and material, and geographical situations.

My own researches have been propelled by a quest to document relationships between the educational and feminist theories in the books and the ways individual feminists and others involved in education think and act in their everyday situations (see chapters 4 and 6). Why do we like or how do we come to like some theories and dislike others? Why, for example, during my own high school teaching days (chapter 3) was my friend converted by B. F. Skinner's behaviorism while I was an open-classroom person? What were the biographical affinities that formed the basis of our choosing—the attractions and revulsions we each felt toward certain theories, ideas, and practices? And why are these personal and emotional affinities bracketed out of so many education courses, majors, and degrees?

My aim in writing this book has been to explore what happens when instead, as Janet Miller (1990) has described it, we base our curriculum on conceptualizations of "the teacher as the researcher of her own underlying assumptions, as connected to her particular biographical, cultural, and historical situations" (p. 17). I have told stories that exemplify what can happen when we conceive of ourselves, our students, and those whose works we study as intellectuals "occupying specifiable locations in social space rather than as free-floating individuals" (Fraser, 1989, p. 108). I have approached the teaching and writing of theory as discourse—described techniques whereby we can make visible and problematize our own and others' positionings within the educational, historical, political, institutional, and other social phenomena that are our objects of inquiry. In this, I have drawn on the kinds of insights that so many postmodernists have discussed but so rarely demonstrated. As teachers and writers of feminist educational theory, "whether the medium be linguistic or visual," we are, as Linda Hutcheon (1989) has argued, "always dealing with systems of meaning operating within certain codes and conventions that are socially produced, and historically conditioned" (p. 143).

The revving engine of a beat-up old Ford belches blue smoke as its young owner tries to start it. It is parked on the grass in front of the state houses near the now-closed Hamilton Girls' Home where George once taught (see Introduction). I wonder how these girls are faring out in the community. George and their other teachers used to speak about them in my class. Some of my students used to visit the home. The girls' voices were audible in my courses. But now we cannot hear them. Government policies of deinstitutionalization have dismantled the kinds of public spaces where we used to come together (Greene, 1988). The two-storied wooden buildings each contain three or four flats for families. Mostly Maori, mostly unemployed. In keeping with its New Right economic theories, the National government has cut their benefits and is raising their rents.

I think about what my students told me about the need for greater visibility of Maori women in my course (see chapter 7). How will it be improved next year? I used to invite speakers in but found that this was adding to the stress loads of already-overworked women. I have—with colleagues—created space for Maori feminist writings by coediting two new texts. One (Middleton & Jones, 1992) is the sequel to *Women and Education in Aotearoa* (Middleton, 1988c)—a set of readings by Maori and Pakeha women. Recent studies on New Zealand education—restructuring, postmodernism, and biculturalism—is a second set text for the "Women and Education" course.

The other is an introductory women's studies text (du Plessis, Bunkle, Irwin, Laurie, & Middleton, 1992). We tried—in our editorial collective, in the readings we included—to be representative of New Zealand feminists and feminisms. We wanted New Zealand women to see ourselves in all our ethnicities, sexualities, political and theoretical diversities, cultural and geographical origins, interests, and themes. We did our best. But inevitably, some will not see themselves in our text. Some will be constituted as "other." When I began work on that text several years ago, I expected to use it in the "Advanced Feminist Theory" course I was teaching in our undergraduate women's studies program. But women's studies, like education, has been restructured. I no longer have a place in the core of the program but have been pushed by this restructuring process out onto its margins.

In chapter 5, I told you how since 1974, feminists on my campus—like those elsewhere—had come together to create an interdisciplinary program that was designed and administered by a voluntary committee of women from various departments. I explained how this cross-departmental structure was an anomaly within the university—what Bernstein (1971) called an "integrated knowledge code" within the encapsulated hierarchies (subject-based departments) of the dominant "collection knowledge code." I know that you, my American readers, will recognize in your own country that kind of structuring of university women's studies.

Our program's restructuring began in 1986, when it was given administrative space within the collection code through the establishment of the Centre for Women's Studies. For the first time, women's studies was allocated its own staffing. It would no longer depend entirely on the voluntary labor of women academics from various departments or on the goodwill of departmental administrators. Although the center had some staffing of its own, some of the core courses and the design of the program still depended on the work of an interdepartmental committee. It remained a structural anomaly that depended on other departments for resources. This pattern, too, will be recognizable to overseas readers.

In 1990, a professor of women's studies was appointed. In New Zealand as in British universities, a professor is a very senior position. Most subjects would have only one or two staff members at that level. Women's studies is in the process of becoming a separate department that will sit comfortably within the compartmentalized subjects of the collection code (Yeatman, 1991). Core feminist theory courses are now to be taught only by the women's studies specialists within the women's studies department. As a capsule in the collection code, women's studies will receive the same treatment as other departments in its funding, its staffing, and its representation on decision-making committees. As a discipline, it is considered mainstream. This structure makes the existence of the subject secure. It is no longer a structural anomaly.

The departmentally based courses, such as "Women and Education," remain as electives that can be chosen to complete the major—as additions to the core requirements taught within the program. Those, like me, who are based within other departments are no longer to participate in the design of the overall program or share in its administrative responsibilities. Those of us based elsewhere who once taught core theory within the program no longer do so. I feel bereaved, sense a loss of community, and experience an intellectual homelessness.

The education department—who had lent me to women's studies in return for equivalent full-time students—responded to the loss of my feminist theory course by putting me into basic sociology of education. I am required to initiate second-year undergraduates into a discipline. I have to get them ready for the third-year and masters courses. Walls are closing in; I feel engulfed. There are encroachments into the spaces I need for my kind of teaching. Where can I make spaces for the new courses I want to develop—on teachers' life histories (Goodson, 1992) and on education and sexuality? I identify closely with the feminist teachers in Kathleen Weiler's (1988) study: Like them, I feel a conflict between my vision of "what teaching . . . *ought* to be, and the reality of working in a large, bureaucratic, organization" (p. 101).

The sun warms my back, soothing my shoulders and neck, healing the cramps that my physiotherapist calls a penalty of the chair-bound society, the desk-bound workplace. I feel the weight lifting from my shoulders as I distance myself from the university and pass through the village of Claudelands. I wait for the lights at the busy intersection by the Claudelands Bridge, which crosses the wide Waikato River. The lights turn green; I pass the bridge and glance over it at the afternoon sun reflecting whitely off the high-rise buildings across the river in the central city. I cross the railway. Ever since the long steam train journeys of childhood holidays—from country to city—I have loved trains. The haunting calls of trains in the night beckon me to faraway places. Twenty years ago—in hippie backpacking days—I travelled the Trans-Siberian. I met and talked with young women in the Russian army. I drank vodka with Estonians and Lithuanians and Latvians and Georgians. I learned of their nationalisms, their resistances, and their hopes. Today, our television screens are filled with images of the disintegration of the Soviet Union. And with it, the collapse of many of the myths and grand narratives of our age.

I pass the harness-racing track and then turn off the main road and into tree-lined Kitchener Street. I like our neighborhood. It has something of an inner-city cosmopolitanism. Some of the smaller bungalows are being repainted. They had fallen into decay as former owners moved to the newer suburbs of gold Huntly brick.[5] Speculators and landlords moved in, tacking incongruously concrete boxes of flats onto the backs of the old wooden houses. Some are now run down; most are tenanted by students, the poor, and the unemployed—many of them Maori or Asian. Scattered among the blocks of flats are what the realtors call character homes—1930s bungalows with leaded glass, timbered floors, and plastered ceilings. They are occupied mainly by professional couples and their children. You have been inside mine and visited me in my little back room (see Introduction).

I feel guilty as I glance at the unweeded tangle that used to be my garden. I love flowers and trees, but weeding is not one of my priorities. We are planting "natives"—trying to return the small garden to the bush—flax, kowhai, and cabbage trees.[6] We are cultivating a wild luxuriance that will not demand of us much labor. As I turn the key in the lock, I hear the stereo pounding. Kate is listening to the digitally remastered CD version of Velvet Underground: Lou Reed, John Cale—shades from my student days. George calls out a greeting from the bedroom. He is watching cricket on TV. I go to make us a drink: coffee for George and me, herbal tea for Kate. I shut myself into the luxurious solitude of my back room. And turn on the computer, the printer, the digital piano, and the tape of Miles Davis.

In the writing of this book, I have shared with you—made visible—the processes of its construction. I have enjoyed the playfulness of what have seemed at times outrageous splicings. I am grateful for what Madeleine Grumet (1988) has referred to as " the promise of word processing" (p. 146)—a technology that encourages intertextuality. It has made practicable my collations and juxtapositions of diverse media: official documents, pictorial images, transcripts of interviews and conversations, and other people's published and unpublished writings. It has helped me in my orches-

trations of multiple voices: academics, artists, teachers, students, administrators, and politicians. The word processor "invites us to use multiple
texts, splicing them, interweaving them with each other, with our commentaries, with our questions" (Grumet, 1988, p. 146).

In my commentaries and questions, you have heard me speak with different voices and write in various ways. You have heard me as a researcher:
the feminist who engages personally with those whose stories she shares,
the doctoral student and writer of formal sociological theory, and the con-
tract researcher. You have heard my voices as a political activist: as someone
who writes submissions to educational policymakers, who works as an official censor of pornographic materials, and who participates in processes of
institutional restructuring. I have spoken as a teacher: a designer of theoretical curriculum content; a white, middle-aged, middle-class feminist in
interactions with students from diverse cultural, generational, and political
backgrounds; and an educational politician engaged in gaining legitimacy
for my courses within the university. As Nancy Fraser (1989) has expressed
it, as feminist academics, "we function in several distinct institutionalized
publics. Necessarily, then, we speak in several voices" (p. xii).

You have also heard me speak in what is commonly known as my private capacity: as a mother, as a wife, and as an individual with everyday
domestic and financial matters to organize. You have glimpsed lights and
shadows from my childhood. You have seen the interpenetrations of work
and home—the intersections of teaching, intimate relationships, institutional and public responsibilities—what Donna Haraway (1990a) referred
to as "the permeability of boundaries in the personal body and the body
politic" (p. 212).

I feel stuck, turn to my digital piano, soar into the delicious freedom of
an improvisation on Kurt Weil's "September Song." September will be
Spring for me but Autumn for you, my Northern readers. The unusual
chord progressions suggest a grammar to my fleeing fingers. After a few
minutes, the singing notes unblock the pathways of my thoughts; I turn
back to the computer and can write again.

I have told you about some of the musical and the visual significances
in my life. You have shared a few of my dreams, my fantasies, and my
desires. There is much that I cannot—will not—tell you. Much that,
although relevant and sometimes important to the projects of this book, is
too personal or too painful to make visible in a public forum such as this.
As teacher educators, it is crucial that we afford such privacy to our students—that we do not demand or pressure them to show us their personal
lives. For, as Patti Lather has argued (1991), even "an intendedly liberatory
pedagogy might function as part of the technology of surveillance and normalization" (p. 139).

I hear Kate on the back deck. She is lying on a cushion, reading *The Diary of Katherine Mansfield* in the late afternoon sun. Although her skin is dark olive like mine, she uses sun-block cream. My generation never had to contend with a hole in the ozone layer. She and her friends are "greenies." Kate is a political vegetarian. She has visions of a nonviolent future. Helping make possible the kind of education that will fulfill her desires is my most important project (Grumet, 1988)—but is submerged, subliminal in this book. Kate needs her privacy, her space. She does not need to be an object of my or others' academic voyeurism. But she is always in my text, fueling and inspiring my educational ideas and projects.

Old dualisms such as public and private sever theories from the lived realities at their base. Our educational theories do not come solely from other people's books or from disembodied ideas but are rooted in all dimensions of our experience. In my classes, as in this book, I have demonstrated a process of theory making in which the educating feminist makes "her direct experience the ground of her knowledge" (D. Smith, 1974, p. 11). My teaching—like this theoretical autobiography[7]—rests on the idea that by keeping to the forefront the rich emotional fullness of our own and others' contextualized personal narratives, we can find ways to resist the encroachments and confinements of oppressive institutional and wider political restructuring—such as reforms that are driven by the narrow, technocratic reductionisms of the New Right.

Notes

[1]The University of Waikato and the Hamilton Teachers College are the first tertiary institutions in New Zealand to amalgamate. In New Zealand, universities are the only degree-granting institutions. Teachers' colleges were institutions that trained teachers. Secondary school teachers usually studied full-time for degrees in a teaching subject and then studied for 1 year full-time at a teachers' college for their teaching credential. This was the pattern of my own training. Primary teaching training was different. Such students studied for 3 years at a teachers' college. Most colleges had working arrangements with their local university that enabled primary teaching students to study concurrently for teaching credentials and degrees. Each university had its own autonomous education department. Students would usually be enrolled in university education classes as well as other university subjects. Although teachers' college education courses were highly vocational/professional in emphasis, university education courses were more academic.

[2]I had in fact been originally appointed as a curriculum theorist. I was later put into sociology. My undergraduate degree was in geography, and my postgraduate studies were in educational theory—all the disciplines equally. My doctoral thesis was jointly supervised by an educationist and an anthropologist located in a sociology department.

³Noncommercial radio funded by public money that is similar to Britain's BBC. It is now under threat of privatization. There was no television in New Zealand until 1960. It was radio that was the media influence on my childhood.

⁴The Tainui are the tangata whenua [literally, people of the land, the local people] of the Waikato region where I live and work. Turangawaewae, the marae complex at Ngaruawahia, is the base of the kingitanga (King Movement). This was a resistance movement that developed in the 19th century to rally the tribes together (King, 1982). The present queen, Dame Te Ata-I- Rangikaahu, lives in Huntly but has her official residence at Turangawaewae. Tainui have a close relationship with the University of Waikato.

⁵Huntly is a small town near Hamilton. Its quarries have provided the clay for the bricks in many houses in the Waikato region. The bricks are a pale honey color and were particularly fashionable during the 1960s.

⁶New Zealand's native rain forests, known locally as the bush, were destroyed over most of the country by white settlers to clear land for farming. Large tracts of bush remain only in the more mountainous—the less affluent—areas; much of this is national parks. The conservation movement is very strong in New Zealand. Many people see the planting of native plants in our gardens as a political act. Some native species such as the cabbage tree are being decimated by mysterious diseases.

⁷I am indebted to Jock Phillips for the term "theoretical autobiography." Personal communication.

References

Acker, S. (1981). No-woman's land: British sociology of education 1960–1979. *Sociological Review, 29,* 77–104.

Acker, S. (Ed.). (1989). *Teachers, gender and careers.* Lewes: Falmer.

Aisenberg, N., & Harrington, M. (1988). *Women of academe: Outsiders in the sacred grove.* Amherst: University of Massachusetts Press.

Alther, L. (1976). *Kinflicks.* Harmondsworth: Penguin.

Althusser, L. (1971). Ideology and ideological state apparatusses. In L. Althusser (Ed.), *Lenin and philosophy and other essays.* London: Monthly Review Press.

Alton-Lee, A., & Densem, P. (1992). Towards a gender-inclusive school curriculum: Changing educational practice. In S. Middleton & A. Jones (Eds.), *Women and education in Aotearoa 2.* Wellington: Bridget Williams Books.

Anyon, J. (1983). Intersections of gender and class: Accommodation and resistance by working-class and affluent females to contradictory sex-role ideologies. In S. Walker & L. Barton (Eds.), *Gender, class, and education.* Lewes: Falmer.

Apple, M. (1979). *Ideology and curriculum.* London: Routledge and Kegan Paul.

Apple, M. (1986). *Teachers and texts.* New York: Routledge and Kegan Paul.

Apple, M. (1989). How equality has been redefined in the conservative restoration. In W. Secada (Ed.), *Equity in education.* Lewes: Falmer.

Arnold, R. (1987). Women in the New Zealand teaching profession 1877–1920. In R. Openshaw & D. McKenzie (Eds.), *Reinterpreting the educational past.* Wellington: New Zealand Council for Educational Research.

Arnot, M. (1981). Culture and political economy: Dual perspectives in the sociology of women's education. *Educational Analysis, 3,* 97–116.

Arnot, M. (1982). Male hegemony, social class, and women's education. *Journal of Education, 164,* 64–89.

Arnot, M. (1989). The challenge of equal opportunities. In P. Woods (Ed.), *Working for teacher development.* London: Peter Francis.

Arnot, M. (1991a). *Feminism, education, and the New Right.* Paper presented at a conference of the American Educational Research Association, Chicago.

Arnot, M. (1991b). Schooling for social justice: A new agenda for British education in the 1990s. In New Zealand Association for Research in Education (Eds.), *1990 Conference keynote addresses.* Auckland: New Zealand Association for Research in Education.

Arnot, M., & Weiner, G. (Eds.). (1987). *Gender and the politics of schooling.* London: Hutchinson.

Aronowitz, S., & Giroux, H. (Eds.). (1987). *Education under seige.* South Hadley: Bergin and Garvey.

Aronowitz, S., & Giroux, H. (1991). *Postmodern education.* Minneapolis: University of Minnesota Press.

Ashton-Warner, S. (1958). *Spinster.* Auckland: Heinemann.

Ashton-Warner, S. (1960). *Incense to idols.* London: Secker and Warburg.

Ashton-Warner, S. (1973). *Teacher.* New York: Simon and Schuster.

Awatere, D. (1984). *Maori sovereignty.* Auckland: Broadsheet Books.

Bates, R. (1978). The new sociology of education: Directions for theory and research. *New Zealand Journal of Educational Studies, 13,* 3–22.

Bates, R. (1990). Educational policy and the new cult of efficiency. In S. Middleton, J. Codd, & A. Jones (Eds.), *New Zealand education policy today: Critical perspectives.* Wellington: Allen and Unwin/Port Nicholson.

Beeby, C. E. (1973). Introduction. In H. C. D. Somerset (Ed.), *Littledene.* Wellington: New Zealand Council for Educational Research.

Beeby, C. E. (1986). Introduction. In W. L. Renwick (Ed.), *Moving targets.* Wellington: New Zealand Council for Educational Research.

Belenky, M., Clinchy, B., Goldberger, N., & Tarrule, J. (1986). *Women's ways of knowing.* New York: Basic Books.

Berger, P. L., & Luckmann, T. (1971). *The social construction of reality.* Harmondsworth: Penguin.

Bernard, J. (1973). My four revolutions: An autobiographical history of the ASA. In J. Huber (Ed.), *Changing women in a changing society.* Chicago: University of Chicago Press.

Bernstein, B. (1971). On the classification and framing of educational knowledge. In M. F. D. Young (Ed.), *Knowledge and control.* London: Collier MacMillan.

Bernstein, B. (1975). Class and pedagogies: Visible and invisible. In B. Bernstein (Ed.), *Class, codes, and control* (Vol. 3). London: Routledge and Kegan Paul.

Biklen, S. (1991, May). *Address to staff and graduate students.* Presented at School of Education, Ohio State University, Columbus, OH.

Bourdieu, P. (1971a). Intellectual field and creative project. In M. F. D. Young (Ed.), *Knowledge and control.* London: Collier MacMillan.

Bourdieu, P. (1971b). Systems of education and systems of thought. In M. F. D. Young (Ed.), *Knowledge and control.* London: Collier MacMillan.

Bourdieu, P., & Boltanski, L. (1971). Changes in social structure and changes in the demand for education. In M. S. Archer & S. Giner (Eds.), *Contemporary Europe.* London: Weldenfeld and Nicholson.

Bowles, G., & Klein, R. D. (Eds.). (1983). *Theories of women's studies.* London: Routledge and Kegan Paul.

Bowles, S., & Gintis, H. (1977). *Schooling in capitalist America*. New York: Basic Books.

Braithwaite, E. (1967). Education, change, and the New Zealand economy. *New Zealand Journal of Educational Studies, 2,* 175–188.

Bunkle, P. (1979, September). A history of the women's movement: Part one. *Broadsheet,* pp. 24–28.

Bunkle, P. (1980). The origins of the women's movement in New Zealand: The Women's Christian Temperance Union 1885–1995. In P. Bunkle & B. Hughes (Eds.), *Women in New Zealand society*. Auckland: Allen and Unwin.

Byrne, E. (1975). *Women and education*. London: Tavistock.

Casey, K. (1988). *Teacher as author: Life-history narratives for contemporary women teachers working for social change*. Unpublished D.Phil. dissertation, Department of Curriculum and Instruction, University of Wisconsin, Madison.

Chodorow, N. (1978). *The reproduction of mothering*. Berkeley: University of California Press.

Christian-Smith, L. (1991). *Becoming a woman through romance*. New York: Routledge.

Clarricoates, K. (1978). Dinosaurs in the classroom: A re-examination of some aspects of the "hidden curriculum" in primary schools. *Women's Studies International Quarterly, 1,* 353–364.

Codd, J. (1990). Policy documents and the official discourse of the state. In J. Codd, R. Harker, & R. Nash (Eds.), *Political issues in New Zealand education* (2nd ed.). Palmerston North: Dunmore.

Codd, J., & Gordon, L. (1991). School charters: The contractualist state and education policy. *New Zealand Journal of Educational Studies, 26,* 21–34.

Codd, J., Harker, R., & Nash, R. (Eds.). (1985). *Political issues in New Zealand education*. Palmerston North: Dunmore.

Codd, J., Harker, R., & Nash, R. (Eds.). (1990). *Political issues in New Zealand education* (2nd ed.). Palmerston North: Dunmore.

Coney, S., & Bunkle, P. (1987, June). An unfortunate experiment at National Women's. *Metro, pp.* 46–67.

Connell, R. W., Ashendon, D. J., Kessler, S., & Dowsett, G. (1982). *Making the difference*. Sydney: Allen and Unwin.

Coyner, S. (1983). Women's studies as an academic discipline: Why and how to do it. In G. Bowles & R. D. Klein (Eds.), *Theories of women's studies*. London: Routledge and Kegan Paul.

Culley, M., & Portuges, C. (Eds.). (1985). *Gendered subjects: The dynamics of feminist teaching*. Boston: Routledge and Kegan Paul.

David, M. (1980). *The state, the family, and education*. London: Routledge and Kegan Paul.

Davies, B. (1989). *Frogs and snails and feminist tales*. Sydney: Allen and Unwin.

Davis, A. (1981). *Women, race and class.* London: Women's Press.

Deem, R. (1978). *Women and schooling.* London: Routledge and Kegan Paul.

Deem, R. (1989). The new school governing bodies: Are gender and race on the agenda? *Gender and Education, 1,* 247–260.

Delmar, R. (1979). Introduction. In S. Firestone (Ed.), *The dialectic of sex.* London: Women's Press.

Delphy, C. (1981).Women in stratification studies. In H. Roberts (Ed.), *Doing feminist research.* London: Routledge and Kegan Paul.

Department of Education. (1944). *The post-primary school curriculum* (Thomas report). Wellington: Government Printer.

Department of Education. (1962). *Report of the Commission on Education in New Zealand.* (Currie report). Wellington: Government Printer.

Department of Education. (1971). *Maori children and the teacher.* Wellington: Government Printer.

Department of Education. (1975). *Education and the equality of the sexes.* Wellington: Government Printer.

Department of Education. (1977). *Growing, sharing, learning.* (Johnson report). Wellington: Government Printer.

Department of Education. (1982a). *He huarahi: Report of the National Advisory Committee on Maori Education.* Wellington: Government Printer.

Department of Education. (1982b). *Teacher career and promotion study.* Wellington: Government Printer.

Department of Health. (1955). *Sex and the adolescent girl.* Wellington: Government Printer.

Devanny, J. (1981). *The butcher's shop.* Auckland: Auckland University Press. (Original work published 1928.)

Dreyfus, H., & Rabinow, P. (1986). *Michel Foucault: Beyond structuralism and hermeneutics.* Chicago: Harvester.

du Chateau, C. (1990, July). Waikato wimmin: Capturing the campus. *Metro,* pp. 78–88.

du Plessis, R., Bunkle, P., Irwin, K., Laurie, A., & Middleton, S. (Eds.). (1992). *Feminist voices: Women's studies texts for Aotearoa/New Zealand.* Auckland: Oxford.

Ebbett, E. (1984). *When the boys were away: New Zealand women in World War II.* Wellington: Reed.

Ehrenreich, B., & English, D. (1979). *For her own good: 150 years of the experts' advice to women.* New York: Doubleday.

Eichler, M. (1980). *The double standard: A feminist critique of feminist social science.* London: Croom Helm.

Eisenstein, Z. (1981). *The radical future of liberal feminism.* New York: Longman.

Eisenstein, Z. (1982). The sexual politics of the New Right: Understanding the "crisis of liberalism" for the 1980s. In N. Keohane, M. Rosaldo, & B. Gelpi

(Eds.), *Feminist theory: A critique of ideology.* Chicago: Harvester.

Elley, W., & Irving, J. (1985). The Elley-Irving socio-economic index: 1981 census revision. *New Zealand Journal of Educational Studies, 20,* 115–128.

Ellis, B. E. (1991). *American psycho.* New York: Picador.

Ellsworth, E. (1989). Why doesn't this feel empowering? Working through the repressive myths of critical pedagogy. *Harvard Educational Review, 59,* 297–324.

Engels, F. (1971). *The origin of the family, private property and the state.* New York: Pathfinder. (Original work published 1891.)

Fahrdi, S. (1992). *Backlash: The undeclared war against women.* London: Chatto & Windus.

Fenwick, P. (1980). Fertility, sexuality, and social control. In P. Bunkle & B. Hughes (Eds.), *Women in New Zealand society.* Auckland: Allen and Unwin.

Fenwick, P. (1983, August). *Feminist research and research on women.* Paper presented at the conference of the New Zealand Women's Studies Association, Christchurch.

Findlay, M. (1974). *Tooth and nail: The story of a daughter of the Depression.* Wellington: Reed.

Firestone, S. (1979). *Dialectic of sex.* London: Women's Press.

Fletcher, B. (1991). *The word burners.* Wellington: Daphne Brasell.

Flude, M., & Hammer, M. (Eds.). (1990). *The Education Reform Act 1988: Its origins and implications.* Lewes: Falmer.

Foreman, A. (1977). *Femininity as alienation: Women and the family in Marxism and psychoanalysis.* London: Pluto.

Foucault, M. (1979). *Discipline and punish.* New York: Basic Books.

Foucault, M. (1980a). *A history of sexuality* (Vol. 1). New York: Vintage.

Foucault, M. (1980b). *Power/knowledge: Selected interviews and other writings, 1972–1977* (C. Gordon, Trans.). New York: Pantheon.

Fox-Keller, E. (1985). *Reflections on gender and science.* Binghamton: Yale University Press.

Frame, J. (1983). *To the Is-Land: an autobiography* (Vol. 1). Auckland: Heinneman.

Fraser, N. (1989). *Unruly practices: Power, discourse and gender in contemporary social theory.* Minneapolis: University of Minnesota Press.

Freire, P. (1971). *Pedagogy of the oppressed.* Harmondsworth: Penguin.

Friedan, B. (l963). *The feminine mystique.* Harmondsworth: Penguin.

Gaskell, J., McLaren, A., & Novogrodsky, M. (1989). *Claiming an education: Feminism and Canadian schools.* Toronto: Our Schools Our/Selves.

Giddens, A. (1982). *Profiles and critiques in social theory.* London: MacMillan.

Gifford, L. (1981). The lesbian as folk witch. In *New Zealand Women's Studies Association Conference Papers 1980* (pp. 117–143). Auckland: New Zealand Women's Studies Association.

Gilligan, C. (1982). *In a different voice.* Cambridge: Harvard University Press.

Giroux, H. (1982). *Ideology culture and the practice of schooling.* Philadelphia: Temple.

Giroux, H. (1983). *Theory and resistance in education.* South Hadley, MA: Bergin and Garvey.

Giroux, H. (1986). Radical pedagogy and the politics of student voice. *Interchange, 17,* 48–69.

Glamuzina, J., & Laurie, A. (1991). *Parker and Hulme.* Auckland: New Women's Press.

Goodson, I. (1988). *The making of curriculum.* Lewes: Falmer.

Goodson, I. (Ed.). (1992). *Studying teachers' lives.* London: Routledge.

Gordon, L. (1991, December). *The bulk funding of teachers' salaries: A case study in education policy.* Paper presented at the conference of the New Zealand Association for Research in Education, Dunedin.

Grace, G. (1990). The New Zealand Treasury and the commodification of education. In S. Middleton, J. Codd, & A. Jones (Eds.), *New Zealand education policy today: Critical perspectives.* Wellington: Allen and Unwin/Port Nicholson Press.

Greene, M. (1973). *Teacher as stranger.* Belmont: Wadsworth.

Greene, M. (1978). *Landscapes of learning.* New York: Teachers College Press.

Greene, M. (1986). In search of a critical pedagogy. *Harvard Educational Review, 56,* 427–441.

Greene, M. (1988). *The dialectic of freedom.* New York: Teachers College Press.

Greer, G. (1972). *The female eunuch.* London: Granada.

Grimshaw, P. (1972). *Women's suffrage in New Zealand.* Auckland: Auckland University Press.

Grossman, E. S. (1908). *Hermione: A knight of the Holy Ghost: A novel of the woman movement.* London: Watts.

Grosz, E. (1989). *Sexual subversions.* Sydney: Allen and Unwin.

Grosz, E. (1990). Conclusion: A note on essentialism and difference. In S. Gunew (Ed.), *Feminist knowledge.* London: Routledge.

Grumet, M. (1988). *Bitter milk: Women and teaching.* Amherst: University of Massachusetts Press.

Haraway, D. (1990a). A manifesto for cyborgs: Science, technology, and socialist feminism in the 1980s. In L. Nicholson (Ed.), *Feminism/postmodernism.* New York: Routledge.

Haraway, D. (1990b). Investment strategies for the evolving portfolio of primate females. In M. Jacobus, E. Fox-Keller, & S. Shuttleoworth (Eds.), *Body/politics: Women and the discourses of science.* New York: Routledge.

Harding, S. (1987). *The science question in feminism.* Ithaca: Cornell University Press.

Harker, R. (1975). Streaming and social class. In P. D. K. Ramsay (Ed.), *Family and school in New Zealand society.* Auckland: Pitman.

Hartmann, H. (1981). The unhappy marriage between Marxism and feminism: Towards a more progressive union. In L. Sergent (Ed.),*Women and revolution*. Boston: South End.

Harvard Report. (1946). *General education in a free society*. Cambridge: Harvard University Press.

Henriques, J., Hollway, W., Urwin, C., Venn, C., & Walkerdine, V. (1984). *Changing the subject*. London: Methuen.

Heron, L. (Ed.). (1985). *Truth dare or promise: Girls growing up in the fifties*. London: Virago.

Hirst, P. (1975). The logic and structure of curriculum objectives. *Journal of Curriculum Studies, 1,* 142–158.

Hollway, W. (1984). Gender difference and the production of subjectivity. In J. Henriques, W. Hollway, C. Unwin, C. Venn, & V. Walerdine. *Changing the subject*. London: Methuen.

Holt, J. (1974). *How children fail*. Harmondsworth: Penguin.

Hooks, B. (1989). *Talking back*. Boston: South End.

Hutcheon, L. (1989). *The politics of postmodernism*. New York: Routledge.

Illich, I. (1971). *Deschooling society*. Harmondsworth: Penguin.

Ingham, M. (1983). *Now we are thirty*. London: Methuen.

Irving, J., & Elley, W. (1977). A socio-economic index for the female labour force in New Zealand. *New Zealand Journal of Educational Studies, 12,* 154–163.

Irwin, K. (1989). Maori, feminist, academic. *Sites, 17,* 30–38.

Irwin, K. (1990). The politics of Kohanga Reo. In S. Middleton, J. Codd, & A. Jones (Eds.), *New Zealand education policy today: Critical perspectives*. Wellington: Allen and Unwin/Port Nicholson.

Irwin, K. (1992a). Becoming an academic. In S. Middleton & A. Jones (Eds.), *Women and education in Aotearoa 2*. Wellington: Bridget Williams Books.

Irwin, K. (1992b). Towards theories of Maori feminisms. In R. du Plessis, P. Bunkle, K. Irwin, A. Lauri, & S. Middleton (Eds.), *Feminist voices: Women's studies texts for Aotearoa/New Zealand*. Auckland: Oxford University Press.

Jaggar, A., & Struhl, P. R. (Eds.). (1978). *Feminist frameworks*. New York: McGraw-Hill.

Jesson, B. (1989). *Fragments of Labour*. Auckland: Penguin.

Jesson, B., Ryan, A., & Spoonley, P. (1988). *Revival of the Right: New Zealand politics in the 1980s*. Auckland: Heinemann Reed.

Jones, A. (1988). Which girls are "learning to lose?" Gender, race, and talking in the classroom. In S. Middleton (Ed.), *Women and education in Aotearoa*. Wellington: Allen and Unwin/Port Nicholson.

Jones, A. (1990). I just wanna decent job: Working-class girls' education: Perspectives and policy issues. In H. Lauder & C. Wylie (Eds.), *Towards successful schooling*. London: Falmer.

Jones, A. (1991). *At school I've got a chance: Culture/privilege: Pacific Islands and*

Pakeha girls at school. Palmerston North: Dunmore.

Jones, A. (1992). Writing feminist educational research: Am "I" in the text? In S. Middleton & A. Jones (Eds.), *Women and education in Aotearoa 2.* Wellington: Bridget Williams Books.

Jones, A., & Guy, C. (1992). Radical feminism in New Zealand: From Piha to Newtown. In R. du Plessis, P. Bunkle, K. Irwin, A. Laurie, & S. Middleton (Eds.), *Feminist voices: Women's studies texts for Aotearoa/New Zealand.* Auckland: Oxford, New Zealand.

Keddie, N. (1973). *Tinker tailor: The myth of cultural deprivation.* Harmondsworth: Penguin.

Kedgley, S. (1987, Autumn). The way we were. *City Magazine,* pp. 84–93.

Kedgley, S. (Ed.) (1989). *Her own country.* Auckland: Penguin.

Kenway, J. (1990). Privileged girls, private schools and the culture of "success." In J. Kenway & S. Willis (Eds.), *Hearts and minds: Self-esteem and the schooling of girls.* London: Falmer.

King, M. (1982). *Te Puea.* Auckland: Hodder and Stoughton.

Klatch, R. E. (1987). *Women of the New Right.* Philadelphia: Temple.

Knight, J. (1985). Fundamentalism and education: A case study in social ambiguity. *Discourse, 5, 19–38.*

Laing, R. D. (1971). *The politics of the family.* Harmondsworth: Penguin.

Lather, P. (1991). *Getting smart.* New York: Routledge.

Lauder, H. (1990). The New Right revolution and education in New Zealand. In S. Middleton, J. Codd, & A. Jones (Eds.), *New Zealand education policy today: Critical perspectives.* Wellington: Allen and Unwin/Port Nicholson Press.

Lauder, H., Middleton, S., Boston, J., & Wylie, C. (1988). The third wave: A critique of the New Zealand Treasury's report on education. *New Zealand Journal of Educational Studies, 23,* 1533.

Lauder, H., & Wylie, C. (Eds.). (1990). *Towards successful schooling.* Lewes: Falmer.

Laurie, A. (1987). Lesbian worlds. In S. Cox (Ed.), *Public and private worlds.* Wellington: Allen and Unwin/Port Nicholson Press.

Lawton, D. (1975). *Class, culture, and the curriculum.* London: Routledge and Kegan Paul.

Lees, S. (1986). *Losing out: Sexuality and adolescent girls.* London: Hutchinson.

Lengermann, P.M., Marconi, K. & Wallace, R. (1978). Sociological theory in teaching sex-roles: Marxism, functionalism, and phenomenology. *Women's Studies International Quarterly, 1,* 375–386.

Lesko, N. (1988). *Symbolizing society: Stories, rites and structure in a Catholic high school.* Philadelphia: Falmer.

Lewis, M. (1990). Interrupting patriarchy: Politics, resistance, and transformation in the feminist classroom. *Harvard Educational Review, 60,* 467–488.

Lingard, R., Knight, J., & Porter, P. (Eds.) (in press). *Contemporary politics, pol-*

icy, and management: The Labor reconstruction of schooling. London: Routledge.

Livingstone, D. (Ed.). (1987). *Critical pedagogy and cultural power.* South Hadley: Bergin and Garvey.

Llewellyn, M. (1980). Studying girls at school: The implications of confusion. In R. Deem (Ed.), *Schooling for women's work.* London: Routledge and Kegan Paul.

Mahony, P. (1985). *Schools for the boys? Co-education reassessed.* London: Hutchinson.

Martin, J. R. (1982). Excluding women from the educational realm. *Harvard Educational Review, 52,* 133–148.

Martin, J. R. (1987). *Reclaiming a conversation: The ideal of the educated woman.* New Haven: Yale University Press.

Marx, K. (1976). *Capital* (Vol. 1). Harmondsworth: Penguin. (Original work published 1867.)

May, H. (1990). Growth and change in the early childhood services. In S. Middleton, J. Codd, & A. Jones (Eds.), *New Zealand education policy today: Critical perspectives.* Wellington: Allen and Unwin/Port Nicholson.

May, H. (1992a). Learning through play: Women, progressivism and early childhood education 1920–1950. In S. Middleton & A. Jones (Eds.), *Women and education in Aotearoa 2.* Wellington: Bridget Williams Books.

May, H. (1992b). *Minding children, managing men.* Wellington: Bridget Williams Books.

McDonald, G. (1980). Education and the movement towards equality. In P. Bunkle & B. Hughes (Eds.), *Women in New Zealand society.* Auckland: Allen and Unwin.

McDonald, G. (1992). Are girls smarter than boys? In S. Middleton & A. Jones (Eds.), *Women and education in Aotearoa 2.* Wellington: Bridget Williams Books.

McDonald, M. (1980). Sociocultural reproduction and women's education. In R. Deem (Ed.), *Schooling for women's work.* London: Routledge and Kegan Paul.

McGeorge, C. (1981). Race and the Maori in the New Zealand school curriculum since 1877. *Australia and New Zealand Journal of History, 10,* 13–23.

McIver, R. (1960). *The elements of a social science.* London: Methuen. (Original work published 1924.)

McKenzie, D. (1975). The changing concept of equality in New Zealand education. *New Zealand Journal of Educational Studies, 10,* 93–110.

McLaren, I. (1973). *Education for a small democracy: New Zealand.* London: Routledge and Kegan Paul.

McRobbie, A. (1980). Working-class girls and the culture of femininity. In Women's Studies Group (Eds.), *Women take issue.* Birmingham: Centre for Contemporary Cultural Studies/Hutchinson.

Middleton, S. (1982). Sexual apartheid or androgyny? Four contemporary perspectives on women and education in New Zealand. *New Zealand Journal
  of Educational Studies, 18*, 57–67.
Middleton, S. (1984). The sociology of women's education as a field of aca-
  demic study. *Discourse, 5*, 42–62. Reprinted in M. Arnot & G. Weiner
  (Eds.) (1987), *Gender and the politics of schooling*. London: Hutchinson.
Middleton, S. (1985a). Family strategies of cultural reproduction: Case studies
  in the schooling of girls. In J. Codd et al, R. Harker, & R. Nash (Eds.), *Political issues in New Zealand education*. Palmerston North: Dunmore.
  Reprinted in G. Weiner & M. Arnot (Eds.) (1987), *Gender under scrutiny:
  New inquiries*. London: Hutchinson.
Middleton, S. (1985b). *Feminism and education in post-war New Zealand: A
  sociological analysis*. Unpublished D.Phil. thesis, University of Waikato.
Middleton, S. (1987a). Feminist academics in a university setting: A case study
  in the politics of educational knowledge. *Discourse* [University of Queens-
  land], *8*, 25–47.
Middleton, S. (1987b). Schooling and radicalisation: Life histories of New
  Zealand feminist teachers. *British Journal of Sociology of Education, 8*,
  169–189.
Middleton, S. (1988a). Dirty books and other secrets: Dilemmas of a feminist
  on the Indecent Publications Tribunal. *Sites, 17*, 22–29.
Middleton, S. (1988b). Towards a sociology of women's education in
  Aotearoa. In S. Middleton (Ed.), *Women and education in Aotearoa*.
  Wellington: Allen and Unwin/Port Nicholson Press.
Middleton, S. (Ed.). (1988c). *Women and education in Aotearoa*. Wellington:
  Allen and Unwin/Port Nicholson Press.
Middleton, S. (1990a). Women, equality and equity in liberal education poli-
  cies 1944–1988. In S. Middleton, J. Codd, & A. Jones (Eds.), *New Zealand
  education policy today: Critical perspectives*. Wellington: Allen and
  Unwin/Port Nicholson Press.
Middleton, S. (1990b). American influences in the sociology of N.Z. education
  1944–1988. In D. Philips, G. Lealand, & G. McDonald (Eds.), *The impact of
  American ideas on New Zealand's educational policy, practice and thinking*.
  Wellington: New Zealand–United States Educational Foundation/New
  Zealand Council for Educational Research.
Middleton, S. (1992a). Developing a radical pedagogy: Autobiography of a
  New Zealand sociologist of women's education. In I. Goodson (Ed.),
  Studying teachers' lives. London: Routledge; New York: Teachers College
  Press.
Middleton, S. (1992b)Equity, equality, and biculturalism in the restructuring
  of New Zealand Schools: A life-history approach. *Harvard Educational
  Review, 62 (3)*, 301–322.
Middleton, S. (1992c). Gender equity and school charters: Some theoretical

and political questions for the 1990s. In S. Middleton & A. Jones (Eds.), *Women and education in Aotearoa 2.* Wellington: Bridget Williams Books.

Middleton, S. (1992d). Towards an indigenous women's studies for Aotearoa. In R. du Plessis, P. Bunkle, K. Irwin, A. Laurie, & S. Midleton (Eds.), *Feminist voices: Women's studies texts for Aotearoa/New Zealand.* Auckland: Oxford.

Middleton, S., Codd, J., & Jones, A. (Eds.) (1990). *New Zealand education policy today: Critical perspectives.* Wellington: Allen and Unwin/Port Nicholson Press.

Middleton, S., & Jones, A. (Eds.). (1992). *Women and education in Aotearoa 2.* Wellington: Bridget Williams Books.

Middleton, S., & Oliver, D. (1990). *Monitoring today's schools: Research report no. 2: Who governs our schools? Educational experiences of members of school boards of trustees.* Hamilton: University of Waikato (prepared for the New Zealand Ministry of Education).

Mill, J. S. (1983). *The subjection of women.* London: Virago. (Original work published 1869)

Miller, J. (1990). *Creating spaces and finding voices: Teachers collaborating for empowerment.* Albany: SUNY Press.

Mills, C. W. (1959). *The sociological imagination.* Harmondsworth: Penguin.

Ministry of Education. (1988). *Tomorrow's schools.* Wellington: Government Printer.

Ministry of Education. (1989). *Charter guidelines for schools.* Wellington: Government Printer.

Mitchell, J. (1973). *Woman's estate.* Harmondsworth: Penguin.

Mitchell, J. (1974). *Psychoanalysis and feminism.* New York: Pantheon.

Mitchell, J., & Rose, J. (Eds.). (1982). *Feminine sexuality: Jacques Lacan and the Ecole Freudienne.* London: MacMillan.

Moss, L. (1990). American influences on New Zealand education 1840–1945. In D. Philips, G. Lealand, & G. McDonald (Eds.), *The impact of American ideas on New Zealand's educational policy, practice and thinking.* Wellington: New Zealand–United States Educational Foundation/New Zealand Council for Educational Research.

Musgrave, P. W. (1965). *The sociology of education.* London: Methuen.

Nash, R. (1981). The New Zealand rural district high schools: A study in the selective function of rural education. *New Zealand Journal of Educational Studies, 16,* 150–160.

Nash, R., Harker, R., & Charters, H. (1990). Reproduction and renewal through education. In J. Codd, R. Harker, & R. Nash (Eds.), *Political issues in NZ education* (2nd edition). Palmerston North: Dunmore.

Neville, M. (1988). *Promoting women.* Auckland: Longman Paul.

New Zealand National Party. (1990a). *National: Investing in achievement.* Abridged version of National's education policy, released by Lockwood

Smith, May 5, 1990.

New Zealand National Party. (1990b). *National Party policies for the 1990s: Creating a decent society.* Election manifesto. Wellington: New Zealand National Party.

New Zealand Treasury. (1987). *Government management: Education* (Vol. 2). Wellington: Government Printer.

Nicholson, L. (Ed.). (1990a). *Feminism/postmodernism.* New York: Routledge.

Nicholson, L. (1990b). Introduction. In L. Nicholson (Ed.), *Feminism/postmodernism.* New York: Routledge.

Noddings, N. (1991). Stories in dialogue: Caring and interpersonal reasoning. In C. Witherell & N. Noddings (Eds.), *Stories lives tell.* New York: Teachers College Press.

Novitz, R. (1982). Feminism. In P. Spoonley, D. Pearson, & D. Shirley (Eds.), *New Zealand: Sociological perspectives.* Palmerston North: Dunmore.

Oakley, A. (1974). *The sociology of housework.* London: Martin Robinson.

Oakley, A. (1982). Interviewing women. In H. Roberts (Ed.), *Doing feminist research.* London: Routledge and Kegan Paul.

O'Brien, M. (1981). *The politics of reproduction.* London: Routledge and Kegan Paul.

O'Brien, M. (1982). Feminist theory and dialectical logic. In N. Keohane, M. Rosaldo, & B. Gelpi (Eds.), *Feminist theory: A critique of ideology.* Chicago: Harvester.

O'Brien, M. (1987). Education and patriarchy. In D. Livingstone (Ed.), *Critical pedagogy and cultural power.* Massachussetts: Bergin and Garvey.

Olssen, M. (Ed). (1988). *Mental testing in New Zealand.* Dunedin: University of Otago Press.

O'Neill, O. (1977). How do we know when opportunities are equal? M. Vetterling-Braggin, F. Elliston, & J. English (Eds.), *Feminism and philosophy.* Tottowa: Littlefield Adams.

Orange, C. (1989). *The Treaty of Waitangi.* Wellington: Allen and Unwin/Port Nicholson.

Pagano, J. (1991). Moral fictions: The dilemma of theory and practice. In N. Noddings & C. Witherell (Eds.), *Stories lives tell.* New York: Teachers College Press.

Papakura, M. (1983). *The old-time Maori.* Auckland: The New Women's Press.

Park, J. (Ed.). (1991). *Ladies a plate: Change and continuity in the lives of New Zealand women.* Auckland: Auckland University Press.

Pere, R. R. (1983). *Ako: Concepts and learning in the Maori tradition.* Monograph, Department of Sociology, University of Waikato.

Pere, R. R. (1988). *Te wheke: whaia te maramatanga me te aroha.* In S. Middleton (Ed.), *Women and education in Aotearoa.* Wellington: Allen and Unwin/Port Nicholson.

Peters, R. S. (1966). *Ethics and education.* London: Allen and Unwin.

Phillips, J. (1987). *A man's country? The image of the Pakeha male: A history.* Auckland: Penguin.

Piercy, M. (1983). *Braided lives.* Harmondsworth: Penguin.

Plummer, K. (1983). *Documents of life.* London: Allen and Unwin.

Poster, M. (1984). *Foucault, Marxism and history.* London: Polity Press.

Postman, N., & Weingartner, C. (1971). *Teaching as a subversive activity.* Harmondsworth: Penguin.

Ramsay, P., CRRISP Team. (1990). *There's no going back* (Final report of the Curriculum Review in Schools Research Project). Hamilton: University of Waikato.

Renwick, W. L. (1986). *Moving targets.* Wellington: New Zealand Council for Educational Research.

Rich, A. (1976). *On lies, secrets, silence: Selected prose.* New York: Norton.

Rich, A. (1980). Compulsory heterosexuality and lesbian existence. *Signs, 5,* 631–660.

Ritchie, J. (1982, November). *A women's studies program in a New Zealand university: The Waikato experience.* Paper presented at the conference of the Australian Women's Studies, Wollongong.

Roberts, H. (1989). *Where did she come from? New Zealand women novelists 1862–1987.* Wellington: Allen and Unwin/Port Nicholson.

Rowbottom, S. (1973). *Womens"s consciousness, man's world.* Harmondsworth: Penguin.

Ryan, A. (1988). The "moral right," sex education, and populist moralism. In S. Middleton (Ed.), *Women and education in Aotearoa.* Wellington: Allen and Unwin/Port Nicholson.

Sayers, J. (1986). *Sexual contradictions.* London: Tavistock.

Schaafsma, D. (1990). *Eating in the street: Teaching literacy in a multicultural society.* Ph.D. dissertation, University of Michigan, Ann Arbor.

Schubert, W. (1991). Teacher lore: A basis for understanding praxis. In C. Witherell & N. Noddings (Eds.), *Stories lives tell.* New York: Teachers College Press.

Schutz, A. (1944). The stranger: An essay in social psychology. *American Journal of Sociology, 49,* 499–507.

Secada, W. G. (1989). Educational equity versus equality of education. In W. Secada (Ed.), *Equity in education.* Lewes: Falmer.

Segal, L. (1987). *Is the future female?* London: Virago.

Seymour, R. (1976). *Abgynaecomnomonicothanasia: Two inter-related methods of counteracting sexism.* In P. Bunkle, S. Levine, & C. Wainwright (Eds.), *Learning about sexism in New Zealand.* Wellington: Learmonth.

Sharp, R. (1980). *Knowledge, ideology and the process of schooling.* London: Routledge and Kegan Paul.

Sharp, R., & Green, A. (1975). *Education and social control.* London: Routledge and Kegan Paul.

Shuker, R. (1986). *The one best system.* Palerston North: Dunmore Press.

Smith, D. (1974). Women's perspective as a radical critique of sociology. *Sociological Inquiry, 44,* 7–13.

Smith, D. (1979). A sociology for women. In D. Sherman (Ed.), *The prism of sex.* Madison: University of Wisconsin Press.

Smith, D. (1987). *The everyday world as problematic.* Boston: Northeastern University Press.

Smith, D. (1990). *The conceptual practices of power: A feminist sociology of knowledge.* Toronto: University of Toronto Press.

Smith, G. (1990). Taha Maori: Pakeha capture. In J. Codd, R. Harker, & R. Nash (Eds.), *Political issues in New Zealand education* (2nd ed.). Palmerston North: Dunmore.

Smith, G., & Smith, L. (1990). Kura kaupapa Maori. In A. Jones, G. McCulloch, J. Marshall, G. Smith, & L. Smith, *Myths and realities.* Palmerston North: Dunmore.

Smith, L. (1992). Maori women: Discourses, projects, and mana wahine. In S. Middleton & A. Jones (Eds.), *Women and education in Aotearoa 2.* Wellington: Bridget Williams Books.

Snow, D. (1991). A politics of university pedagogy: Inserting the self into the disciplinary text. *New Zealand Sociology, 6,* 110–134.

Somerset, H. C. D. (1973). *Littledene.* Wellington: New Zealand Council for Educational Research. (Original work published 1938.)

Spender, D. (1978). Notes on the organization of women's studies. *Women's Studies International Quarterly, 1,* 225–275.

Spender, D. (1980). *Man made language.* London: Routledge and Kegan Paul.

Spender, D. (1981). The gatekeepers: A feminist critique of academic publishing. In H. Roberts (Ed.), *Doing feminist research.* London: Routledge and Kegan Paul.

Spender, D. (1982a). Education: The patriarchal paradigm and the response to feminism. In D. Spender (Ed.), *Men's studies modified.* New York: Teachers College Press.

Spender, D. (Ed.). (1982b). *Men's studies modified.* New York: Teachers College Press.

Spender, D. (1983). *Invisible women: The schooling scandal.* London: Writers and Readers Co-operative.

Stanley, L., & Wise, S. (1983). *Breaking out: Feminist consciousness and feminist research.* London: Routledge and Kegan Paul.

Steedman, C. (1986). *Landscape for a good woman.* London: Virago.

Taskforce to Review Educational Administration. (1988). *Education for excellence* (Picot report). Wellington: Government Printer.

Taylor, S. (1984). Reproduction and contradictions in schooling: The case of commercial studies. *British Journal of Sociology of Education, 5,* 3–18.

Taylor, S. (1990). *Battlers and bluestockings: Women's place in Australian educa-*

tion.. Australia: Australian College of Education.

Te Awekotuku, N. (1984). Conclusion. In P. Spoonley, C. McPherson, D. Pearson, & C. Sedgewick (Eds.), *Tauiwi.* Palmerston North: Dunmore.

Te Awekotuku, N. (1988). He whare tangata, he whare kura? What's happening to our Maori girls? In S. Middleton (Ed.), *Women and education in Aotearoa.* Wellington: Allen and Unwin/Port Nicholson.

Te Awekotuku, N. (1992). Kia mau, kia manawanui—we will never go away: Experiences of a Maori lesbian feminist. In R. du Plessis, P. Bunklen, K. Irwin, A. Laurie, & S. Middleton (Eds.), *Feminist voices.* Auckland: Oxford, New Zealand.

Thompson, C. (1971). *On women.* New York: Mentor.

Tilly, L. (1979, Summer). Individual lives and family strategies in the French proletariat. *Journal of Family History,* pp. 37–160.

Tobias, S. (1978). Women's studies: Its origins, its organisation and its prospects. *Women's Studies International Quarterly, 1,* 85–97.

Vetterling-Braggin, Elliston, M. F., & English, J. (Eds.) (1977). *Feminism and philosophy.* Ottowa: Littlefield Adams.

WACE. (1988). *National policy for the education of girls and women in New Zealand.* Wellington: Women's Advisory Committee on Education/Government Printer.

Walker, R. (1985). Cultural domination of taha Maori. In J. Codd, R. Harker, & R. Nash (Eds.), *Political issues in New Zealand education* (1st ed.). Palmerston North: Dunmore.

Walkerdine, V. (1984). Developmental psychology and the child-centred pedagogy: The insertion of Piaget into early childhood education. In J. Henriques, W. Hollway, C. Urwin, C. Venn, & V. Walkerdine, *Changing the subject.* London: Methuen.

Walkerdine, V., & Lucey, H. (1989). *Democracy in the kitchen.* London: Virago.

Watson, H. (1988). The impact of the second wave of the women's movement on policies and practices in schools. In S. Middleton (Ed.), *Women and education in Aotearoa.* Wellington: Allen and Unwin/Port Nicholson.

Watson, J. (1966). Marriages of women teachers. *New Zealand Journal of Educational Studies, 1,* 149–161.

Watson, J. (1973). Foreword. In H. C. D. Somerset. *Littledene.* Wellington: New Zealand Council for Educational Research.

Weedon, C. (1987). *Feminist practice and post-structuralist theory.* New York: Basil Blackwell.

Weiler, K. (1988). *Women teaching for change: Gender, class, and power.* New York: Bergin and Garvey.

Weiler, K. (1991). Freire and a feminist pedagogy of difference. *Harvard Educational Review, 61,* 449–474.

Weiner, G. (1991). *Shell-shock or sisterhood! Ideology in the British National curriculum: School history and feminist practice.* Paper presented at a conference of the American Educational Research Association, Chicago.

Weiner, G., & Arnot, M. (Eds.). (1987). *Gender under scrutiny: New inquiries.* London: Hutchinson.

Willis, P. (1977). *Learning to labour.* Westmead: Saxon House.

Wilson, T. (1971). Normative and interpretive paradigms in sociology. In J. Douglas (Ed.), *Understanding everyday life.* Chicago: Aldine.

Witherell, C., & Noddings, N. (Eds.). (1991). *Stories lives tell: Narrative and dialogue in education.* New York: Teachers College Press.

Wollstonecraft, M. (1978). *A vindication of the rights of women.* Harmondsworth: Penguin. (Original work published 1792.)

Wolpe, A. M. (1978). Education and the sexual division of labour. In A. Kuhn & A. Wolpe (Eds.), *Feminism and materialism.* London: Routledge and Kegan Paul.

Woolf, V. (1978). *A room of one's own.* London: Granada. (Original work published 1929.)

Yates, L. (1987). Theorizing inequality today. *British Journal of Sociology of Education, 7,* 119–134.

Yates, L. (1988). Does "all students" include girls? *Australian Educational Researcher, 15,* 41–57.

Yates, L. (1989.) Review of S. Middleton's *Women and education in Aotearoa. Gender and Education, 1,* 309–311.

Yates, L. (1990). *Theory/practice dilemmas: Gender, knowledge and education.* Geelong: Deakin University Press.

Yates, L. (1991). *A tale full of sound and fury—signifying what? Feminism and curriculum policy in Australia.* Paper presented at a conference of the American Educational Research Association, Chicago.

Yeatman, A. (1991). *A vision for women's studies at Waikato.* Address presented for the Centre for Continuing Education, University of Waikato.

Young, M. F. D. (1971). An approach to the study of curricula as socially organized knowledge. In M. F. D. Young (Ed.), *Knowledge and control.* London: Collier MacMillan.

Index

Index

About the Author

SUE MIDDLETON is a New Zealander. She has taught in elementary, junior high, and high schools; and has taught in the Department of Education Studies at the University of Waikato, Hamilton, since 1980. She is editor of *Women and Education in Aotearoa* and is coeditor of *New Zealand Education Policy Today: Critical Perspectives; Feminist Voices: Women's Studies Texts for Aotearoa/New Zealand;* and *Women and Education in Aotearoa 2.* She has published in many academic books and journals, including the *British Journal of Sociology of Education, New Zealand Journal of Educational Studies,* and *Harvard Educational Review.* She loves to travel, loves all kinds of music, and plays jazz piano. She is married and has a teenage daughter.

DATE DUE

DE 17 '93			

DEMCO 38-297